Inner Yoga

Selected Writings of Sri Anirvan

There is no greater Yoga than to be perfectly natural.

INNER YOGA

Selected Writings of Sri Anirvan

MORNING LIGHT PRESS

Published by Morning Light Press, Copyright © 2007
Edited by Margaret Case

Printed in Canada on Acid-free Recycled Paper

ISBN-13: 978-1-59675-019-7

Library of Congress Cataloging-in-Publication Data

Anirbana, 1896-1978.
Inner Yoga : Selected Writings of Sri Anirvan.
p. cm.
ISBN 978-1-59675-019-7 (alk. paper)
1. Yoga. 2. Spiritual life. I. Title.
B132.Y6A525 2007
294.54'36--dc22

2007033260

MORNING LIGHT PRESS

Morning Light Press
323 North First, Suite 203
Sandpoint, ID 83864

morninglightpress.com

CONTENTS

Introduction

Sri Anirvan was born on 8 July 1896 in the town of Mymensingh in East Bengal (now Bangladesh). It was a typical small Bengali town of that era, natural and lovely, with thatched-roofed houses and yards hedged by flowering creepers. Palm trees stood everywhere, on the outskirts lay paddy fields, and nearby flowed the mighty Brahamaputra. In this setting the child imbibed the beauty of nature. His knowledge of plants in later life was almost that of a botanist.

Sri Anirvan's original name was Narendra Chandra Dhar. His parents, Raj Chandra Dhar and Sushila Devi, were cultured middle-class Hindus of the Kayastha caste. They were pious and affectionate, and the child grew in an environment of love and harmony. By the age of eleven, the boy knew Panini by heart and daily recited a chapter from the Gita. There was nothing unusual in all this—it was a part of the traditional teaching at home for most boys of his age and caste. He also went to a newly established school recently opened by the British Government of India, where the teaching was nontraditional.

From his childhood, Narendra was introspective and loved solitude. Once, when he was only nine years old, he had an inner experience which profoundly affected him. He *saw* that the sky with its myriad stars entered into him. He felt wide, free, and detached, like the sky. The experience left its mark behind. In later life, he became the sadhaka of the Void.

At the age of sixteen, having completed his secondary education, Narendra left Myemsingh to live in Assam with the guru to whom his whole family was devoted, Swami Nigamananda. The Swami was building a new ashram on virgin land near Jorhat. Narendra joined the other disciples in clearing land, digging wells, plowing, and constructing. The one call was to work for the guru, and Narendra served him ungrudgingly. A few months later, news came that he had been awarded a state scholarship based on the results of the matriculation examination he had taken before he left home. Swami Nigamananda told him to continue his education. For six years, first in Dhaka and then in Calcutta, he pursued his study of Sanskrit and Indian philosophy, specializing in the Vedas. A brilliant student, Narendra stood first in the University of Calcutta Sanskrit examinations at both the bachelor's and master's levels.

At the age of twenty-two, the young scholar returned to the ashram, which had grown rapidly after the initial labor. The number of inmates rose to fifty. Narendra taught in the ashram's school, Rishi Vidyalaya; edited its journal, *Arya Darpana*, and in time assumed many other responsibilities as well. Swami Nigamananda was, in fact, preparing Narendra to succeed him. He initiated him into sannyasa and gave him the new name Nirvanananda. Eventually retiring to Puri, the Swami left Nirvanananda in charge of the ashram. But after twelve years of service, new forces were stirring in the disciple. His soul sought release from the cares of the ashram which, as it developed, involved many administrative activities; it sought freedom to express itself in its own way. One day in 1930, at the age of thirty-four, he left the ashram never to return, and began a new life. Events proved him right. It was a gain for the cause of Indian religious culture, of which he became a great interpreter and exponent. In due course, he also gave up the saffron clothes of a sannyasin. He changed his name from Nirvanananda to Anirvan, a name by which he was to be known later to the larger world. It signified a change in approach, philosophy, and life-goal. It was also a declaration that he was no longer bound by the vows of sannyasa and that he was free from the ties which even sannyasa forges.

Not much is known of his life during the next twelve years of wandering. Traveling widely in the Himalayas and Assam, he spent much time alone in quiet retreats, meditating, studying, writing. By disposition he was a lover of solitude and nature, but Sri Anirvan also believed in accepting the world and sharing his life with others. Even during his wandering years, he lived for long stretches in cities, often as the guest of an old friend, Biren Sen, a government officer who was posted at the time in Delhi, Allahabad, Lucknow, and mainly Ranchi. Wherever Sri Anirvan stayed, a small number of fellow-seekers gathered around him. He shared with them what light he had, but at the same time was careful to remain unassuming and informal; he wished to keep others and himself free. In the winter, it was his custom to travel about India, visiting friends in the towns and cities, going to historical sites and places of pilgrimage. This winter tour was a way of keeping in touch with things.

In 1944 Sri Anirvan began living in a house near Almora, in the Himalayan foothills of Uttar Pradesh. There he made a translation of Sri Aurobindo's great philosophical work, *The Life Divine*, and also started writing his own great work, *Veda Mimamsa*, for which he would receive the Rabindra Puraskar award. It was during this time that Sri Anirvan fully realized the meaning of a brief but momentous childhood experience. At the age of seven he had a revelatory vision of a young girl of radiant beauty, whose charm and mystery had haunted him ever after. At Almora he recognized her as the presiding deity of his life, "the Divine Mother born of perfect wisdom" who, he felt, was unfolding to him the secret of the Veda, the meaning of India's philosophical systems and the essence of her heritage. In her, he recognized the Uma Haimavati of the Kena Upanishad who led Indra, king of the gods, to the Supreme Godhead. Throughout his life Sri Anirvan remained a devotee and interpreter of this Haimavati principle.

It was also here at Almora that Sri Anirvan met Madame Lizelle Reymond, who became his pupil, biographer, and interpreter of his philosophy to the West. She remained with him for five years and kept intimate contact with him throughout his life.

In 1953–1954, Sri Anirvan moved from Almora to Shillong in Assam; and again finally in 1965 to the vicinity of Calcutta, which remained the field of his activities during the rest of his life. He continued writing and also started giving systematic lecture courses to a small group of disciples.

Still active even in his seventies, he took long walks and exercised regularly. Then in July 1971, a tragic fall altered his way of life forever. Sri Anirvan's legs were paralyzed by the fall, and examination revealed that in addition he was suffering from tuberculosis of the backbone. Bedridden for the last seven years of his life, he was dependent upon others for everything. Sri Anirvan bore this condition with equanimity. His body, always lean, became emaciated and weak, but his mental powers remained strong till the end. And always there was a light and smile on his face. During these long years, he was devotedly tended by his disciples, Srimati Rama Chaudhuri and Dharmapala, who joyously shouldered the main burden.

Sri Anirvan passed away on 31 May 1978, at the age of eighty-two.

"My ambition is not very great," he once said. "It is to live a life rich in impressions, luminous to the end; to leave behind a few books embodying my lifelong search for Truth, and a few souls who have caught fire. My aim?

Simply to inspire people and give them the most complete freedom to live their own life. No glamor, no fame, no institution—nothing. To live simply and die luminously."

Sri Anirvan is the author of twenty books, most of them commentaries on the scriptures and philosophical systems of India. His first major published work was a two-volume Bengali translation (1948, 1951) of Sri Aurobindo's *The Life Divine*. Sri Anirvan's *Veda Mimamsa,* an exposition on the Vedas, came out in three volumes in 1961, 1965, and 1970. His commentaries on the Isha, Kena, and Aitareya Upanishads appeared in the late 1960s, and a three-volume commentary on the Gita between 1968 and 1970. Other books include several volumes of letters and a few smaller works such as this one. All but one were written in Sri Anirvan's mother tongue, Bengali. The exception is *Buddhiyoga of the Gita and Other Essays* (1983), a collection of most of his writings in English.

II

After this brief biographical note, we should now say something about the book in hand and its subject, antar-yoga. Through this book, the reader will become acquainted with Sri Anirvan as a poet, religious thinker, and a yogi. He will see for himself that the author is both an analyst and a synthesizer. He places Patanjala Yoga in the larger spiritual tradition of India rooted in the Vedas and the Upanishads and brings out its intimate links with other disciplines and traditions like Buddhism, Vaishanavism, Tantras, Mantra Yoga, and so on.

The synthesis is a necessary task and has to be performed by great teachers again and again. The mind divides a subject for convenience and as an aid to better understanding, but it soon loses the underlying unity and begins to treat sections as autonomous systems. Those who restore the lost unity render a great service, but it can only be done by those who have a larger and deeper view of the subject.

The subject of this book is transformation of life and awareness of a larger life that surrounds us. In ordinary course, a man looks outward, but when he learns to turn his gaze inward he becomes aware of a secret life, a larger life buried within. Through earnest endeavor and devout invocation, this life can become dynamic and manifest.

The method and discipline by which this is done is called Yoga. Yoga is a multi-significant word and it covers many disciplines. One of the most celebrated of them is the *Patanjala Yoga-Darshana*, a section of which is discussed in the present volume, the discussion enriched by frequent cross-references to other disciplines.

The sage, Patanjali, defines Yoga as chittavritti nirodha, or stoppage of the mind. But looked at from another angle, it could also be defined as *atma-prabodha*, or self-awakening, awakening of the great life of the Spirit that lies beyond the mind. For receiving this higher truth, a man has to develop a new receptivity, new powers and new channels. He has to develop new organs of truth—virya, shraddha, smriti, dhyana, samadhi, viveka, and prajna—organs which are already there but are in a dormant state and have to be quickened.

The task is not easy. It requires weakening the negative forces and nourishing the positive ones. It requires fighting with settled habits of the mind, with ingrained dispositions, with deep-rooted nescience, ego, desires, and aversions. By the same token, it requires opening out the mind to the higher truth, the cultivation of a heart that waits and watches and receives in wise passiveness.

For the two related tasks, Patanjali proposes the discipline of kriya-yoga, of devotion to one's chosen deity, of the eight-limbed yoga, of higher orders of samadhi, of discrimination and intuition. Bhagvan Buddha also prescribes a closely similar three-tier discipline of sheela, samadhi, and prajna.

As the aspirant takes up the practice of Yoga and advances on the path, he experiences an inward and upward movement. This movement is more than an allegory; it is felt even physically. The sadhaka becomes aware of a new subtle-physical body; he can feel that his life-forces have moved into the spinal channel (*sushumna*); he also feels that he is now stationed in the upper region of the body, particularly at the heart center or the forehead center. It is different from the feeling of the ordinary man—if he has a feeling at all in the matter—who lives in the lower region of the body.

A man's awareness of his mind is even dimmer than his awareness of his body. Man's mind is at the disposal of his vital forces and it is dragged down by various lower pulls. The ordinary mind is scattered, dispersed; in that state it neither knows its object properly nor knows itself. But through Yoga it illumines the object of its attention and also becomes self-aware. The sadhaka also begins to realize that he is more akin to mind than to matter. He becomes aware of a larger mind whose working is more direct and untrammeled.

As the mind advances in purity and power of concentration, it develops the capacity of reflecting the Self. Man becomes Self-aware. In his ordinary and even in his scientific thinking, he thinks that his material existence is in the first term. But as he grows in Yoga, he begins to see differently. He finds that the objects belong to the sense-organs, the latter belong to manas, and manas to buddhi; and buddhi itself is an instrument of the soul.

All this forms part of yogic development. The process, method, and concepts connected with this development have been discussed with great scholarship and insight by Sri Anirvan. But there is one thing which could still be discussed with great advantage, something which is traditionally left out altogether from discussion. Vyasa, the great commentator of *Patanjala Yoga-Darshana*, tells us that the mind has five habitual states or planes (*bhumis*): *mudha*, dull or inert; *kshipta*, restless (or probably it is *samkshipta* and means contracted); *vikshipta*, scattered; *ekagra*, one-pointed; and *niruddha*, stopped. He makes a further pregnant statement that samadhi is natural to mind and it can take place on all bhumis (*sarvabhaumika*); but he adds a warning that the samadhis of the first three bhumis are non-yogic and only the samadhis of the last two bhumis are yogic. Only the yogic samadhi leads to spiritual development.

Traditional commentators concentrate on expounding only the yogic samadhi and make only the barest reference to samadhi on the first three bhumis. *Vishuddhi-Marga*, the great Buddhist treatise on Yoga, does the same. After observing that samadhi is of many kinds but discussing them all would cause distraction, it limits itself to the elucidation of the samadhi of the kushala chitta, or purified mind.

This self-limitation is good for the purpose in hand, but it has a serious disadvantage too. Considering that the two kinds of samadhis are often confused with each other, it would have served the cause of clarity if both were discussed and their differences pointed out. After all, the Gita does it; in its last two chapters, it discusses various spiritual truths like austerity, faith, duty, knowledge in their triple expressions, and sharply distinguishes their sattvika forms from their rajasika and tamasika imitations.

The elucidation of non-yogic samadhis or ecstasies has also its positive value and peculiar concern. It could help to explain quasi-religious phenomena which, sadly, have been only too numerous and too important in the spiritual history of man. Many creeds seemingly religious sail under false labels and spread confusion. As products of a fitful mind, they could but make only a temporary impression, and their life could not but be brief. But as projections of a mind in some kind of samadhi, they acquire unusual intensity, a strength of conviction and tenacity of purpose (*mudhagraha*) which they could not otherwise have.

Developing Vyasa's hint, we may say that even the lower bhumis (*kama bhumis*) have their characteristic trances or samadhis, their own revelations, prophets, and deities. They project ego-gods and desire-gods and give birth to dvesha-dharmas and moha-dharmas, hate religions and delusive ideologies. All these projections have qualities very different from the qualities of the projections of the yogic bhumi.

For example, the God of the yoga-bhumi of Patanjala Yoga is free, actually and potentially, from all limiting qualities like desire, aversion, hankering, ego, and nescience; free from all actions, their consequences, present or future, active or latent. Or in the language of Patanjala Yoga, he is untouched by klesha-karma-vipaka-ashaya. But the God of the ecstasies of non-yogic bhumi or kama-bhumi is very different. He has strong likes and dislikes and has cruel preferences. He has his favorite people, churches, and ummas, and his implacable enemies. He is also very egoistic and self-regarding; he can brook no other god or gods. He insists that all gods other than himself are false and should not be worshiped. He is a "jealous god," as he describes himself in the Bible. And he "whose name is Jealous" is also full of "fierce anger" (*aph*) and cruelty. He commands his chosen people that when he has brought them to the promised land and delivered its people into their hands, "thou shalt smite them, and utterly destroy them; thou shalt make no covenant with them, nor show mercy unto them . . . ye shall destroy their altars, and break down their images, and cut down their groves. . . . For thou art an holy people unto the Lord" (Deut. 7:1–6).

The Allah of the Qur'an exhibits about the same qualities. He is god of "wrath" (*ghazab*); on those who do not believe in him and his prophets, he wreaks a "terrible punishment" (*azab alazim*). In the same vein, he is also a "mighty avenger" (*aziz al-intiqam*). He is also a god of "plenteous spoils" (*maghnim kasirat*). He tells the believers how he repulsed their opponents and caused them to inherit the land, the houses and the wealth of the disbelievers (Qur'an 33.27). He closely follows the spirit of Jehovah, who promised his chosen people that he would give them great and goodly cities they built not, and wells which they dug not, vineyards and olive trees they planted not (Deut. 6:10–11).

No wonder this kind of god inspired serious doubts and questions among thinking people. Some of his followers like Philo and Origen allegorized him to make him more acceptable. Some early Christian Gnostics simply rejected him. They said that he was an imperfect being presiding over an imperfect moral order; some even went further and regarded him as the principle of

Evil. Some Gnostic thinkers called him "Samael," a blind God or the God of the blind; others called him "Ialda baoth," the son of Chaos.

He continues to offend the moral sense of our rational age. Thomas Jefferson thinks that the "Bible God is a being of terrific character, cruel, vindictive, capricious and unjust." Thomas Paine (1737–1809) says of the Bible that "it would be more consistent that we call it the work of a demon than the word of God."

Hindus will buy any outrages if they are sold as gods, saints, or prophets. They have also a great weakness for what they describe as "synthesis." In that name, they will lump together most discordant things without any sense of their propriety and congruity, intellectual or spiritual. However, a few names like Bankim Chandra, Swami Dayananda, Vivekananda, Aurobindo, and Gandhi are exceptions to the rule. To Bankim, the God of the Bible is "a despot," and Jesus's doctrine of "eternal punishment" in the "everlasting Fire" (Matt. 25:41) is "devilish." Swami Dayananda, remembering how the biblical "Lord sent a pestilence . . . and there fell seventy thousand men of Israel" (1 Chr. 21:14), His Chosen people, observes that even "the favor of a capricious God so quick in His pleasure is full of danger," as the Jews know only too well. Similarly, the Swami argues, in his usual unsparing way, that the Allah and the Shaitan of the Qur'an, according to its showing, are about the same.

But to reject is not to explain. Why should a god have to have such qualities? And why should a being who has such qualities be called a god? And why should he have so much hold? Indian Yoga provides an answer. It says that though not a truly spiritual being, he is thrown up by a deeper source in the mind. He is some sort of psychic formation and carries the strength and attraction of such a formation. He also derives his qualities and dynamism from the chitta-bhumi in which he originates.

Yoga will explain that the biblical God is not peculiar and he is not a historical oddity. He has his source in man's psyche and he derives his validity and power from there; therefore he comes up again and again and is found in cultures widely separated. This god has his own ancestry, his own sources from which he is fed, his own tradition and principle of continuity, self-renewal, and self-validation.

Not many know that a similar god, Il Tengiri, presided over the life of Chingiz Khan and bestowed on him revelations. Minhajus Siraj, the mid-thirteenth-century historian, tells us in his *Tabqat-Nasiri* that "after every few days, he [Chingiz Khan] would have a fit and during his unconsciousness he would say all sort of things. . . . Someone would write down all he said, put [the papers] in a bag and seal them. When Chingiz recovered consciousness, everything was read out to him and he acted accordingly. Generally, in fact always, his designs were successful."

In this, one can see unmistakable resemblance with the revelations or wahi of the Semitic tradition.

In actual life, one seldom meets truths of the kama-bhumi unalloyed. Often they are mixtures and touched by intrusions from the truths of the yoga-bhumi above. This, however, makes them still more virulent; it puts a religious rationalization on them. It degrades the higher without uplifting the lower. The theories of jihad, crusades, conversions, and da'wa become spiritual tasks, commandments of God, religious obligations, vocations and duties of a chosen people. "See my zeal for the Lord," says Jehu, an army captain anointed as king at the command of Jehovah. Bound to follow His will, he called all the prophets, servants, priests, and worshipers of rival Baal on the pretext of organizing his service, and when they were gathered, his guards and captains "smote them with the edge of sword," and "they brake down the house of Baal, and made it a draught house [latrine] unto this day" (2 Kings 10:25, 27).

Like intrusions from above, there could be and are also eruptions from below unless the life is purified by a moral and spiritual discipline. Hence the insistence of Indian Yoga on purification. In fact, the whole Indian Yoga could be summed up in one word: purification or chitta-prasada or chitta-shuddhi. Indeed, without purification, even Yoga could be put to a negative use. In fact, in certain creeds, the initial limbs of Yoga are used not for liberation but for the intensification of certain fond ideas and beliefs, for theological self-conditioning.

Therefore the Indian Yoga insists that the aspirant should first be established in sheela, yama, and niyama, (harmlessness, self-restraint, and truthfulness.) Indian Yoga cares only for such samadhi which is built on the foundation of a developed ethical life. Next it insists on the purification of samadhi itself through the purification of antah-karana, manas, and buddhi, of smriti and dhyana. The mind should expand by constantly dwelling on benevolence, compassion, sympathetic joy, and equanimity (*maitri*, *karuna*, *mudita*, and *upeksha*).

As we have learnt to distinguish yogic samadhi from the non-yogic one, we should also remember that even yogic samadhi is not something fixed and given once for all. It has many grades and stations, and each grade has its characteristic qualities and flavor. If the mind is sufficiently purified, it automatically moves from one stage to its next deeper one, different both in what it contemplates and in the qualities of that contemplation.

The subject is large, but we shall here do with a briefest reference. *Vishuddhi-Marga* describes this movement very clearly. It divides the movement into several dhyanas and samapattis. Put roughly, it tells us that the first three or four (depending on one's enumeration) dhyanas are characterized by vitarka (reflection), vichara (sustained application), priti (joy), sukha (felicity), ekagrata (one-pointedness), and smriti (mindfulness), in the ascending order of yogic subtleness. In the fourth dhyana, the coarse limbs leave or go into abeyance, leaving behind only "mindfulness purified by upeksha," or equal-mindedness or samata of the Gita. This equal-mindedness opens the door to many kinds of infinities and universalities (*anantyas*). Beyond these infinities lies the nirodha-bhumi of Patanjala Yoga or the nirvana-bhumi of the Buddhists.

We need not go into this larger yoga at all. Suffice it to point out that the higher Indian spirituality begins with the fourth dhyana, which is characterized by equal-mindedness.

This elucidation should help to throw light on the fact that even scriptures which contain the truths of the yogic bhumi differ from each other in their ethos and feel. For example, the New Testament, even in portions where it contains the truths of the yogic bhumi, includes only the qualities of the first three dhyanas: zest, zeal, piety, belief, faith, joy, promise, confidence, and fervor. But even in these portions we find nowhere the mention of samata, equal-mindedness, and of further truths based on the edifice of samata, like atma-jnana, advaita, nirvana or moksha, or liberation—the staples of Indian spirituality.

There is another point. The truths of the initial dhyanas are not secure unless they develop into a settled seeing (*drishti*) or prajna (wisdom) of higher dhyanas. This explains why the Church lost them so soon. Almost from the beginning, its zeal became zealotry and persecution, its faith blind and dogmatic, its confidence arrogant self-assertion and sectarianism. In the absence of a true science of interiority, it took to the ideology of physical and outward expansion.

The West has provided a rationalist critique of Semitic and other allied religions. But what is needed is also a spiritual critique, which the Indian Yoga is best fitted to do.

The present volume is Sri Anirvan's second publication in English. It is a translation from the original Bengali, which was first published in 1980 by

Haimavati Anirvan Trust. This itself reproduced the still older matter which first appeared in a quarterly journal, *Ananda Varta*, Varanasi, in 1956–1958.

From its informal tone, it appears that it was first presented as a series of talks to small interested audiences.

The subject matter of this book is sadhana. There are not many books like this on the subject showing such mastery and insight. Sri Anirvan lived a life of dedication and reflection, and he speaks as an insider. He takes his readers onto unfamiliar grounds, and there is no doubt that they will find in him a sure guide on this unusual pilgrimage.

The subject of Yoga is vast. Therefore, even though Sri Anirvan's treatment of the subject is comprehensive, it is still possible to look at it from many more angles. In fact, he himself does it in his various writings. He gave another course of lectures on *Patanjala Yoga-Darshana* in March 1964 in Calcutta. Notes of these discourses were taken by Sri Gautam Dharamapal in longhand, but these have yet to be edited and published.

Ram Swarup
Dhulivandana Day
4 March 1988

Section I

INNER YOGA

Chapter 1

The Eight-Limbed Yoga

The Outer Practices

The eight limbs of Yoga[1] may be divided into two parts. Yama, niyama, asana, pranayama, and pratyahara are the five outer disciplines or practices (*sadhanas*); dharana, dhyana, and samadhi[2] are the three inner ones. Through the outer practices the mind is gradually turned inward. Calmness, clarity, and inwardness of mind—these three qualities are closely interrelated.

In the depths of my being, the subtle substance of mind appears in the form of tiny points or rays of electric light. It is this light, spreading outward, that creates my world—my outer as well as my inner world. But in both these worlds, disturbing movements of various kinds are constantly taking place. For, as the Upanishad says, "The soul of a man gazes outward and not at the Self within." Observing an object, it sees only its outer aspect, but fails to see the Self within. To turn the gaze inward—this is the practice of Yoga.

It is necessary, first of all, to set in order the things outside ourselves, for only when the mind is somewhat freed from outer disturbances can it go within. But in establishing order in our external circumstances, we must not depend on others. Instead of trying to change the actions of others, we must try rather to change our own reactions to them. In all our contracts and relations with the world, we must strive to maintain equality of mind. The discipline for attaining this equality is called *yama*.[3] As a result of it, my relations with outside life become harmonious from an inner point of view. Then, in the language of Yoga, the light that spreads from my mind to the outer world becomes calm and clear and glad.

And what is niyama? It is the discipline aimed at making this light within me clear and calm and glad. Of its aspects, the three most important are austerity, study of the scriptures, and devotion to God.[4] Indeed, it is said that through these three alone even ordinary people can attain to the highest goal of Yoga, the state of samadhi.

Once yama and niyama have been mastered, the mind becomes full of joy, and full, too, of goodwill toward others. False motives and intentions do not arise in it, nor any thought of personally benefiting from the fruits of Yoga. The heart is filled with exceptional power and inspiration. One clearly perceives the task that the divinity within has set one to do. The energy of the body and senses becomes clear and irrepressible. One's cherished object of contemplation (*ishta*)[5] is felt in the center of the heart. Into all one's activities a wonderful concentration settles. When these signs begin to manifest, one can be sure that one has the capacity to do Yoga, for one's inner and outer life will have become clear and pure.

At this point the mind's attention must be interiorized more deeply, and to this end the discipline of the body, life-force, and mind must be taken up. To make the physical body clear and still, the next step is the practice of asanas, fixed postures.[6] Its two aids are relaxation and expansion. And if, along with the asanas, a few locks (*bandhas*) and gestures (*mudras*) are used, one can obtain results more quickly. Jalandhara Bandha and Yoni Mudra are especially recommended.[7] Keep in mind that, as the Gita advises, the head, neck, and body should be held in a straight line during the sitting posture.

By mastering asanas, stillness, stability, and sense of clarity and well-being develop within the body and pervade it. One feels the beloved One as ever-present and at play in the heart. One clearly feels too the twin streaming of Agni and Soma—the Fire in the heart—rising up, the Nectar from above flowing down. As a result, the breathing becomes slow, deep, and rhythmic. One feels as if with every breath one were drawing in the nectarous Breath of Life, as if every cell of the body were being filled with the nectar of immortality.

Next, one should turn one's attention directly to the breathing and become aware of it; not a single round of breath should escape one's notice. To maintain this attention it is helpful to combine the practice of japa, continuous repetition of a mantra, with the breathing. And to succeed at japa, it is necessary to control one's speech. Never utter a single unnecessary word if you can help it; if something must be said, say it in a few words, in succinct, well-chosen speech. I mention this because control of speech has a great bearing on the practice of pranayama, the control (*yama*) of the breath and life-energy (*prana*). If the breathing and the japa can be made to fall into a rhythm and harmonize—if, as a Baul saying puts it, one can "get into the boat of the mind-wind"—then pranayama becomes easy.

Pranayama here means nothing more than to pause for a short while after each inbreath and outbreath. If by yama and niyama the mind has been cleared of disturbance and by asana the body has developed a feeling of stability, clarity, and well-being, then this pause of breath is effortless and deep. One feels as if one were living in another realm of existence, a realm in which everything is clear and bright and buoyant. This inner realm seems to be filled with an invisible light, as when the globe of a neon lamp is filled with burning gas. This, precisely, is the result of pranayama. I shall not speak of the numerous methods of pranayama, for they are unnecessary here and at times even harmful. Through the practice of this easy, natural pranayama, a deep sense of emptiness engulfs the being. At this point a suspension of the breath sometimes occurs automatically. But this arrestation of breath is not, after all, the main thing.

Through asana and pranayama the body-consciousness (*deha-bodha*) becomes clear and pure; the mind then begins to find its delight within and no longer needs to run about outside in search of it. At this point the practice of pratyahara—the withdrawal of the mind and senses from outward things—becomes easy. The keynote of pratyahara is this: "Abide, O mind, in thyself alone." The mind, attracted toward things, is ever running outward. We lose ourselves then, we are borne away by the current of activity and become wholly immersed in it. Yet it is possible, even in the midst of this stream of events, to retain self-awareness, to separate ourselves from outer objects, and maintain an inward poise. These are the characteristics of pratyahara.

But we cannot develop a capacity for pratyahara unless there is also some practice of detachment (*vairagya*). The mind should always remain detached; nothing should hold it fast. The mind should become like that of a young boy: open, empty and at the same time alert. Such is the character of an indrawn mind, a mind in which pratyahara has been established. While sitting in a moving train, I observe through the window all the sights that pass before me; I enjoy them, yet I feel no attachment to them; at every moment I leave them behind. In the depths of my mind I know that I am traveling to Vrindavana and all that I see is but a sight on the way. To possess at every moment of life this sense of freedom from the world and its activities—this is a pratyahara. As a result of it, the senses are brought under control.

This, in brief, is a description of the outer limbs of Yoga. When one has mastered them, one has established control over one's outer and inner life, and over the center of one's inner world, the mind, life and body fashioned by nature. They still remain, but they do not, as before, disturb or obscure. It should be noted, however, that to remain unaffected and undisturbed are not only the signs of a yogi; along with them there must also be an awareness of the Self. Therefore, as is stated in the Samkhya, after purifying the body, restraining the senses, and quieting the mind, it is necessary to purify the ego. The sadhus and sannyasins do this with the aid of the Great Word (*mahavakya*). Ceaselessly they do japa, repeating such words as *Shivoham* (I am Shiva), *Ayam atma Brahma* (this Self is Brahman), and *Tat tvam asi* (Thou art That). The bhakta, the lover of God, continually repeats, I am Thine, I am Thine. This practice of japa is included as part of kriya-yoga, with its purificatory processes of svadhyaya, the study of scripture, and Ishvara-pranidhana, devotion to God.

When one has an abiding sense of clarity and purity within, and a sense also of being united with the vastness around, the impurities of the ego are strained out and the being becomes pure. It is as when a woman is suddenly awakened by the touch of someone's love. Her being is filled then with a sweet self-consciousness; inwardly and outwardly she becomes, as it were, attuned to a new melody; her mind, life, and body become clear and pure and fragrant. Such a mood may be likened to what is achieved through mastery of the outer limbs of Yoga.

Truly though, there is no need for us to place too much emphasis on the technical aspects of Yoga. Within our own being, movements of a Yogic nature are regularly taking place quite naturally; I would like to draw particular attention to them. There is no greater Yoga than to be perfectly natural.

Notes

1. Yoga: union; the union of the individual soul with the supreme Self. Spirit, divine; the conscious seeking for this union.

2. These eight terms will be defined in the course of the text.

3. Patanjali, in whose Yoga Sutras the eight-limbed yoga is enunciated, lists five yamas (restraints): noninjury, truthfulness, nonstealing, continence, and noncovetousness.

These rules of moral self-control purify the character and, as the author notes, establish equality in the mind.

4. The other two aspects mentioned by Patanjali are purity and contentment. These five "observances" purify and elevate the mind.

5. Ishta: chosen, cherished, beloved. The ishta is usually a deity (*ishtadevata*) or a person, such as one's guru or a great spiritual figure.

6. The principal asana in Patanjali's Yoga is the seated posture. One must be able to sit firmly and comfortably for a long period of time.

7. In the Jalandhara Bandha or chin lock, the chin is contracted and pressed down into the chest. In the Yoni Mudra (literally, womb gesture), as the author uses the term, the anal and abdominal muscles are contracted and drawn upward and inward toward the spine. These contractions are usually applied in the seated posture when the breath is suspended; they "seal off" the ends of the trunk, aiding the retention and increase of life-energy (*prana*) in the body.

Chapter 2

THE EIGHT-LIMBED YOGA

The Inner Practices

The introduction is over; we come now to the inner Yoga. First we want to arrange its limbs in a schematic way for our comprehension, though in fact all the different limbs are intimately related to one another; at times their action may even reverse our imagined order. The real aim of Yoga is for the Observer, the Seer (*drashta*) in us to discover its true nature (*svarupa*). If we keep this in mind, the relationships between the different limbs will become clear.

The first limb of the inner Yoga is dharana, the fixing of the mind for some time on a single thought, feeling, object, or place. The writer of the Sutra says, "When the mind can be fixed in one place, that is dharana." Let me note at the outset that the principal idea behind dharana is to create a clear and pure state of awareness in the body-consciousness (*deha-bodha*). Dharana is thus the basis of the Hatha yogin's practices. Indeed, no Yoga is possible without some disciplining of the physical instrument. Through asana, pranayama, and pratyahara, we have been disciplining the body. Through asana the body-consciousness has become stable and stilled; in the words of Sri Ramakrishna, "One becomes like Mount Sumeru—immobile and steadfast." This feeling should always be with us. Whether we walk or sit or lie down, whatever we do, there should be physical stability, a stable poise in all our limbs. Through pranayama, a lightness, buoyancy, and limpidity have come into the body-consciousness. And through pratyahara, this body-consciousness has become luminous and bright. These qualities—stability, lightness, and luminosity—now have to be brought together and concentrated at one spot. This is dharana.

But where shall we do it? First within our three and a half cubits, the space of our own body. Our world is centered around our body, so let us try to become conscious of that center. Through the outer Yoga we have already acquired a physical sense of luminosity; now we must possess its center by diving into the body. This is one kind of dharana, the kind that is done in the body.

There is a deep connection between dharana and the practice of asana. In asana there are three characteristics of mastery: calm stability, a joyous feeling of well-being, and a sense of infinite expansion. All three are bodily sensations. When we are seated somewhere engaged in work, we ought to check from time to time to see whether our body-consciousness is pervaded by these three feelings. They help us, in fact, to bring about the purification of three of the five elements (*bhutas*), the elemental states of material energy. The Upanishad says, "The natural, physical qualities of the elements are gradually replaced by the supra-natural yogic qualities which start manifesting in them." The quality of the Earth element is solidity; its corresponding yogic quality is the feeling of calm, steadfast well-being. The quality of the Water element is fluidity; its yogic quality is relaxation, as if upon this stable feeling of well-being waves of gracefulness were flowing; the body then feels like that of a little child brimming with happiness. The quality of the Air element is pervasiveness, movement everywhere; its yogic counterpart is infinite expansion; it gives the feeling that the body is not solid; there seems to be no gulf between the inner and the outer: the whole body seems to be spread out like gas on all sides.

When to these three feelings, the feeling developed by pranayama[1] is added, the yogic quality of the element Fire begins to manifest within. Its characteristic is radiance, radiating heat, and light. It brings to the human instrument, the "vessel" (*adhara*) of mind, life and body, a marvelous feeling of radiant warmth and clarity. Special mental endowment, genius, is a quality of pranayama. Control your breath and your intelligence will flourish.

What has been said thus far may now be summarized. Through asana and pranayama, we have been able to acquire a feeling of all-pervasive expansion and a body-consciousness which is peaceful and clear. As the sun shines bright in the sky—"filling earth and sky and heaven," as a Vedic rishi says—so shines our subtilized being, filling the universe with life and light. A sense of complete harmony pervades us, harmony between our inner nature and the outer nature around us.

It is now necessary, with the aid of pratyahara, to draw into ourselves the whole spiritual world centered around our body. This is the primary purpose of inner dharana, the fixation of the mind at a center of the body.

As the earth has an axis, so has our Yoga-body an axis—it is the spinal column. And as the earth's axis is ever pointed toward the Pole Star, so is our body's axis ever pointed toward a Sun that burns in the Great Void (*mahashunya*). This inner sun and the outer one are actually two forms of the same spiritual reality. They become co-axial when the outer sun reaches its zenith at midday and falls directly on top of the head, especially during uttarayana, the northern phase of the sun's yearly cycle. There is reference in the Vedas to the greatness of this midday moment; at noontime especially, it is advantageous to draw upon the solar energy of nature.

There is, too, a fixed and permanent Sun at the heart of the universe; it is above and beyond the outer physical sun. This highest Sun has been called Ishvara, the Lord, Hiranyagarbha, the Golden Embryo, and other names as well. A ray from this Sun has penetrated us; entering us through the brahmic opening (*brahmarandhra*) at the crown of the head, it courses down the channel in the spinal cord (*sushumna*).[2] This ray is called in Veda the *sushumna suryarashmi*—the spinal sunray; it is the support, the pillar of inner dharana.

How then is dharana, this stationing of the mind in a center, to be done? The answer is: through bhavana, the power of mental conceptualization in which the mind dwells upon an idea or image in order to realize its truth or essence.

There is a connection, let me note, between dharana and pranayama, for one result of pranayama, mental capacity, is also the fruit of dharana. As Patanjali says, "Through the fixing of the mind, mental capacity develops." As for pranayama, there is no need to turn it into a difficult performance. The vedic method of pranayama is a most natural and easy technique. The Buddha too has referred to it as *anapanadipani*. There is a close connection between this kind of pranayama and the ajapa japa of Tantra. This will be easier to understand once the tantric system of practice has been explained a little. In the japa-yoga of Tantra, dharana, pratyahara, and pranayama have been joined together into a beautiful, easy, and sovereignly effective method of spiritual practice. I shall now give a brief account of it.

Notes

1. The Upanishad speaks of the nectarous breath of life. With each breath the finite draws in the nectar pervading the universe, then throws it back out again into that universe (author's note).

2. This spinal channel, though spoken of as if it were in the gross material body, is in fact located in the subtle body. The same is true of the brahmic passage (*brahmarandhra*) and the centers of consciousness (*chakras*).

Chapter 3

Japa Yoga

The Four Limbs

The Tantra says: "Shiva, Shakti, Manas, Marut—these four must be united while doing japa."

Shiva, the Supreme Being, is seated above the head in the Great Void (*mahashunya*).

Shakti, the Supreme Power, is seated in the center of consciousness at the base of the spine (*muladhara*). Shakti flows upward through the subtle nerve channel in the spine (*sushumna*).

Manas, mind, is our chosen mantra. The mantra is a bhava, an emotion, mood, or attitude of heart expressive of our feeling toward the object of our concentration; the mantra is also a bija, a seed-sound expressive of the core and essence of its being. The practice of mantra-japa, continuous repetition of a mantra, is a means of concentrating the mind and making it one-pointed. It can form part of the practice of pratyahara, the internalization of the mind and senses. When, through constant awareness of the mantra, our mind has become so deeply absorbed in the inner consciousness that whatever we see and hear outwardly only serves to awaken the mantra within, it may be said that we have mastered pratyahara in Mantra Yoga.

Marut, wind, the life-power that supports the action of thought, is our breath. Among our vital activities, breathing is prominent, easy to apprehend, unceasing, and rhythmic; therefore it is easy to use it to tame our vital nature and so make our mind clean and pure. There is another vital activity which is prominent in us—the heartbeat; and it too is ceaseless and rhythmic and takes place inside us. But the breath has this advantage over the heartbeat: at every moment our breath is joining the existence outside us with the existence within us, and thus with its aid it is easy to awaken the universal consciousness. For this reason the rhythm of the breath is more advantageous to spiritual practice than the rhythm of the heart.

Let me add something more, for it may help to understand the relation between the body-consciousness and the fixing of the mind. Our natural being is composed of body, vitality, and mind. They may be regarded as three different mediums through which quality of consciousness is manifested. When the consciousness is dull and inert, it is the body; when it is clear, it is the mind. Our spiritual effort has to be made with the help of the mind, but how rarely that mind is pure! Almost always its purity is adulterated by restlessness and inertia. Yet inertia does have its corresponding yogic quality—calm steadiness—and restlessness likewise has a yogic counterpart—forcefulness. If the mind can be made steadfast and at the same time forceful, then one can have a pure mind, the mind of the yogin.

In our natural being, the body alone is steadfast; its functions occur with almost mechanical quality and surety. The activity of the vital nature is more dynamic, and as for the mind we can hardly grab hold of it. But if the stable quality of the body can be instilled in the mind, the mind is more easily tamed. And this is only one side of the matter; the other is that when the clear quality of the mind pervades the body-consciousness, it makes it light and clear. This association of mind and body helps to make possible the establishment of spiritual consciousness. In bringing about this clarity of mind and body, pranayama is a big help. And through the combined action of body, vital-force, and mind, dharana becomes easy.

Let us now return to the subject of Ajapa Yoga. First, the mantra has to be woven together with the breath. Never take a single breath without repeating the mantra. Whether that mantra be a seed-syllable (*bija*) or a Name, one should add to it the customarily used syllable OM. Patanjali says that OM is the syllable of the divine. The root mantra one uses should be enfolded on both sides with OM. Suppose that the root mantra is Hrim or Hari or the Gayatri. When enfolded, it will become *OM Hrim OM*, *OM Hari OM*, or *OM tat savitur . . . OM*. The first OM should be contemplated with the aid of pure or permanent memory (*shuddha khyati*, *dhruva khyati*). The final OM should simply be repeated. This must be practiced a little at the beginning.

In the first verse of the Mandukya Upanishad, it is said that OM is everything.[1] In the language of philosophy, the eternal Sound that fills the ether is OM. Our body-consciousness having become lighter and more pervasive through the practice of inner expansion, it should not be difficult for us to keep alive, both within the body and outside it, a constant awareness of this all-pervasive ether, this luminous space or sky called the akasha.[2] The akasha is vibrating with energy (*shakti*), and the vibration of this energy is the sound OM. It is as if the akasha were ceaselessly droning, "OM, OM, I, I, I am that I am." This self-declaration of the Void is the sound OM. OM is the Word of Brahman, OM is the Sound, and OM too is the unstruck sound at the heart of our being; again, OM is the ego-sense. The contemplation of the akasha as ever vibrating with the sound of OM should form the backdrop of our consciousness. "The akasha is my eternal companion": to carry this feeling (*bhava*) always in ourselves is what is implied, really, in the contemplation (*bhavana*) of OM with the aid of pure or permanent memory. Arriving at this conception is facilitated by sensing in the akasha the living presence of God.

The root mantra and the final OM should be repeated, audibly or inaudibly, moving the lips and tongue; this is how the japa is to be done. While drawing in the breath, the root mantra, such as Hrim, is to be pronounced; while releasing it, only OM. If the Gayatri mantra is used, while drawing in the breath say *OM: tat savitur varenyam bhargo devasya dhimahi*; while releasing it, say *dhiyo yo nah prachodayat OM*. This is the rule for japa.

First, observe the movement of the breath. Notice that while inhaling, a current or stream of wind courses downward until it reaches the heart. This must be felt very concretely. Again while exhaling, the stream rises from the heart, passes through the eyebrow center, emerges through the opening and the crown of the head, and spreads out into the Void. This too must be felt. Next, along with this two-way stream of wind, a two-way stream of awareness must be felt coursing up and down. And all this time the repetition of the mantra will go on continuously—while inhaling, it is the root mantra; while exhaling, OM. The Bauls speak of this as "rowing the boat of the mind-wind." Thus rowing, the boat of the mind-wind gradually moves upstream; bypassing all the knots and eddies of the stream, it reaches the Great Void and dissolves into it. This description is also to be found in the Veda.

So much for the technique regarding mind and wind, manas and marut. They must now be joined with Shiva and Shakti. The seat of Shiva lies above the head in the Void. The first OM I have mentioned, is Shiva. He is spread out above us, around us, on all sides, like the kadamba.[3] His countless rays of light-power (*jyoti-shakti*), are entering us on all sides and converging at the heart-center, which is the seat of the individual Self (*jiva*). At present, this power should be held and concentrated in the heart. For the heart is the center of our universe; from it countless rays are radiating forth, above, below and all around. And from the ocean of consciousness surrounding us, Shakti, the power of the universal Lord, is at every moment entering us along the same ray-lines.

Let us imagine our body as if it were the earth floating in the Void and engulfed in an ocean of light-power. As the earth has an axis, so has our body an axis, a central channel through which the power pours in from the ocean of light. This channel extends from the Brahmic opening in the head to the center of consciousness at the base of the spine; and in the middle of the channel lies the "heart-knot" (*hridaya-granthi*), the seat of the Self in the individual. The main channel itself is the sushumna, the corridor in the spinal column. Parallel to and in front of this channel is the channel of the breath. While inhaling and exhaling, it is through this breath-channel that we feel the current of the breath.

While doing japa of the mantra, we ought to have the conception (*bhavana*) and the feeling (*bhava*) that is from the all-enveloping sphere of Shiva: he or his power (*shakti*) is entering us. Piercing the top of the head, borne downward on the in-breath, he enters the heart, seat of the Self, and there awakens the sleeping consciousness of the Self. Then on the out-breath, this awakened Self-consciousness ascends with him, breaks out through the top of the head, and dissolves into the Void. The in-breath is life, the out-breath is death. With the in-breath the being is charged with Shakti, with the out-breath it is filled with Shiva (*shivamaya*). When Shakti filled with Shiva (*shivamayi shakti*) returns again to the heart with the in-breath, she comes back enriched in divine content and transforms the atoms and molecules of the body into spiritualized consciousness.

In this way the gulf between inner and outer, consciousness and matter, Shiva and Shakti, is gradually removed. Little by little, one's whole experience is filled with Shiva-Shakti, one's whole universe is pervaded by the profound and intimate union of Shiva and Shakti. This state of consciousness is termed samarasya, equal delight. This feeling of equal delight is the first OM of the mantra; I have referred to it as the backdrop of the base mantra, and so it is to be conceived in the mind.

Let us take a less subtle example—the love of a man and a woman who long for each other. At first this yearning is nothing but a passionate craving of body and mind, a craving expressed through various efforts to get physically close to each other. But once the union of these lovers is consummated, the passion fades, there is no longer any restlessness or disquietude. Each dissolves into the other, and all that remains is a sublime feeling like "the delicate tremor in the heart of a tuberose."

When we are deeply absorbed in japa, this is the kind of feeling we experience. That feeling then plunges into the fathomless depths of the emotion (*bhava*) in our heart; the functioning of our breath is no longer noticed, nor any descent and ascent of the Shakti; all that remains is the radiation of innumerable rays from our heart. Then we are at once Shiva and Shakti seated at the heart of the universe.

Notes

1. "OM is the imperishable word, OM is the universe. . . . The past, the present and the future, all that was, all that will be, is OM. Likewise all else that may exist beyond the bounds of time, that too is OM."

2. Usually translated as ether, space, or sky, akasha has also been rendered by the author in English as luminous Void. Its roots are *kash*, to shine, and *a*, pervasion, extension.

3. The kadamba is a golden-yellow globe-shaped flower which looks like a sun. From its small round core, numerous yellow filaments shoot straight out, like sunrays, to form the globe.

Chapter 4

Dharana Yoga

The Three Regions and Four Centers

I have spoken of the practice that is to be done with the aid of the breath. As the practice of japa and mental contemplation deepen, our awareness of breathing recedes from the foreground to the background. We clearly feel, then, that the movement of breathing is a gross physical activity. The real thing is the subtle vital or nervous current which, behind the breath current, ascends and descends through the spinal channel (*sushumna*). At this point we should forsake our concentration on the breathing and direct our attention to that nervous current. The nature of our emotional attitude (*bhava*) remains the same as before, but our mind retires from the outer realm and enters into the spinal channel, where it is held. This is the beginning of the true working of dharana.

In breathing we normally have only an external awareness of its process; now we must turn our attention within and become inwardly aware. This we can do with the aid of the spinal channel. Ordinarily, the actions and reactions of our consciousness create waves in our bloodstream and we feel their impact in our heartbeats. But as we become conscious in the spinal channel, our blood flow becomes soft and gentle. We discover that every thought and movement gives rise in the nervous current in the spinal channel to a vibration which is subtle and deep, yet full of ecstatic power. At present the spinal channel in us is insensitive and unfelt, and as a rule human beings are seldom ever aware of it except at the climax of the sexual experience; the spinal channel opens briefly at that time, which is why the sexual hunger in human beings is so strong. When the spinal channel is open and "awake," our inner consciousness is flooded with samarasya, an equal delight in all things; we feel then, in the words of Sarada Devi, "as if the heart were a pitcher filled to the brim."

When this feeling of equal delight is experienced, the mind becomes quiet and indrawn; in other words, a deep and natural state of pratyahara is achieved. When this occurs, the seeker is ready to practice dharana, the stationing of the mind in one or more of the body's subtle centers of consciousness (*chakras*); which center will depend on his temperament.

In the ancient Yoga three broad regions for the practice of dharana have been suggested: the heart, the spot between the eyebrows, and the crown of the head. In the Gita, in its discussion on the Yoga of Dissolution, it is advised to fix the life-force and mind in these three regions. But along with them, a fourth may be added—the throat region, by which is meant the region just behind the jaw. In the practice of dharana, one begins by focusing on a center at the front of the body, then gradually moves backward toward the spinal cord. The Upanishads speak of this as *antarvritti*, the inner movement. This movement inward is not limited to the mind; the sensation in the body too must be shifted toward the spinal column.

In Hatha Yoga, four chakras, centers of consciousness and energy, have been pictured in the four regions of the body. Some, instead of calling them chakras, prefer the term padmas, lotuses. The chakra is not conceptualized in terms of form, whereas the padma is, and in it there is a suggestion of sensuous enjoyment. The Shakti or divine power is conceived with the aid of yantras, geometric figures.

Each of the chakras corresponds to a mental activity in man and is its container, vessel, holding place (*adhara*). For example, the heart is the container of emotion (*bhava*); its yogic name is *anahata*. The throat is the container of willpower; its yogic name is *vishuddha*. The eyebrow center is the container of intelligence (*buddhi*) or knowledge (*jnana*); its yogic name is *ajna*. The center just above the crown of the head is the containing center of spiritual knowledge (*vijnana*); its yogic name is *sahasrara*.

The breath and mind should be fixed in one of these places, depending on one's temperament and aim. But it is also possible to practice dharana by taking them all together. Those with a clear intellect and strength of character can obtain good results by practicing fixation at the center between the eyebrows. This center may be called the seat of the Witness. A ray of light descends from it and illumines the heart; another rises above and diffuses itself in the Void. It is not really difficult to hold the mind at this point between the eyebrows and at the same time develop a feeling of expansion into the regions above and below. From the standpoint of the Yoga of Knowledge, the advantage of this center is that it allows one to simultaneously combine in a harmonized contemplation the three realities of Brahman, Atman, and Jagat—Supreme Being, Self, and World. The vast expanse (*mahakasha*) of consciousness above the crown of the head is the Brahman. The point of consciousness between the eyebrows is the Atman. The ocean of consciousness in the heart is the Jagat. Seated in the center of the eyebrows, we are able to take the whole world into us and at the same time perceive that the world-ocean in the heart is but a reflection of the expanse above the head.

This type of conceptualization and contemplation is most suitable to women, owing to their mental and physical constitution. The woman in whom the delight of a love transcending physicality has been awakened can easily concentrate at the eyebrow center and experience these two felicities (*rasas*): the love of a mother in the heart center and the bliss of communion with Shiva in the crown center. The world is then like a child cradled upon her breast; from above Shiva pours down his serene delight into all her being, even as her consciousness rises up and dissolves in the Void.

This, then, is the principal idea behind the dharana that takes all four higher centers together; of them, the heart, eyebrow, and crown centers are the most important. When fixing the mind in them has been established through practice, fixation in the throat center comes about naturally. There is a relation between the concept of dharana set forth by Patanjali and the bodily locks or contractions (*bandhas*) practiced by the Hatha yogins. I shall speak of this later, for the idea of dharana at the throat center will then become clear.

Having discussed the knowledge of the centers and their corresponding regions, let us now return to the subject of stilling the mind with the aid of japa.

Chapter 5

Mantra Yoga

The Mystery of Ajapa

The practice of Yoga proceeds with the help of three streams or currents of energy—the air or breath current, the nervous current, and the mental current; of these, the air and nervous currents together may be called the vital current. Just as the inflow and outflow of the breath goes on continuously, impelled by the laws of nature, so the nervous and mind currents go on continuously with the same ebb-and-flow movement. Ordinarily we are unaware of these currents because our mind is habitually turned outward. But if we become aware of the breath current in us—aware, that is, of the outer aspect of the vital current—and if through mental conceptualization (*bhavana*), we press that current inward toward the spine, we then perceive the flow of the nervous current. This is the development of spinal awareness or spinal consciousness (*sushumna-chaitanya*). Once this spinal consciousness is awakened, we can faintly feel the mental current flowing within the nervous one. In a way it may be said that the nervous and mental currents are the same; indeed, all three currents are but different qualities or modes of a single nature-force.

Once we grasp the basic character of the mind-current, we can more clearly understand the science of japa. When we closely observe the activity of the mind, we see that it is outward-directed and dissipated; all in it seems confused, disorganized, incoherent. The activity of such a mind may be likened to the attempt of an untrained shooter to hit the bull's-eye of a target. The mind's impulse is to run toward its object, but it fails to hit the mark; all that happens is that the area around the bull's-eye becomes perforated like a sieve full of holes.

But what is the bull's eye, the center of our target? It is sat-chit-ananda, infinite existence, consciousness, and bliss—the one true Object. In Patanjali's sutras it is called the one Reality. In truth it is this one Object we are always seeking in things, but we are never able to find it; and this is why the mind is ever upset and unhappy. When the mind gets hold of an object attractive to it, it thinks it has found the real thing; but of course it has not. This intense and unending search is the reason for the mind's restlessness. Anyone who has gone deeper and looked into himself knows what a tremendous dissatisfaction this brings. But as the mind grows disenchanted with its own unsatisfied state and turns further inward, it finds that what it was seeking for outside in fact lies within itself. Then, even while outwardly the soul (*jiva*) continues to play the game of blind man's bluff, inwardly another mental substance is being awakened, though it falls back again and again into somnolence. The vedic seers have called this inner mental substance *madhvada*, the honey-eater, and *pippalada*, the eater of the sweet pippal fruit. To further understand it, it can be named *gopi*, after the cowherdesses of Vrindavana who were so enamored of Krishna. As soon as the gopi hears the flute of Shyama, she wakes with a start and finds—yes, it is Shyama! and spontaneously throws herself upon his breast. The same thing is in fact happening within us with every cycle of our breath, but because we are turned outward we are unaware of it.

The vedic seers have described this breath cycle in terms of the twin streams of Agni and Soma, the Fire of aspiration and the Nectar of bliss. A stream of Nectar is ceaselessly flowing down into us from the Void; pouring down into the heart, it touches there the Fire, which at once leaps up. A small spark at first, it flames up as it rises and burns like a sun, then rises yet higher and spreads out into the sky (*akasha*), into the sweetness of the moonlight. In philosophic language, the Brahman-consciousness descends and coils itself up in the jiva, individual soul or self; then the jiva ascends and unfolds itself into the Brahman. This process goes on continuously, in fact, with every round of the breath. The oscillation of this rhythm is our waking and our sleep, our activity and our rest, our life and our death. In the outer world it is day and night, in the Void it is the blossoming of creation and the withering of dissolution. In all our thoughts and actions this process of contraction and relaxation goes on incessantly; the contraction is creation, the relaxation is dissolution. This indeed is our mind-current, and we possess it just as we possess a heartbeat. It is hidden within our own self. Discover it and we are liberated.

During our spiritual practice, the existence of this mind stream is at first accepted as a hypothesis. Assume that it is there, and proceed. After a time you will discover for yourself that indeed it is there. You may say, "But this is auto-suggestion; I have created it by auto-suggestion." But the truth is that you have not created it, you have only discovered it. Besides, in spiritual life, auto-suggestion is a fundamental power. What you think, that you become; and if this be so, then all can be done, and what you discover in this way is the very Truth. This will be confirmed when you find that with the aid of this Truth everything can be resolved. Even the scientist would say that if all the facts of nature could be explained through a single principle, that principle would be the highest Truth. If you can discover it through auto-suggestion, what is the harm?

In spiritual practice, bhavana—conceptualization and dwelling in mind upon what is conceptualized in order to realize it—is of the highest importance. In fact, through your thought-conception you are creating yourself at every moment. Once you have grasped this law of your inner nature, it may be said that the foundation of your practice has firmly been laid. "What you dwell upon, that you realize. Bhavana is a spiritual power."

I have spoken here of certain things not directly related to our discussion, but it has been necessary. The modern mind, in the boasting of its rationality, sometimes loses everything.

The ebb-and-flow movement of the mind-current or vital current has been described beautifully in a verse in the Tantras:

Hamkarena bahiryati sahkarena vishet punah
So'ham hamsah rupenaiva jivo japati sarvada

As the sound "Ham" it [the life-breath] goes out,
as the sound "Sa" enters in again.
Repeating "So'ham Hamsa", in this form
the individual Self continually does japa.

"Ham" in the Tantra is the seed-sound of Shiva; with a bindu (·) added to it, its force is toward dissolution, for with it the rising life-force (*prana*) goes out. "Sa" in the Tantra is the seed-sound for Shakti; with a visarga (:) added to it, its force is toward creation, and through the attraction of the downward-moving life-force (*apana*) it enters in. Thus we have "Hamsa."[1]

When "Hamsa" is reversed, it becomes "So'ham" (He am I), which is the mantra continually repeated by the individual Self (*jiva*) as its japa. "Hamsa" in the Vedas is the sun or Aditya. "So'ham" is the self-assertion of the Self. At every moment, in every work and act and thought, we are declaring and asserting our own existence. This declaration, inseparably linked with "So'ham," gets distorted and deformed and then takes on various aspects in the ego (*ahamkara*). Unable to hit the mark, this self-declaration, "So'ham," (He am I), gets deflected, goes astray and cries out, "This am I, that am I." But the true Self, the jiva, is the madhvada purusha, the self who eats honey, and always it is repeating within, "I am Thou and Thou art me." Or again, the gopi-consciousness, adoring the Beloved, is saying, "I am Thine and Thou art mine."

The conceptualization of the Hamsa mantra, which is by nature the ebb-and-flow movement of the mental current, will be slightly different when practiced by women and by men. Women can conceive it quite easily because in their essence (*svarupa*), they are prakriti, nature. Their mind, life, and body move spontaneously in accordance with their natural function (*vritti*). Because the functions of her body, life, and mind are naturally attuned to her consciousness, a woman is truly chinmayi, full of consciousness. Thus, the true form (*svarupa*) of the Self in a woman's heart is a womanly form.

While taking in the breath, a woman ought to imagine that Shiva (*Ham*), dwelling above in the Vast, is coming down into her heart and flooding her being in an inundating downpour. Through his spiritual touch, her Power of Self (*atmashakti*) is awakened and it cries out, "Sa!" At that moment she truly becomes Great Nature (*mahaprakriti*) with all her twenty-four cosmic principles manifested. Thus experiencing her true Self during the in-breath and Sa, she then goes out with the sound Ham and dissolves in the Void, the breast of Shiva. In this way a woman develops a rhythmic thought-conception which involves her whole being.

In the case of a man, this same thought-process will be followed, but it should be in harmony with the feeling that his true nature (*svarupa*) has the qualities of the Purusha. The Purusha, Conscious Being or Self, is pure consciousness without any body or form. The body of a man, and not only his body but his life-force, mind, and intelligence, are in fact Prakriti, Nature, and therefore of the woman; in his true Being he is spread out in the Void. When, with the Sa mantra, the breath enters into him, it awakens in him not the Purusha, but the Shakti, the power of Self (*atmashakti*), which is woman (*nari*). The woman is not outside man, but within him; that is why in the Tantras man has been called an *Antah Shakta*, one who has the Shakti within him. Thus with the in-breath and Sa, a man is in truth embracing his own power of Self in delight of Self. When he rises upward again, with Ham, he takes with him his own inner power, spiritualized, into the emptiness of the Void. The whole movement, from beginning to end, is really just a kind of blissful play of the One with Itself—the One dividing into Two. In the case of the woman, it is the Two that are united to become One. For the ordinary man, however, this subtle distinction is difficult to grasp; he begins with the assumption that his body, life, and mind are his real Being, Purusha. And the result of this error has been disastrous, for not only has he created a mess for himself, but also he has dragged down woman along with him.

From what I have just said, it should now be easier to understand why the conception of ajapa is ingrained in the nature of a woman. This is not so in the case of a man, who can only experience its ineffable sweetness when by brachmacharya, sexual purity, he has arrived at a consciousness free from identification with his body. There are even some men who conceive of themselves as women in order to make the practice of ajapa easier; there are others again who through bhakti, love for the Beloved, become woman-life in nature, and they too find the ajapa practice easier for them.

Indeed, it is not even possible to wholly become the Purusha, the He, the Pure Conscious Being, until one has succeeded in detaching oneself from everything. But can everyone do this? Obviously not. The easiest way for a man, then, is either to become like a little child or a woman. The nature of a little child and a woman are very near to each other, for both in their essence are Para Prakriti, Supreme Nature. The difference in gender is not so strong a factor here; though the umbilical cord has been cut, the inner cord that binds the child to its mother is never really severed; hence the child remains very natural. Actually, in spiritual practice, the difference between man and woman is not so much one of body as of thought. When there is a sense of surrender and dependence in the seeker's practice, he is identifying his being with Para Prakriti, the true She. When he relies solely on his own Self, then only he is truly the Purusha, the He; but such an attitude is rare and difficult, as I have said. The little child knows no one else but his mother; she is both father and mother to him. When I call upon the Mother as her child, the Mother is for me the very embodiment of the sweetness and beauty of the Supreme Purusha. If I can find Her, perhaps I can also discover Him in me. And if I should fail, what does it matter? After all, the last word of all spiritual endeavor is fulfillment, the filling of one's vessel, by whatever means it is done.

There is another form of the Hamsa mantra: it is OM Hrim.[2] While drawing in the breath, it is Hrim or Shakti; while releasing it, it is OM or Shiva. If we look closely at OM Hrim, we find that its conception is the same as for Hamsa—it is the same cycle of creation and dissolution. Shakti is the Creatrix, Shiva is the Destroyer. In the Tantra this duality is again expressed in the visarga and the bindu. The visarga is creation; its symbol is two points (:) signifying that the One has become Two. The bindu is dissolution; its symbol is a single point (·). In the Bengali script the bindu is combined with nada (ঁ).

Symbolically, Shakti streams down from the bindu at a slant. Why at a slant? Because if Shakti were to come straight down, there would be no deflection, no divergence or deformation. But the Unmanifest can manifest itself only when it is deflected. In the language of Samkhya, this is termed *visadrisha parinama*, meaning a dissimilar resultant or development.

Let me say something more about Hrim. It is also called *maya-bija* and *lajja-bija*, the seed-form of maya and lajja. (OM is the *Brahma-bija*, the seed-form of the Brahman.) In Sanskrit *hri* also means lajja—shyness, bashfulness, modesty. Woman is the embodiment of lajja. This is a very great truth. In our country the feminine nature has been developed in accordance with this principle. The psychology behind lajja is this: in the overpowering spell of love, there is a partial concealment of form. When Sati in her love for Shiva has become all-Shiva, possessed of him, there is no lajja, only ananda, pure bliss. But when this love tries to express itself in form, nature seems to behave a little oddly: she reveals only half of herself; the other half remains hidden. For this reason creation or manifestation has been called *maya*, illusion, meaning that it is illusive, veiled, imperfectly expressed. A Tantra tells us that this manifestation is like the sweetness and charm of lajja of Shodasi Prakriti—the sweetness and charm of the shyness of a sixteen-year-old girl in full bloom. This shyness is in fact the inexpressible ananda. The little of it that has been expressed in the manifestation is surrounded by various hints of the unexpressed, the unmanifested. And if were not so, the sap of life (*rasa*) would not be there, the sweetness and charm would be lacking. Lajja is the deflected sweetness of love.

This, then, is the fundamental sentiment or emotion (*bhava*) implied in Hrim, the seed-form of lajja. If we analyze the seed-form, we first have "H" or Shiva (*akasha, sat*: ether, being). "R" is the seed-form of Agni or Fire (*chidagni*: consciousness). "I" is the seed-form of Rama (*shri, ananda, prema*: beauty, bliss, love). "M" (or \˙) represents sound. Hrim is therefore also a symbol of sat-chit-ananda, being-consciousness-bliss. What distinguishes Hrim from OM is that Hrim is the mantra of the self-creation of Shakti, the divine power. When doing japa with Hrim, think of yourself as the Shakti as you draw in your breath. Then with OM and the out-breath, dissolve yourself into the being of Shiva.

Let me now offer some hints for doing ajapa japa while using the Gayatri mantra. This will conclude almost the whole of the subject. While doing japa of the Gayatri, the mantra should be enclosed at both ends with OM. The sound of OM will form the background. (Some recommend including the vyahritis[3] with the Gayatri, but this is not necessary at the beginning. Once one has realized the conception of the fundamental Gayatri, the conception of the vyahritis naturally follows of itself.) First, divide the mantra into two parts: *Tat savitur varenyam bhargo devasya dhimahi* in the first part, *dhiyo yo nah prachodayat* in the second.[4] The first part should be said with the in-breath, the second with the out-breath. While conceptualizing the mantra, stress should be placed on the two verbs *dhimahi* and *prachodayat*. Dhimahi, "We meditate upon"—"we," not me alone, for the seeker is a representative of everyone in the universe and his effort is not done merely for his own sake. Upon what, then, are we meditating? Upon the light of the divine Sun. And where are we meditating? In the heart. That effulgent light is coming from the sphere of the divine Sun down through the passage in the crown of my head and entering my heart. There it takes the form of intelligence (*dhi* or *buddhi*). My work is done.

The verb used during exhalation is *prachodayat*, "May He direct." It is He whom we request to direct the intelligence; may our intelligence lose itself in His Light. Thus we see that the Gayatri mantra, too, is cast in the rhythm of ajapa.

The method of ajapa japa is the central secret of Mantra Yoga. It can be applied to all mantras in the same manner.

There is a close connection between ajapa and the Yoga of the Dissolution mentioned in the Gita. (Hints of it are also given in the Gita's eighth chapter.) The practice of dissolution has to be done throughout our life by this ajapa. Then only can life become immortal. Death is the ultimate zero.

The Void is the ultimate principle. If you do not accept this, you can never realize the divine life; it simply cannot happen.

Let us now return to our discussion of dharana.

Notes

1. Pronounced Humsuh (short "u" m); in northern India, often pronounced Hunsuh or Hungsuh.

2. Pronounced Hreem; in northern India, often pronounced Hreeng.

3. *Bhur, bhuvah, svah.*

4. "We meditate upon the effulgent Light of Divine Sun. May He direct our intelligence."

Chapter 6

DHARANA YOGA

Fixation within the Body and Outside It

From our discussion of the practice of dharana with the aid of mantra, it should now be clear that the true purpose of dharana is to fix and hold in one's being the conscious power (*chetana-shakti*) and delight (*ananda*) of the Vast. To do this it is helpful to open the spinal channel (*sushumna*) through the power of conceptualization (*bhavana*). As this Yoga of the spinal channel becomes firmly established, dharana becomes easier.

This technique belongs, of course, to the Hatha yogins. Patanjali has not explicitly referred to it, and there is a reason. Patanjali has analyzed the question from a purely scientific viewpoint and therefore has not allowed any extraneous concepts to enter in. In this view spiritual practice ought to be centered on the Self (*atman*); thus if one is able to fix his mind in the heart center or any other center without taking the help of a mental image or concept, that too is dharana. In each of the body centers there is a particular kind of energy (*shakti*) lying asleep; through dharana that energy is awakened. We have already discussed the special characteristics of the different energies of consciousness (*chit-shakti*), so we need not repeat them.

I should now like to put in a word of caution. If you wish to master dharana by conceptualizing the movement in the spinal channel, you may bring the current of energy as far down as the heart, but do not allow it to go below that point. It is only when, in your practice, the light in the heart (*vishoka jyoti*) has appeared that you can safely, with the aid of that light, lead the energy down into the three lower centers—the navel, abdominal, and basal chakras. The deep-sea diver goes down to the bottom of the sea, but all the while a cord is bound to his waist; that cord is held at the other end by sailors on the deck of the ship above, and if there is any sign of danger, they haul the diver up. In the same way, when the light in the heart has been firmly established, that light itself gives the indication when it is all right to flow down with the current of enjoyable sensation; no separate effort is needed to do it. But if the seeker fails to take note of this and suddenly goes down to the navel center, he may find himself in serious trouble.

Thus far, what I have said about dharana has dealt with the technique of concentration, of withdrawing or gathering in the mind and senses. And the methods of fixation I have mentioned have all been bodily ones. But there is another kind of dharana, which Patanjali calls *videha dharana*, fixation outside the body. It belongs to the Jnana yogins, those who practice the Yoga of Knowledge. The essential idea behind it is to convert the five physical elements into their nonphysical yogic qualities.

Videha dharana, like the inner dharana, begins with the body, but whereas in the latter the mind remains focused on some part of the body during practice, in videha dharana the mind is not centered solely on the body; indeed, the body is only a secondary support of the practice. To do this nonphysical dharana, it is necessary to have knowledge of two things first: first, a clear understanding of the physical elements or qualities (*bhutas*); second, a thorough knowledge, gained through self-observation, of the developments and changes that occur in the body-consciousness (*deha-bodha*).

The Buddhist yogins have beautifully described the nature of the physical qualities. According to them, the quality of earth is solidity; of water, fluidity; of fire, heat and radiance; of air, expansiveness; and of ether, voidness. These concepts will be easier to understand with the aid of science.

Physical science speaks of three states of matter: solid, liquid, and gaseous. In the solid state of substance, the molecules remain dense and compacted. With the application of heat, they begin to break apart and their rate of vibration increases; at this stage solid matter is changed into liquid form. With the application of still more heat, the rate of vibration further increases, and at the same time the volume of substance expands considerably; as a result, even a small quantity of gaseous substance is able to occupy the space of the vessel containing it.

In this description we find four of the five physical qualities: the solidity of earth, the fluidity of water, the heat of fire, and the expansiveness of air. Heat is the fundamental energy of change and transformation. As long as the body-consciousness is there, these four qualities will be active;

when the body becomes empty, so to speak, the fifth quality, the voidness of ether, appears.

There are two aspects to the qualities of the elements. The five elements which constitute the outer world give us the five subtle properties or qualities of sound, touch, form or sight, taste, and smell, which are apprehended by the five senses of knowledge. These again, upon entering our body, are converted into the five subtle properties of matter (*tanmatras*). The disciplines which use them as their means of practice will be taken up later in reference to dhyana.

Our body is made up of the five elements, but their qualities are not apprehendable by our senses; we can only feel them. In other words, I do not see myself inside, I do not taste myself, and so on, but still I am able to feel the change that takes place in my body-consciousness when one or another of the physical elements predominates in my body. The Hatha yogins refer to this as the rise of tattva, inherent quality. They say that the rise of tattva goes on all the time in us, and that due to it a change is always taking place in our body-consciousness, though ordinarily we fail to perceive it because we are turned outward.

In any event, the practice of dharana can be done by incorporating the yogic quality of the physical elements into our body-consciousness. This is bhuta dharana, fixation of the elements. We have already come across the idea of this kind of dharana in our discussion of the practice of asana, fixed posture. While sitting in an asana, I begin by imagining that my body has solidified and turned to stone. My body has become one with the earth upon which I am sitting; it is like an anthill or a hump of earth. When this feeling develops, the sensation is one of utter stability and stillness in the body. This is the yogic counterpart of solidity or firmness. When it appears in the body-consciousness, the finer, subtler qualities of that consciousness can be felt; at a certain point one even loses awareness of the gross body and feels as if another body has come into existence within oneself.

The first inner body to appear is the apya sharira, the liquid, fluid or, literally, the water body. It feels like the body of an adolescent boy. This fresh young body, says a Vaishnava poet, has a grace that seems to be flowing through the sky. When this water body appears, rasa chetana arises, a deep enjoyment and felicity of consciousness. The quality of suppleness also arises, and the body loses its rigidity. The mind too seems to melt and flow; as a result one can easily enter into and experience the feelings of others. This condition may be called the melting movement of the mind.

Yet even in the melting condition, the earth principle of solidity is maintained. One has a feeling as of waves playing upon a rock. It is not really so difficult to have this feeling while sitting in an asana. On the one hand the body is stable and motionless, on the other it is relaxed and at ease; the feelings of firmness and fluidity are experienced together at the same time. Note, however, that it is important to retain the feeling of firmness, for otherwise, with the appearance of the fluid body there may be a pervasion of the enjoyment in the consciousness. The Upanishad speaks of the earth as the foundation: "The earth is my footing"; this secure foundation or pillar must never be allowed to loosen. Indeed, all the qualities of the elements must be kept in control. They will appear and develop their play, but always one must remain an unmoved witness. Keep this in mind at all times.

If this witness consciousness is maintained, then after the water body, the taijasa sharira or fire body will appear. The water will, as it were, catch fire. This has been described by a vedic rishi as the appearance of fire out of water. "Whence," he says, "has appeared this child of light on the bosoms of the water maidens? This child of light is indeed the Youth!" When this fiery body appears, the mind seems to be radiant, blazing; the body seems to be filled with Yoga-fire.

The domain of the earth, the realm of form, extends up to this point. Beyond it, through the expansion of the fire body, the vayavya sharira or air body appears. As a vedic rishi says, the fire in the individual becomes universal. It is this aerial body which is the vehicle, the container, and the carrier of the cosmic consciousness. Here form becomes formless, and all that remains is an all-pervading sense of conscious energy (*shakti*). Afterward, this energy becomes still and motionless; then air is transformed into ether (*akasha*), energy into being, body into the bodiless. Patanjali calls this condition *mahavideha dharana*; in it the mind is fixed in the ether and there is no awareness of body.

This, then, is a rough sketch of an all-extensive dharana. It will be seen that its real object is to transform the microcosmic into the macrocosmic body. Our body is composed of the five elements, but they do not exist there in their pure form. Not only are they intermingled with one another but they are constantly at war, ever clashing and struggling. And due to this clash and struggle, our vital energy (*prana*) is diminished and enfeebled; then disease, decay, and death come to visit us. The yogins of India have been trying for thousands of years to conquer these maladies of the life-force through a discipline aimed at attaining a state beyond decay and death, not only in the consciousness but in the vital and physical nature as well. Many names have been given to this discipline. The Upanishad in one place calls it the practice of dhatuprasad, the clarifying of the elemental substance of the being. In another place it refers to the practice of filling the body with Yoga-fire; this discipline is even greater than that of dhatuprasad because in practicing it one must not only follow the lines of nature (*prakriti*) but have an acute discriminative knowledge of the Self (*purusha*). Patanjali goes further still in speaking of the practice of bhutajaya, the mastery or conquest of the elemental substance through the full awakening of the discriminative knowledge of the Self, leading to the mastery of the five elemental qualities. This discipline is very difficult, but its results are more lasting.

Through all these disciplines, yogins have tried to give practical shape to the possibility of immortality in the physical body. Many yogins, by mastering the etheric element, have been able to establish themselves in the mahavideha dharana in which the mind is fixed outside the body and functions from there. It is also possible, by universalizing the consciousness, to establish oneself in the fire body; but to establish oneself permanently in the water body or in the rocklike stability of the earth body has thus far proven impossible.

Let us end our discussion of dharana at this point. The concept has many other subtle variations, but we need not enlarge this work by delving into them. One thing alone must be kept in mind: the whole object of dharana is to awaken the body-consciousness and illumine it. The process begins with pratyahara, the drawing in of the mind and senses; actually, this practice has two movements or rhythms, to withdraw inward and to expand outward. Both must be mastered in order to make the practice complete and perfect. When one practices expansion outward, one arrives at a feeling of imperturbable peace; the impartial attitude of a witness develops toward the world. This is the course followed by the vedantins, and through it one can even get beyond the feeling of death. But when one has to deal with the physical elements, which is necessary if we would realize life as full of power and delight—then one must also practice inner dharana, fixing the mind within the body. For if one does not draw the world and one's experience of it into oneself, draw them deeply into one's being, how can one possibly experience the Self in All and All in the Self? Only when each contact with outer existence resonates inwardly in the spinal channel (*sushumna*) can one truly become one with others. The practice of inner fixation is therefore indispensable.

The Brahman is not only spread out in the Infinite; He is also gathered in the individual Self (*jiva*). As He is greater than the greatest, so is He smaller than the smallest. This is why one ought to practice dharana within the body as well as outside it. Only when the two have been harmonized can the practice of dharana be said to be perfect. It is the unification of the microcosm with the macrocosm.

Chapter 7

Dhyana Yoga

The Three Limbs

After dharana, fixing the mind, the next step is dhyana, meditation, in which there is a prolonged absorption in the object of one's contemplation. Actually, the practice of dhyana has already begun with that of dharana, and so it is said that as dharana deepens it turns into dhyana. Indeed, all the limbs of Yoga are interconnected; it is only for convenience of understanding that we arrange and analyze them in a particular pattern; it helps us to observe the characteristics of the various limbs and thus to regulate our practice.

Regarding the character of dhyana, Patanjali says, "There where the perceptions of the mind become continuous is dhyana" (*tatra pratyayakatanata dhyanam*). "There" (*tatra*) refers to the region where the mind has been fixed through dharana—for instance, in the heart, between the eyebrows, at the crown of the head, in the spinal channel, or outside the body in the ether. One feels then, while moving, walking, sitting, lying, talking, or working, that one's true abode is the center in which one is fixed: "I am actually there." "Pratyaya" refers to the perceptions of the mind. The mind (*chitta*) in its natural state is like an expanse of pure light, but as soon as it comes into contact with objects, waves arise in it, as ripples arise on a pond that has been blown by the wind. These rising waves are the chittavrittis, the modifications, movements, activities of the mind. But beneath these movements, the expanse of mind remains as still as always. Ordinarily, however, we are unaware of this; for though the mind is the cause and its activities the effects, our minds are not aware of the cause at the same time as they are aware of the effects; and for this reason we are constantly being thrown outward. But once we have mastered dharana and are able to fix our mind within, an awareness of the cause comes easily, and a feeling of clear peace fills out inner being with an immutable sense of repose. Then we are able to remain in a state of full awareness, an awareness that is not lost even when we are drawn outward.

Due to the impact of winds from without, waves are forever rising on the waters of the mind. But how long does a wave last? Not even a few seconds. Consequently, the sense-bound, outward-looking mind is ever bouncing from one object to another. But during this activity the discriminative intelligence (*buddhi*), due to its interest in the process, tries to bring some kind of regularity and coherence to it. We call this mental attentiveness. Through it the mind is concentrated and the waves are arranged in a somewhat orderly way; even so, they do not cease from rising and falling, but at least the mind becomes interiorized to an extent.

Through attention, then, the ingathered mind tries to grab hold of its object, and by doing so a degree of regularity is brought to its movements (*vrittis*). This naturally happens by focusing on an object. In this process, however, an awareness of the subject, the Self or I, is secondary; but so long as an awareness of the subject is not gained, the mind cannot be said to be fully interiorized. Nevertheless, as the mind is drawn inward by concentration on an object, there occurs a progressive regularization of its movements; and with increasing interiorization, these mental movements become more and more regular and persist for longer and longer periods of time. The result is a mind which is ekatanata: continuous, even, unbroken in the flow of its movements.

In the ordinary mind, we find that this continuous flow is virtually absent in the waking state of consciousness (*jagrat*); such is the case too in the dream state (*svapna*). It is only in the sleep state (*sushupti*) that the continuity of mental flow is at is maximum, though in that state the mental movements take place in an objectless manner and the self-consciousness too is veiled. Still, in this deep-sleep state, a great clue to Yoga is hidden. For if we can develop the sleep-state experience and bring it into our waking consciousness, or if we can bring the clarity of the waking consciousness into the sleep state, we shall then be able to grasp the fundamental key to the continuous flow of the mind's movements.

Let us try to understand this through a little more analysis. On the plane of nature, our consciousness is able to maintain itself only through constant dispersion, through an absence of continuity in mental activity. This is why we feel bored when life becomes monotonous. If the same thing occurs again and again, our consciousness droops. But this drooping is actually a return of the mind to its source. It is a kind of inner ekatanata or unbroken mental flow. There is, however, no witness to this continuous flow: as soon as I droop, I fall off to sleep and no longer exist. But we do not wish to cease to exist, we do not want to be finished off in this way; we want to remain awake—in other words we want to remain outward-turned. For time hangs heavy on our heads when we are deprived of the chance to stay awake and alert by constantly responding to external stimuli.

The yogin, on the contrary, seeks just the opposite condition. He would rather be asleep to the world without and awake to the world within. This is why, incidentally, it is advantageous to yogic life if there are relatively few causes for distraction from the outer world, and one's daily living is kept simple and well-ordered. From time immemorial this has been the ideal of life in this country, and as a result the yogic life has fully flowered here. Unless the complications of one's outer life are reduced, Yoga cannot progress smoothly. To maintain a yogic attitude even on the battlefield is a distant goal, and it can be attained only after long practice. As an ideal it sounds very fine, but remember, one cannot leap to the top of a tree all in one bound; one has to climb up branch by branch and gradually get there.

When an ordinary person receives a severe jolt and is inwardly excited by it, it has the effect of waking him up within. If the cause of excitation is undesirable, something one would like to avoid but cannot, this inner awakening is an affliction. But if the exciting thing is enjoyable, the awakening is a pleasure. Pain and restlessness are associated with suffering (*duhkham*), as expansion and peace of mind are associated with happiness (*sukham*). A happy mind naturally spreads itself out like a radiating light—a condition helpful to Yoga. This is why contentment (*santosha*) has always been regarded as an integral part of Yoga. To remain satisfied with whatever comes to one is an aid to attaining peace of mind.

It should be noted, however, that this contentment must not depend on outer things. If you make your contentment depend on externals, you are inviting sorrow and suffering its wake; for if your contentment depends on an outward object, then when it is withdrawn sadness will follow inevitably. Happiness is possible, in that case, only by obtaining the thing desired; its absence can only result in unhappiness. Therefore you must try to be happy, as far as possible, without depending on any outer object, but relying solely on yourself. One way to do this is to go within yourself when you come into contact with something pleasant; instead of focusing your attention on an outer object, try to perceive the pleasurable movement as something occurring *within* you.

An example will make this clearer. It is an accepted fact that tasting good food is enjoyable. But really the sense of enjoyment is not in the thing eaten, but in yourself. If your body or mind were unwell, you would not enjoy the food even if it were tasty. Thus, while tasting something pleasant, if you remember that the pleasure of the taste is not in the food but in yourself, you will not have to eat a great deal in order to prolong the pleasure. The outward thing—the food—is simply a means of giving pleasure; the real current of pleasure is flowing within you. In this way, self-restraint and refinement of taste will develop even in your enjoyment of things; you will feel ashamed to enjoy things as would a greedy man.

We can see that this practice belongs to pratyahara, the withdrawal of the mind and senses from outer objects. The fact is that until pratyahara becomes natural the mind cannot achieve the meditative state. A poet says, "A little touch, a fragment heard—with this alone I weave in mind my springtime moonlit night." Is this not a beautiful description of an indrawn mind? A little touch fills one's heart to overflowing; an inner sea of sweetness rises up. We find here on the one hand a sign of deep love and on the other a meditative mind. But unless one's being becomes clear as crystal, this does not happen. As I have mentioned before, the being is clarified through dharana.

Let me now say something else. Unless one has a meditative mood, meditation does not come easily or naturally. By meditation (*dhyana*) is meant making the movement of the mind one-pointed (*ekatana*) for a time. But in order to do this, it is necessary to maintain an atmosphere conducive to meditation throughout the whole day. When I meditate, I come deeply and intensely into contact with my chosen Object of meditation, my Beloved, my Ishta. I meet Him exclusively in solitude. But at other times? Even then the mind must be kept on the Ishta. Mahaprabhu has given a beautiful example. A wanton woman, though busy with her housework during the day, all the while savors in her mind the prospect of union with her paramour. In the same way you must carry in yourself a feeling of closeness with the Object of your love, so that remembrance of the loved One takes possession of your mind like an intoxication. This spell of intoxication is the meditative mood, and only when this mood is continually kept in mind can your meditation become deep and intense for any length of time. Again, this mood must linger in the mind even after the meditation has ended, thus deepening further the meditative mood.

As I meet Him in solitude, so I also meet Him in the multitude. Thus does meditation become a sovereign law, a natural function (*dharma*) of the mind.

To create an atmosphere conducive to meditation, a few things are necessary. You must make your lifestyle simple and disciplined, so that there is no unnecessary cause for restlessness or dispersion of the mind. You must develop the habit of remaining satisfied with whatever comes to you, so that your mind remains filled with a radiant gladness. You must keep a watchful eye on what happens in your mind when it comes into contact with external objects, so that this awareness of objects may be transformed into an awareness of self. And always you must cultivate a continuous stream of meditativeness, so that the mind never forgets its chosen object of seeking. To these disciplines, one more may be added—control of speech. Shankara says that restraint of speech is the first door to liberation. One who babbles all the time has hardly any chance of succeeding in meditation. This restraint of speech can be achieved through ajapa japa, the automatic repetition of a mantra in consonance with the breathing.

Next it is necessary to unite these three together: pratyahara, dharana, and dhyana—the drawing in of the mind and senses, the fixing of the mind at a single place, and meditation, one-pointed absorption of the mind for some length of time on the object of its concentration. Pratyahara is the natural inwardness of the mind. We ought not to run after things for the happiness they seem to bring us, but rather draw into the depths of our soul the feeling (*bhava*) awakened through contact with them. And then too, there ought to be a little love; whether it be love for nature, love for mankind, love for an individual or love for an ideal, there ought to be some love. Love is the mind's movement of delight (*ananda*), and by this movement alone the mind can become meditative. But in loving, try to separate the object of your love from the delight that comes from loving; in other words, try to transform the outer object of your love into an inner emotional condition (*bhava*) and get accustomed to savoring its essence. Then your mind, instead of turning outward towards the object, will rather turn inward toward its own state of being; the external object will merely be a means of awakening the inner state. The Buddhist theory of knowledge and the Vaishnava concept of devotion both have this principle as their basis. All things perceived by the senses are only symbols of their true reality. That which is loved is not actually outside you, but within; its material form is only a shadow, its true body is its spiritual form.

Whatever is pleasant (*preyas*) should thus be associated with what is good (*shreyas*). All good is united with a Supreme Good, and it is He who is your chosen One, your Ishta. He is the Good beyond all good; all that is good and pleasing is but His manifest becoming. The Cause is He, His becomings are only the effects; one must go beyond the effects to reach the Cause. This causal knowledge must be brought into bold relief in the consciousness. It is He alone, the One, who has become all these many forms. This is deductive knowledge and it must be firmly grasped in the inner perception; otherwise it is not possible to securely establish the inductive movement of pratyahara in the mind. Even if it is easy to withdraw the mind from the pleaṣant, it is not so easy to withdraw it from the unpleasant. But once the deductive knowledge has become rooted in you, you can taste the delight of His presence in both the pleasant and the unpleasant. This enables the mind to become free of all fear and thus removes a great source of mental obstruction. Keeping the causal knowledge in the background, the Ishta must be awakened and fixed in one spot, either within the body or outside it. This is the adding of dharana to pratyahara. The aim of dharana within the body is to spiritualize the body-consciousness; the aim of dharana outside the body is to spiritualize one's sense of spatial consciousness. It is an indispensable step for dhyana, meditation.

Of the nature-parts of the being, the body is the most stable, and of course it occupies space. Thus there is a connection between body-consciousness and spatial consciousness, between one's awareness or sensation of the body and one's awareness or sensation of space. Both these sensations must be clarified—made clear and pure—through mental conceptualization and reflection (*bhavana*); when this is done the body-consciousness becomes clear and light, full of sattva. If one then centers one's feeling (*bhava*) inside the body, the body-consciousness in addition becomes solid and stable. Again, since the body-sensation is such an intimate one, by concentrating one's inner feeling on it, that feeling itself will be more intimately and profoundly experienced. Then it is possible to extend the feeling beyond the body and experience it as pervading all space, though at the beginning this experience is difficult to sustain for long. In any event one can see that by first practicing fixation of the consciousness inside the body, it is then comparatively easy to fix it outside. That is why in this country so much stress has been laid on the discipline of the physical body. Through asana and pranayama, the body's stiffness and rigidity are broken down and the qualities of stillness and stability are developed in it; the body then becomes light and clear and blissful. In such an enlightened, blissful body, the fixation of consciousness in an indrawn condition becomes easy; then taking hold of this happy state of the body, a continuous, unbroken flow of mind comes about effortlessly, making one's meditation deep and absorbing.

This is the fundamental idea underlying the practice of Dhyana Yoga. The body becomes light and yet remains solid, the life-force is freed from its customary restraints, the mind is turned inward. Then, and only then, can the flow of mental perception become even and continuous. This is a basic principle of yogic practice.

Next we shall take up the idea of the even flow of mind from the standpoint of mental perception (*pratyaya*).

Chapter 8

Samadhi Yoga

Bhava and Bhavana

The awareness that arises in the mind when it comes into contact with an object is called *pratyaya*, mental perception. The object may either be within us or outside us. We know external objects through the senses, internal objects through the mind. When the senses come in contact with an external object, we feel a sensation in ourselves; in the language of Yoga, the substance of our self or consciousness undergoes modification. The fact is that when our self-substance comes in contact with a not-self substance, the self-substance tries to assimilate the substance that is not-self. This is why the yogins and the Upanishadic seers have compared knowing to eating. As the body is nourished by eating, the mind is nourished by taking in objects through the senses. And just as in eating there are differences in taste, so there are differences in the mind's reception of objects. Not every object is helpful to everyone. The mind is pleased when it finds an object congenial to it, but what is not congenial is considered unpleasant. What is congenial or uncongenial to a particular person is determined by his past habits and mental impressions (*samskaras*). Naturally, what is congenial and therefore pleasing to the mind will hold its interest for a longer period than what is not. For this reason the contemplation of an object pleasing to the mind is conducive to achieving continuous flow (*ekatanata*) of mental perception. Patanjali, while offering various methods for stopping the activity of the mind, ultimately suggests that mental movements most easily subside when the mind meditates on an object for which it has a natural predilection.

Here let me note something else on this point. The conscious awareness of movements in the mind and the cessation of those movements are both a part of Yoga, for from both of these a kind of absorption, loss of self, can result. This is the effect and the ultimate aim of meditation (*dhyana*); it leads to a total absorption in one's object of meditation and an identification with it—to samadhi. But the yogins say that samadhi is an inherent quality of mind, and this means that samadhi can be attained in all the states of mind.

These states or planes of mind (*chittabhumi*) are five: mudha, the dull or inert state; kshipta, the restless or excited state; vikshipta, the dispersed or scattered state; ekagra, the concentrated, one-pointed state; and niruddha, the arrested, stilled, motionless state. Of the five, only the last two are truly yogic states. Nevertheless, samadhi can take place in all the states of mind. Every day, when we go to sleep, the activity of mind is slowed down; sleep, we may say, is a kind of samadhi on the mudha plane. There the quality of tamas, of dullness and inertia, is prominent, and as a result the mental activities are somewhat arrested. That is why people normally have no self-awareness in the state of sleep. But if one can learn the technique of inwardly remaining awake during sleep, it is possible to retain one's self-awareness. We shall come to this later. In point of fact, we find that when a person wakes up from sleep, he is still the same person; there has been no change in his nature.

Similarly, a kind of self-forgetful absorption can be experienced during a period of intense rajasic excitement. This is the samadhi of the restless state of mind, kshipta. But in this state also there is normally no self-awareness.

Again there is the samadhi of the dispersed state of mind, vikshipta. It can occur when one becomes fully absorbed in an emotional mood (*bhava*) while dwelling upon some thought or sentiment. This kind of self-loss may be observed in the philosopher, the scientist, the thinker, or the poet who sometimes becomes temporarily lost to himself. In this case, the qualities of tamas and rajas have been depressed and the quality of sattva has arisen. It is sattva that makes the mind clear and bright, a condition that is obviously favorable to Yoga; but even this sattvic state may not lead to self-knowledge. For though in the dispersed state, the mind's activities may become concentrated or arrested for a time during the spell of self-absorbed intoxication, afterwards rajasic restlessness or tamasic dullness will overtake it again. Aided by sattva, the mind is on the verge of reaching the self, but it does not make contact; the mind has caught a glimpse of pure consciousness and being, but it has not been able to recognize and take hold of it.

The point to note here is that without the knowledge gained through inner discrimination (*viveka-jnana*), self-realization is not possible. As I have mentioned before, objects are of two kinds, those belonging to the self and those belonging to the not-self. The not-self objects are outside you, the self-object is your own self. By your "self" I mean your pure awareness or consciousness. This self-consciousness (*atma-chaitanya*) is luminous, serene, blissful, self-immersed, turned within. All beings have consciousness, even birds and beasts and insects, but not all have self-consciousness. This consciousness of self has to be discovered through the aid of discrimination (*viveka*). I must find not the "I" that is involved in objects, but the "I" that stands apart from them and abides in itself alone. That I is my true self; it is the I of the yogin. It may be the I of the man of knowledge (*jnani*) or the man of love (*bhakta*); whichever it is, its special characteristic is a profound inner feeling of pure and uninvolved being. Such a person is a child of the Mother. His delight lies in the discrimination between what is self and not-self, and always he is detached from the entangling coils of life (*samsara*). Clear as a crystal, no taint from outside can ever stain him. But this state is not easy to achieve. Only when the movements of mind are gathered up and concentrated immovably on the single perception of the pure self-consciousness, or when they cease altogether, can the samadhi of Yoga be attained—not otherwise.

Let us return again to the object of our inner quest, the object of meditation which attracts us and is in accord with our nature. If, taking pure self-consciousness as our basis, our mental activity is directed toward an object in consonance with our inner search, there naturally arises in us a sentiment toward it, a feeling, an emotion, a bhava. When this happens, the yogins say, the quality of sattva rises in the mind. What is this emotional mood called *bhava*? It is like a luminous aura around our consciousness. But we must feel this aura as something radiating from the self-consciousness itself. In other words, the bhava, the emotional attitude arising from our contact with an object, must be turned from the object and focused on the subject, on our self-consciousness. We must experience the bhava as a quality not of the object but of the self. Only then is the bhava helpful to meditation.

This point may be illustrated with an example. Suppose you experience delight (*ananda*) at the sight of a beautiful flower. Your impulse will naturally be to prolong that delight. But if you have assumed, at the outset of the experience, that your delight is due to the flower, then to prolong the delight you will have to keep the flower alive. There are various means of doing this, and by adopting them you will be able to continue to enjoy the flower outside yourself. This kind of enjoyment is that of the sense-enjoyer (*bhogi*).

But the truth of the matter may actually be other than you have assumed. The delight you experience is not really in the flower—it is in you. The flower is merely a means by which you experience the delight of your own self. In reality the flower has bloomed not in your garden, but in your mind. What you must do then is to turn your gaze from the flower in the garden to the flower in your mind; then you will experience the pure emotion, the bhava, of the delight in itself. And to perpetuate that delight, it will not be necessary to employ a host of external measures. All that is required is to withdraw your mind from the outside and fix it within yourself. This holding (*dhriti*) of the mind is a quality of dharana, fixation. If one practices this fixing of the mind within and if one's being is clear and pure, then the flower of delight will blossom in one of the centers of consciousness (*chakras*)—in the heart center, for instance, or the eyebrow center, or the spinal channel. The gross flower will thus become a subtle flower, the subtle flower a flower of delight, and that flower of delight will be full of consciousness.

It is by this method that the sense-awareness of an object must be led step by step toward pure awareness. In the language of Yoga, this is called *samapatti*; it is the absorption of mind gained through identification with the bhava of a thing.

The yogin's delight, we have seen, lies in the enjoyment of the pure delight in the essence of the object. The technique for this kind of enjoyment has to be mastered. And that technique is not to run after the objects apprehended by the senses, but to draw into the depths of one's self-consciousness the experience and feeling received from the senses. This practice is made easier if the spinal channel (*sushumna*) is used as a passageway leading to those inner depths. In front of the breast lies the great world of activity; behind it, in the spinal cord, lies the vast, illimitable, unfathomable ocean of consciousness, motionless and peaceful. The waves of the world are hurling themselves upon the breast, breaking there and sinking down into the deep peace of the ocean within. This clue of Yoga is profoundly expressed in the image of Lord Narayana lying in eternal repose upon the many-headed serpent Sheshanaga. That serpent is the spinal cord of the universe.

Purification of the bhava, the inner mood of the mind and heart, gradually leads the yogin toward a meditative state of mind (*dhyanachitta*). This mood can easily be awakened if one gazes at some grand aspect of nature, such as the view of a valley seen from a mountaintop, the flow of a large river, a vast expanse of sea, the infinite sky, a bright sunny day. Such sights energize the mind. Weary and anxious due to the troubles of life, the mind suddenly becomes peaceful and quiet. A clarity and contentment come upon it as if, delivered from the constriction of the day's pettiness, the mind finds release in the freedom of the Vast. In such a release there is a simple and natural feeling of happiness. When it grows in the mind through contact with some aspect of nature, one can easily attain a continuous flow of mental perception.

There is something deeper at the root of this. The yogins say that for perfection in asanas, the immobile postures of the body, two things must be mastered: relaxation and expansion into the infinite. In fact, these two may be said to be fundamental to all yogic practice. In the ordinary cycle of life, we always move under stress, in a constricted and unnatural manner. When a bow is strung, there is tension on the string, a lack of rest. But when the bow is unstrung, the tension is released, the string is relaxed and at rest. In ordinary life our body, vital force, and mind are always under tension; and when the ego is strong the tension is increased. But this condition is obviously not favorable to Yoga because it begets us in restlessness and fatigue. Our environment itself creates obstacles for us; we live cramped up within four walls and walk along narrow lanes. Nowhere do we find a little elbow room to stretch ourselves. And that condition, likewise, is not favorable to Yoga, for in the yogic consciousness there is no such rigidity and constriction.

The same truth applies conversely to nature. Being in contact with the vast earth, the sublime sky, the meditative mountains, the flowing rivers, there is a tendency to loosen up, to spread out naturally, and be at ease. This tendency, this feeling is often inspired in the minds of men who come in contact with nature. Among these aspects of nature, the one most conducive to mental contemplation (*bhavana*) is the sky (*akasha*)—the daytime sky resplendent with light or the nighttime sky full of stars. When the mind spreads itself out into the infinite expanse of the sky, the two qualities of relaxation and expansion are easily realized. Such was the ancient method of vedic practice. There are also references to it in the Upanishads. Dwelling in mind upon the sky (*akasha-bhavana*), the outer sky should be brought down into the heart (*hridaya*), freeing it from rigidity and constriction. There rises then in the heart a faint illumination as of dim moonlight or of starlight. That glow gradually intensifies until it becomes the effulgence of the sun, until there shines in the heart the vishoka jyoti, the radiant sun, which is the size of a man's thumb; its light is the light of sattva, of clarity and illumination. Then, just as there is a sun in the outer sky, so there is a sun in the sky of the heart. The sun outside represents the universal Self, the sun within the individual Self. And, as the Upanishad says, both are one "The Purusha there and here, He am I."

When the mind comes in contact with nature, it becomes serene and happy—a condition helpful to meditation. This fact was known and accepted even by those yogins who believed in severing all ties with nature (*prakriti*) and arresting its activities altogether. Even though their object was to go beyond nature and plunge their minds into the depths, still, in selecting places for spiritual practice, they always advised choosing places with a calm and peaceful atmosphere. This fact is also a confirmation of a process already noted: closing my eyes, I see the calm vastness of the sky in my heart, opening them I see the same thing outside; gradually both my inner and outer worlds are filled with this tranquil vastness and always there abides in my mind the presence of the one infinite Brahman.

Nature and man, these two constitute our world. Nature is the backdrop of man. Our problem as men lies in our relationships with other men, and often we can find release from this problem only when we are able to lose ourselves in nature. But if a current of peace were flowing always through our mind, then taking our station upon that background we would be able to deal smoothly and harmoniously with our fellow men. We would see them not as something separate from nature, but as part of her light and air, mountains and rivers, plants and trees. Seeing man in the perspective of the Vast, we would no longer be so affected by his pettiness.

All this belongs properly to the dynamic side of Yoga, the Yoga that goes on in our daily activities, our sitting, moving, and working. Not all can renounce everything and go off to do Yoga in solitude; but this dynamic Yoga can be done by all. And it brings the same result that is gained by practicing the eight-limbed Yoga. Indeed, Patanjali says that by doing this dynamic Yoga (*Kriya Yoga*) the five great obstructions (*kleshas*) to consciousness are weakened, thus making easier the contemplation leading to samadhi.

A fundamental aim of Yoga is to make the mind serene, clear, luminous, and blissful. One way of doing this, as I have said, is to contemplate the sky. But this practice can be carried on effectively only when one is alone; and when one comes into contact with people again, the mind tends to lose its felicity; the sky becomes overcast. We cannot afford to neglect this aspect of things. The yogic consciousness must abide unhindered and at ease both in nature and among men. Its serenity and happiness must not be diminished anywhere, for then life and Yoga will never become one.

The way to keep the mind happy in relating to men, is to move about in the Brahman (*brahamavihara*). It includes the fourfold practice of maitri, karuna, mudita, and upeksha: friendship, compassion, joyfulness, and indifference. This concept must be elaborated a bit.

Our human life is full of opposites. They may be divided into four: the opposites of pain and pleasure and of vice and virtue. The first two belong to the field of psychology, the second two to the field of ethics. And according to the nature of the four, humanity may be divided into four categories: the happy, the unhappy, the virtuous, and the sinful. Entering into contact with these types of men, the mind experiences certain reactions. Among the ordinary ones are these: to feel envious at another man's happiness and sorrow at his suffering, or again, to feel elation due to either of them; to feel doubt and skepticism about another man's work, or envy and contempt because of it; to feel disgust or annoyance or anger upon witnessing another man's evil deed, especially if it is done to oneself!

Needless to say, none of these natural reactions are feelings of peace and happiness. Therefore, to obtain a happy and serene state of mind, the yogin must completely reverse the order of the natural reactions. The reactions favorable to creating peace and happiness of mind are: friendship (*maitri*) toward those who are happy: as one feels happy when a friend is happy, so one should feel happy when anyone is happy; to feel compassion (*karuna*) toward those who are unhappy and suffer: here there must be sympathy, but no self-delusion or loss of inner poise; to feel joyfulness (*mudita*) toward the virtuous; and to feel indifference (*upeksha*) toward the sinful (this unmoved neutral attitude is referred to in the Gita).

Through contemplation of the sky (*akasha-bhavana*), holding the image of the sky in mind and dwelling upon it, the image of the sky eventually becomes firmly imprinted on the mind; and when this happens, the mind's poise of calm wideness remains unimpaired even when one comes into contact with others. This is one way that a universal relationship with other men can be established. But there are other ways too, other types of relationship with men, which are helpful in developing serenity of mind. The Vaishnavas speak of five such relationships, or bhavas: shanta, dasya, sakhya, vatsalya, and madhura. The first is the relationship of peace with another; the others are the relationships of service, friendship, parental affection, and love. The middle three may be considered as human relationships. Knowing another to be greater than myself, I bow down to him: this is dasya, the reverential relationship of a servant; the reverence one feels toward one's parents and elders belongs to this emotional relationship or attitude, this bhava. I open my heart to someone sincerely and unreservedly, as if both of us were of one heart: this is sakhya, the relation of friendship or companionship; the relation between a husband and wife belongs to this bhava. I feel that I am nurturing someone, fostering his or her growth as a parent fosters the growth of a child: this affectionate attitude is vatsalya.

It is possible to have all three of these attitudes simultaneously and express them toward someone; it all depends on the largeness of one's mind. But with all of them, the one thing essential is that there must be no separateness or egoism in the mind, no hesitation or reservation. The heart must open and give itself. There must be a spirit of service: where there is selfish hunger, there is poverty, want, lack of feeling (*abhava*); where there is service, there is feeling (*bhava*). Even if the object of this feeling be something of nature (*prakriti*), still, if there is a spirit of service toward it, it can be a means of lifting the mind above nature to the heights of greater felicity. And if the emotion one feels is directed toward some god or a guru, this elevation of mind is even easier to achieve. Through the practice of bhava, the cultivation of beneficial emotional attitudes, absorption of the mind takes place naturally and easily because the mind is fixing itself on something already dear to it. This fostering of pure and intense inner emotion is most conducive to developing a meditative mind.

Chapter 9

Yoga

From the Outer to the Inner

We have seen that the means of lifting the mind into a state of clarity and gladness are three: first, to expand the mind into the peace and light found in certain grand aspects of nature; second, to release the mind by idealizing someone you love, turning him or her into a god; and third, to make the mind content by feeling love and friendship toward all men. The first method of practice is vedic, the second Vaishnava, the third Buddhist. Of them the vedic method is the least complex. I have already spoken about the value of contemplating the sky (*akashabhavana*), so there is no need to elaborate on it. When you study the Vedas and enter into the mysteries of vedic practice, you discover that there is no parallel in the history of spiritual endeavor to the way in which the vedic seers succeeded in awakening the universal Mother-power (*mahashakti*). We hear nowadays about the supramental descent.[1] Even the spiritual effort toward it will become easier if you succeed in grasping this vedic method of contemplating nature; otherwise the intellectual and psychological aspects of the practice will loom large and delay the realization. The discipline of the intellect belongs to the conscious self (*purusha*), and only through it can one have vision. But it is only nature (*prakriti*) that can make that vision concrete by bringing it down to the planes of intuition and sensation. That is why the vedic contemplation of nature (*prakritibhavana*) is indispensable for supramentalization. Here I am speaking symbolically; try to understand it in the deepest sense. Then you will be able to understand the mission of Savitri, the divine Mother, who came down to earth to uplift men.

The Buddhist contemplation of friendship and love for all beings (*maitribhavana*) is also indispensable for attaining a meditative mind. Of the four qualities—benevolent love and friendship (*maitri*), compassion (*karuna*), joyfulness (*mudita*), and detached indifference (*upeksha*)—the Buddha laid greatest emphasis upon the first, because once it is gained the rest follow naturally. In the Buddhist method of meditation, this fraternal kindness toward all has been recommended as one of the primary disciplines. You must think of yourself as a dynamo of inexhaustible love and benevolence, then feel that love as radiating from you and spreading out in all directions. There are days when the mind is reluctant to settle down and concentrate; if one dwells then upon this thought of universal love, the mind soon becomes buoyant and happy and concentrated of itself.

The contemplation of nature and the contemplation of benevolent love are both fairly easy because they are abstract and universal. The Vaishnava practice of bhava—the cultivation of an emotional attitude or relation—is somewhat more difficult, especially if the object of the emotion (*bhava*) is an individual. But if from the beginning you make the object of your emotion abstract and idealize it, the difficulty is resolved. An example is Sri Ramakrishna, who developed the attitude of a child who loves his mother (*maitribhava*) and directed his love toward the goddess Bhavatarini. But if that feeling of love for one's mother is directed toward a woman, the matter is not so simple! Even for Ramakrishna it was not simple; at one point in his practice the Brahmani was his mother-preceptor, but finally he had to go beyond her.

Here we can see both the advantage and the disadvantage of guruvada, the practice of making a human guru into the supreme object of one's love and devotion. By devoting oneself to the guru, there may take place a general blossoming of that particular emotional relationship (*bhava*); but it will not be pure unless one has been able to give up attachment. Just as in the ordinary life of ignorance one gets tied down to family and friends, so in the larger life of ignorance one can get tied down through attachment to guru, ashram, and all the rest thrown in. This is why I repeatedly warn, in regard to guruvada, that you should fix your sight not upon the human guru, but on the consciousness in him. Do not make the guru bigger than God himself. To realize God is the supreme object, after all; the guru is a means to that end.

You should now be able to understand why the practice of bhava is helpful to attaining a meditative state of mind. Yet there is the difficulty I have just pointed out. How to overcome it? We shall know the answer when we discuss the technique of meditation. I come to that now.

First, let me mention some fundamental principles of meditation (*dhyana*).

Already I have discussed the subject from various angles because when one looks at a thing from several perspectives the mind can grasp its truth more firmly and deeply. By now you ought to have a fairly clear understanding of these three limbs of Yoga: asana, steadily held posture; pranayama, regulation of the breath and vital force; and pratyahara, the indrawing of the mind and senses. The purpose of these limbs is to create stability, clarity, and inwardness of mind, life, and body. They may be practiced at certain times of the day, especially at the junctures of sunrise and sunset, but the feeling gained by them has to be maintained throughout the day in all your movements and activities.

A full mastery of asana has been achieved not simply when you are able to sit quietly in one place, but when in all your movements there is harmony, balance, and rhythm, as in the case of soldiers who have perfectly mastered their marching drills. You must observe whether the body movements you make in the course of the day are rhythmical. Some races possess this quality naturally—the Japanese, for instance. In our country there is a similar grace among our women when they serve food. In the physical education program at Pondicherry, much stress has been laid upon making the movements of the body graceful and rhythmical. This too is the practice of asana—its dynamic side. You should keep this in mind and try to develop this quality. We in India are presently so undisciplined in our movement, speech, and behavior—I wonder how we can boast of being a race of yogis. It is precisely this drawback which prevents Yoga from establishing the right regulating rhythm (*ritam*) in our life; instead we flee from life, go off and hide in a cave, and consider this to be the only path of Yoga.

Pranayama, too, has a natural rhythm which goes along with dynamic asana. When the movement of your limbs is rhythmical, you will observe that your breathing is also rhythmical. But to achieve this condition, you have to devote some attention to it. The kind of deep and rhythmic breathing that takes place during sleep should also occur in the waking state. It is not such a difficult thing, but it has to be practiced, and by doing so you can make your physiological functions rhythmic. A stableness and depth will come to your mind, you will not get upset upon receiving a shock or blow, and even in a crisis you will have the power to take an immediate decision. These are the very characteristics of the true personality. I maintain that Yoga is not only meant to stop the mind's chaotic activity but also to develop the personality and to perfect life. Indeed, Yoga is the only scientific way to bring out the Person in you.

You should now be able to see that even the outer limbs of Yoga can be adapted to daily life. And if you can do it, you will be able to do all your work in the state of Yoga—"fixed in Yoga," as the Gita says. Yoga will bring grace and beauty to your life.

From the outer, let us move to the inner. The three inner limbs of Yoga are dharana, the stationing of the mind at one spot; dhyana, meditation, the continuous absorption of the mind in the object of its concentration; and samadhi, the complete immersion (identification) of the mind in that object. The three are inseparably linked; from dharana to samadhi is one continuous process. And the purpose of that process, as I have stated, is the assimilation of the object, just as one assimilates the food one eats.

By mastering the outer disciplines of Yoga, the whole being is pervaded by a light, clear, luminous, and expansive feeling. The next step is to concentrate that feeling in one of the centers of consciousness (*chakras*), which is the purpose of dharana. It may be helpful if a luminous image is visualized in the center. In the heart, for example, visualize the sun of consciousness in the forehead, the moon between the eyebrows, a star at the crown of the head, a moonlit sea in the spinal cord, a lightning bolt. The region where you fix your attention is your natural dwelling place, your home; the whole universe has to be gathered up there. Suppose you are practicing dharana in the center between the eyebrows. Gradually you will come to be stationed in that center, as if you were always sinking into it. Eventually there will not even be this feeling of sinking in, of plunging inside; only a deep, clear, expansive feeling will remain. To abide always in that condition is to be fixed in Yoga.

Next, while stationed in that state, you will have to practice two things: self-control of the will and self-control of the emotions. Will arises in you from within, emotion enters from without. You have to establish such a control and mastery of them that they are unable to throw you out of your yogic poise. The first thing to remember is that you must not allow any will to arise in you. Will nothing. These days it is a great obsession with us to do good for the world. This notion has to be eliminated completely. Yes, even this must be given up. Before you ever thought of doing good for the world, He to whom the whole world belongs must surely have thought of it and surely due to His Truth-Will, the world is moving toward its good. Is it not overdoing it a bit on your part to suddenly be so concerned about it? Does this mean that you will do nothing? Of course not. But before doing, you ought to learn to recognize His Will and accept it.

Another point. You have read in the book *Yogic Sadhan* "Learn to distinguish between will and desire." Desire, with us, is in fact a kind of restlessness; it is, in the language of Samkhya, a quality of tamas and rajas, dull obscurity and feverish activity. Far greater than these is the will of pure sattva, the quality of harmony and light. That will is the will of pure existence. He wills what IS. He said, "Let there be Light," and there was Light, because He *is* the Light. In the same way, you can only be your own self. Therefore, first know yourself. Then your self-knowledge will naturally blossom forth into a wealth of creativity. You will come to realize that whether you notice it or not, He through His divine Will moves all that goes on in the world, just as the light of the sun keeps all things moving in the world. To know that Will and to feel yourself to be its instrument, that much is your concern. To give a shattering blow, through an intense force of will, to the dull inertia of incontinence to carry all the suffering of the world in your breast to suffer on the cross—yes, there is a truth in these things, but even so, they belong to the realm of ignorance. All your dramatic battling and suffering is nothing but a farce unless you know in the depths of your being that you are only willing what IS, and unless that knowledge and silence keep you always unperturbed. Even here, this rule should be applied: three-fourths of your being should remain gathered inside you, only one-fourth should be put out into feeling and action. Whose destiny is it, after all, to undergo the divine suffering? Only the Son of God. First become a daughter of the Light. Then feel "I am that I am." Then will.

I have said enough now about the will to do good for the world. There is another kind of will that is concerned with worldly gain, with getting and having—what the Scriptures call *yogakshema*. This kind of will makes you think about getting and having the things which may bring you well-being and happiness. Needless to say, this kind of will must also be given up. What will happen will happen. Why worry about it, why be concerned? This is an obvious point and I will not elaborate upon it.

There is yet a third kind of will. It is the will behind our day-to-day activities, the will to make things happen in a certain way. Here one must take a detached and balanced attitude; one must be an onlooker. Do not place undue emphasis on getting anything. You have chalked out a program in broad outline according to how you foresee things. But suppose events take a different turn and go in a different direction? Well, let them go. Take it calmly. Everything is but a play, after all. Again and again, come back to your yogic center. If you do this you will find that inwardly you are becoming well organized and orderly. The truth-will in you is in fact taking shape, though it may be following a somewhat circuitous course. But what of it? Unerringly the stream flows down to the sea, and so it is with inner things. Outwardly, too, you will notice that after a time your outer world is getting arranged in conformity with the truth-will in you. This only happens somewhat later, but all the same it does happen. His artistry is at work both on your inner and outer worlds, and it brings them together. He wants you to blossom like a flower. If you get impatient, it only delays His action.

We come then to the following advice. Remain inwardly still and unmoved, stationed at the center between the eyebrows. Do not allow any will to arise in the mind. Wait for the command to do something; it will come either from within or without. You have only to carry out that command. When the work is over, return to your spot at the center of the forehead, just as an office boy returns to his stool after completing his allotted task. Shankaracharya has beautifully expressed this idea in one of his sayings: "No desire, no effort; abide always in yourself."

Another necessity is to still the emotions. The Gita says that one must be without duality, without conflict. Blows may fall on you from outside, but you will not get upset. Suffering may come, but you will not get worried or anxious. Pleasure may also come, but you will not be attracted by it. Always remember it is pleasure that corrupts us and plays the greatest havoc with our lives. There is even a fiery kind of pleasure which is derived from spiritual fervor, but it too brings disaster in the end. All this excitement and commotion over the guru. Then after a few days it collapses, like a punctured balloon. The euphoria fails to stay. Yet often we indulge in this kind of excitement, thinking it to be good—that is why I am making special note of it. As with the obsession about doing good for the world, so with this unseemly hullabaloo over the guru; in both cases it is ignorance that has come to deceive us by wearing the mask of knowledge. So beware, seeker, beware.

The two austerities, the two types of self-control I am speaking of are beautifully summed up by Sri Krishna in a verse of the Gita: "Free from dualities, ever based in the true being, above getting and having, possessed of the self." There will be no duality of emotion in you, no tension between will and effort always you will remain stationed in your unmoving center; and you will be self-possessed. Such is the perfect mastery of dharana in daily life. It implies that you will keep hold of yourself, remain centered in yourself in all the movements of life. You can see that I am placing great emphasis on the practical, dynamic processes of Yoga. Practice in seclusion by all means; undoubtedly you will do it. But until Yoga is brought down to the level of daily life, it is not an integral Yoga.

Let us suppose that your present level of attainment is something like this: You have developed a harmonious rhythm in all your movements. The regulation of your breathing has become easy and natural for you. Your mind, dwelling within, is full of gladness. You have learned to remain centered in a state of Yoga by fixing the mind in one of the subtle centers of your body. (If the mind is fixed outside the body, it should be in the center just above the head, in the Void; this results in an overhead consciousness.) If all these conditions have become natural to you even in your common daily movements, then the Yoga of meditation will be easy and fruitful for you.

Now let me speak about meditation (*dhyana*). First we must understand what the term *samyama* means in the language of Patanjali. It is the perfect self-control by which, through concentration upon an object, one becomes aware of all that is in the object, its meaning, content, essence. Patanjali states that dharana, dhyana, and samadhi together constitute samyama; that is, when the mind is fixed on an object and becomes absorbed in it to the point of total immersion and identification, that is samyama: one enters the object and becomes aware of its content in a knowledge by identity. Patanjali says further that the mastery of samyama leads to spiritual illumination, to the light of knowledge (*prajna*). We shall again speak of samyama when we discuss his aphorism on samadhi. Here I wish to draw your attention especially to this point: although dharana, dhyana, and samadhi are considered as separate limbs of the Yoga, in fact they constitute a single inseparable whole.

Dhyana, absorbed one-pointed meditation, is not possible unless, through dharana, an awareness of the self has been awakened; this is an important point to remember. This awakened feeling of one's self is in fact the subtle but clear perception of the body-consciousness (*deha-bodha*). Whether at the center or the periphery of the body-consciousness, a clear feeling of stability and stillness has to be experienced; this is the central idea of dharana.

The awareness of self that is awakened through dharana provides the background of dhyana; this too is a very important point. Samadhi is the result of dhyana, and prajna is the result of samadhi—this we know well. But if we try to meditate without first preparing our instrument, our vessel (*adhara*) of mind, life, and body, our meditation becomes merely a kind of wrestling. Hints about preparing the instrument have already been given in discussing the outer limbs of asana, pranayama, and pratyahara. Naturally they presuppose a certain amount of effort, and indeed it is because of this effort that they are called outer limbs. As for the inner limbs, the practice must be effortless, the attainment of total absorption easy, the radiation of knowledge spontaneous and natural. What are the signs that we are ready? When the endeavor to interiorize the mind has become easy and natural, and when a feeling of clarity and stillness pervades the body-consciousness, then the meditative state of mind is there.

The logicians say that to gain knowledge of a thing, it is first necessary to perfect the means by which that knowledge is acquired. The final word of all knowledge is knowledge by identity, in which there is no longer any separation between knowledge and knower, between what I am trying to know and myself. This knowledge cannot be gained by the mind or senses alone, but only by the whole being, and this is possible only when the self-being, the self who essentially I am, is made empty. But this is the very opposite of our ordinary way of knowing things! When we try to know an object through the eye, we observe it minutely, we intensify the power of our eye and concentrate our sight. This is one-pointedness (*ekagrata*), and to so restrict our field of knowledge by mental concentration is undoubtedly a part of yogic knowledge.

Just behind this one-pointed vision, however, there must also be the vast and sublime background of the knower-consciousness. An effortless expansion of our consciousness is needed; we must learn to spread ourselves out into a skylike expanse of peace and tranquility, and then, on the background of that expanse, to allow the knowledge of our object of concentration to rise up of itself. It is a double movement of concentration and expansion. There must be a concentration on the object of knowledge, but at the same time there must be in the knower a calm and motionless sense of expansion. If these two aspects are not combined and balanced, our meditation will not be smooth and effortless. Let me give an image of this. Just as the evening star appears at sunset in the wide and peaceful sky, so the object of our concentration reveals itself in a wide and peaceful mind. This is the ideal of meditation.

The mind may decide upon an object of meditation, but let us remember that it is only an intense and one-pointed concentration of mind which results in true meditation. This one-pointed concentration is the outgoing movement (*pravritti*) of the mind; behind it there should also be an ingoing movement (*nivritti*). The outward movement is the mind's motion, the inward movement its immobility. The secret of effortless meditation is to establish a harmony between the two.

I am not sure if I have made this point clear enough yet. Normally we do not look at meditation in this way; I have tried to speak of it from several angles, so that you may have a clear idea of it. Let me give another example to illustrate what I mean. Suppose you are meditating on a particular deity. You look at it and then close your eyes, trying to see that outer image in your mind. We call this meditation. At first you can see nothing when you close your eyes, but gradually, by repeatedly invoking the memory of the image, you are to awaken in yourself an inner form of the external image. After prolonged effort, it may even happen that the form of the one you worship appears in your heart. At first this form reveals itself only for an instant and then vanishes, but gradually it becomes stationary. Then, closing your eyes, you are able to see it for quite a long time in the heart; the fixed image remains for longer and longer periods. Finally, your mind becomes so totally absorbed in the image that no other image remains in your mind. It seems so simple, but in fact it is not.

Note

1. The term "supramental" is that of Sri Aurobindo; by it he means the highest divine Truth, Consciousness, and Power operative in the universe.

Chapter 10

Yoga with a Support

We are discussing dhyana, meditation. I have said that unless the meditative mood has been awakened, meditation cannot be smooth and effortless. If we wish to absorb our mind in a certain object at a particular time of day, we must cultivate, throughout the day, a readiness and eagerness for it. During the day I shall work and walk and talk, but all the while my mind will cherish a remembrance of its chosen object of meditation (*ishta*); this is the proper attitude. Ramakrishna used to give the example of a toothache which remains in the mind, constant and unforgotten, amid all activities.

It is not so difficult, really, to keep alive this remembrance of one's object of contemplation. The consciousness has two parts, mind (*chitta*) and awareness (*bodha*). We have discussed what the mind is and how great an obstacle its restlessness is on the spiritual path. We have seen how strenuous an effort is required to remove that restlessness and fix the mind on an object. We usually call this the effort of meditation. But if we try to meditate not with the mind, but with the awareness, the effort becomes easier.

The mind works through some wave, modification, movement (*vritti*), the awareness through some emotional state (*bhava*). The mental movements are distinct, separate, and turned outward; the emotional mood is continuous, one-pointed, and turned inward. Suppose I am angry with someone. This anger is an emotional state, its effect pervades my whole body. But accompanying the emotion are wave after wave of bad thoughts; these thought-waves are the fluctuating movements (*vrittis*) of the mind. The mental movements, then, are restless, whereas the emotional mood is comparatively settled and stable. The emotion of anger persists, and with it a sort of burning sensation smolders in the heart. The thoughts, however, are never stable; they continually cast themselves forth in all directions. When the emotional state expresses itself outwardly, the mind is scattered to the winds in the form of diverse thoughts.

We know that meditation means one-pointedness of mind. Now when we meditate, upon what shall we concentrate—on an object of the emotion or of the mental activity? The mind's restless, dissipating activity takes place on its surface. Normally, in our effort to quiet the mind, we at once try to grab hold of that activity and stifle it. This a mistake. The complaint is often heard, "When I sit for meditation, my mind won't settle down; it wanders off in all directions and pursues whatever useless thought invades it." But in truth, that is not the mind's defect—it is its natural function. The mind is nothing but an office boy forever running around doing odd jobs. It runs about at the command of the intelligence (*buddhi*) or the emotion (*bhava*) in order to bring back this or that item to its master. Until the intellect or emotion is satisfied, it is bound to run about, but as soon as its master is satisfied its work is over.

We forget this essential truth each time that we forcibly try to restrain the mind as it scurries about. I have taken my seat for meditation, but do I have some feeling (*bhava*) in me, some tenderness, kindness, love? No—my love is for outer things. All day long I am engrossed in them, for in them I find my pleasure. My inner feeling, therefore, is dependent on outer things for support. And since my mind is nothing but a servant of my feeling, what else can it do but think about things? There is no love, no yearning in me. Forcibly, out of a sense of duty, I seat my body in my place of meditation, then command my mind "All right, now keep quiet!" Maybe I even perform some exercises to quiet it. But really, as long as the inner feeling has not been awakened, why should my mind suddenly become quiet merely because of a verbal order?

The question arises, then: How to evoke the inner feeling, the emotion, the bhava? Unfortunately, there is no simple answer. A popular adage says "Beauty comes forth by polishing and cleaning, love by capturing and compelling." But that will not do here. If the time is not ripe, the mind and heart simply will not abandon worldly things in order to seek Him. Moreover, this seeking is not very strong or well defined at the beginning. This fact is nicely illustrated by an analogy given in the Bhagavata. There is light within a log of wood, but it is not manifest. Brought into contact with fire, the log ignites, but at first there is much smoke and little fire. Only when the smoke is dispelled does the fire leap forth and with it light. In the same way, only when the pure light of sattva emerges does one have the vision of the Brahman.

The period of smoke is excruciating for the seeker, but it is inevitable, it is bound to come. We have spoken before about the five planes or states of mind. In the first state, the dull and stupid mind is sunk in tamas, whose quality is inertia and obscurity. To bring out of that tamasic darkness the light of sattva, it is necessary to pass through the state of rajas, with its excitement and activity, its effort and struggle. Only when the spell of rajas is ended does the sattvic condition of mind emerge, and for that condition to be stabilized an even longer time is needed. Sattva is the quality of light, harmony, happiness and peace. Only when the sattva in a being has become pure can the mind attain to a state of one-pointedness. Then the remembrance of one's object of seeking (*ishta*) will possess the mind like an intoxication, and in that state the mind will cease from movement, at least for a time. There will be then, as it were, a rowing movement in which there is a plying back and forth between the state of one-pointedness (*ekagrata*) and that of cessation (*nirodha*) of mental activity. Little by little, a habit of cessation will imprint itself in the mind, creating a vast formless and colorless backdrop and upon its bosom light will play.

To rise from the tamasic state of mind to that of pure sattva, one must pass through the state of rajas; this fact had better be recognized from the outset. The seeker must be prepared to face a lot of difficulties. But under no circumstances should he ever lose faith and give up the effort as a hopeless task. One must enter upon the path of spiritual endeavor with the determination of one who is ready to empty the whole ocean with a tiny seashell. The Gita says, "This Yoga is to be resolutely practiced without yielding to any discouragement." Yoga must be done with a rocklike resolution of will. Never give any scope to depression. As Patanjali says, "The foundation of Yoga will be firm if the practice is done for a long period of time without intermission and with enthusiasm." Ramakrishna once said, "Spiritual practice must be done with vigor and stubbornness; it should not be weak like a soupy porridge of flattened rice." And the Buddha said, "Practice with faith and heroic strength." "I shall succeed, come what may"—this is faith. "I shall not retreat"—this is the dynamic strength of the hero. In the Upanishads it is written, "The Self is not realized by one who is weak; he who lacks strength can never attain to the Self."

Firm determination, then, and due to it a tremendous forward push which says, "I must reach the goal. As the river cuts its way through the mountains as it rushes to the sea, so shall I push forward." Such is the irrepressible force of will demanded of one who takes up the spiritual endeavor. Will is the foundation of spiritual discipline. The firmer the will (*samkalpa*), the purer and intenser the emotion (*bhava*). Every seeker possesses a little fund of emotion, otherwise he would never even feel like taking up the spiritual effort, but at the beginning this emotion is diffused like a gas; unless it is consolidated and channeled, the divine power (*shakti*) cannot manifest.

You will find that while meditating with firm resolve of will, the spine automatically becomes straight and the power manifests itself. The yogic explanation is this. When the spine is straight and the chin is pressed down, a tension is created whereby the vital current (*prana*) flows upward through the nerve channels and gathers at the throat center, which is the center of the will; at the same time the emotion (*bhava*) in the heart center rises up to the throat and mingles with the will. This confluence of emotion and will is the source of all Yoga power.

The mind has three faculties: emotion (*bhava*), will (*samkalpa*), and knowledge (*jnana*). Using the division of Samkhya, we might say that emotion and will fall into the category of nature (*prakriti*), while knowledge falls into the category of self (*purusha*). Nevertheless, the three faculties are inseparable, because nature is in fact the self's own, its self-nature and self-power. Consequently, the activity of nature is subordinate to the self.

Let us now look at meditation (*dhyana*) in terms of fixing the mind at a certain spot (*dharana*). We find that the three faculties of mind have three corresponding centers of activity. The place of emotion is the heart center; the place of will is the throat center (just above the throat, behind the jaw); and the place of knowledge is the center between the eyebrows. Knowledge, as we have said, is the governor of the other two. Each faculty, in its own domain, acts freely and naturally and is pure in quality. For this reason, to experience and appreciate the pure nature of each faculty, it is helpful to fix the mind for a time at each of the three centers associated with them. To hold the mind firmly at a point, one should take the support of some mental conception (*bhavana*). In this case the best support, in my opinion, would be to dwell upon the image of the infinite sky (*akasha*) or the Void (*shunya*).

In the ancient Yoga, the contemplation of the sky (*akashabhavana*) was considered to be the most effective support to meditation, and there is a reason for it. First, by dwelling upon the image of the sky, an expansion of mind takes place automatically; it brings a pleasant sense of relief and ease. The opposite of expansion is contraction, which brings discomfort and uneasiness. The many contradictory impacts of daily life make us contract; we shrink back, our mind suffers, a constant tension strains our nervous system. By dwelling upon the image of the sky, this tension is relieved, the mind, life-force, and body relax, the consciousness regains its self-possessed status. These are the benefits of the pleasant experience of expansion and relaxation.

Second, by contemplating the ethereal Vast, our mind gets rest, and this rest is truly a source of energy and power. Energy manifests itself in the mind both through an outgoing movement toward action (*pravritti*) and an ingoing movement of withdrawal from action (*nivritti*). The first is the tendency to move outward and forward, the second to withdraw inward and backward. If the restraining tendency does not hold back the outgoing one, the result is an excited energy which soon spends itself, tires, and flags from exhaustion. This slackening is a form of the ingoing movement, but because the outgoing movement has not received its full play, there remains a sense of dissatisfaction and frustration. Then, due to this lack of fulfillment, a renewal of enthusiastic action again takes place. Thus an alternating rhythm goes on, of excitement and exhaustion, excitement and exhaustion; it is a continual mechanical recurrence. And it is one of the principal reasons for the restless distraction that plagues the mind.

In truth, all impetus toward action issues forth from the immense Void behind. In the mind, there is normally a ceaseless bubbling of thought, feeling, and desire, but in reality this is just like the foam on the surface of the ocean. We see only the bubbles, the foam on the ocean, but not the ocean itself; and yet it is there. By dwelling upon the image of the infinite sky, the mind becomes conscious of the ocean. This ocean is in fact the infinite consciousness of which I have spoken; the bubbles are the mental consciousness. In the language of Samkhya, the one is purusha, conscious self or conscious being; the other is prakriti, cosmic energy or nature. The activity of nature goes on—let it go on. But at the same time rise above nature by awakening an awareness of the self. And it can be awakened if, remaining motionless within, one is able to feel and keep hold of the natural continuous flow of vital force (*prana*) in the body. This sensation of a constant stream of life-energy in the body is something like what one experiences when the whole body is relaxed and stilled in the dead-body posture (*shavasana*). With a little practice, one finds that it is possible to feel and remember this sensation of life-energy inside. It is a feeling as of the sky or ocean. The vedic seers have spoken both of a heart-sky and a vessel containing the vast consciousness of the sky or ocean. Why the heart? Because there it is easy to establish this wide expansive consciousness. And yet the heart remains empty in that Emptiness (*shunya*), bubbles arise, foam gathers, but all the while I am leaning upon the Emptiness, not pursuing the bubbles, not chasing the foam.

Once someone asked Ramakrishna, "Where should I meditate?" "Why not in the heart?" he replied. "The heart is the place proclaimed by its own beats." Indeed, for most seekers, the heart is the best place for fixing the mind because it is the center of emotion (*bhava*). Ordinarily it is with the help of emotion that the natural consciousness is illumined. But even while trying to hold the mind in the heart, one should not forget the entire body-consciousness, which must be made the background and larger container of the heart's emotions.

In fixing the mind in both time and space, equal attention must be given to concentrating it at a point and expanding it infinitely. As I have mentioned, to arrive at an absorption of the mind at a fixed hour, one has to maintain some feeling of inner absorption throughout the whole day. This rule for time applies also to space. The emptiness in the heart, intensifying itself, must take into itself the emptiness pervading the entire body. Indeed it is often better to establish an all-pervasive feeling of emptiness first in the body-consciousness, for it is then more easily experienced in the heart.

At the beginning of this book, while discussing the outer limbs of Yoga, I said something about asana. I mentioned that the main components of its practice are relaxation and expansion. These two conditions are in fact the basis of any kind of attempt to fix the mind at a particular place. The bodily sensation in oneself must be relaxed, made subtle and buoyant, then spread out like an ever-widening sphere into the infinite. The center of this global expansion should be the heart.

Next, just as there is a natural rhythm of contraction and expansion in the cycle of the breath, so there is a similar, but subtler rhythm emanating from the heart. This inner rhythm of the heart has to be awakened and then expanded, through conceptualization (*bhavana*), into the infinite Void. The seer of the Upanishad says, "That luminous sky (*akasha*) in the heart has gone beyond the earth, beyond even the heavens." In this statement lies a deep key to spiritual practice. Heaven and earth have first to be drawn into the sky of the heart, then released again and spread into the Infinite. In conceiving this, it is helpful to imagine a brilliant source of light in the heart, such as the sun or moon. Again, it is helpful if this thought of contraction and expansion in the heart is synchronized with the rhythm of the breathing. As I inhale, with the inflow of the vital current I draw down the infinite Sky above into the sky of my heart. As I exhale, with the upward flow of the vital current I rise up and expand into the Infinite. This is how one should conceptualize the movement.

Here let me note something else. The impression (*samskara*) which form (*rupa*) makes upon us is very strong and deep-rooted. That is why we consider the seeing of Ishta, our chosen object of meditation, to be so highly desirable. Meditating in the heart on the image (*murti*) of our cherished object has long been a widely accepted practice. But often we find that the image does not easily come to mind, or if it comes, it is not very clear or complete. The object that attracts us and easily evokes our feeling (*bhava*) becomes an object of heart-breaking toil when we try to conceive it in our mind (*bhavana*). My advice is this. Instead of trying to grasp the form, rather allow it to reveal itself from out of the bosom of the formless; then it arises more easily and remains for a longer time. Moreover, this method resolves the conflict between inner feeling and outer form, for by it the play between the form and the formless goes on unhindered on the background of feeling. The form appears and then disappears, but since this happens on the firm background of feeling (*bhava*), the soul does not suffer any loss of feeling (*abhava*) even when the form is absent.

The foundation of all feeling is the self-feeling (*atmabhava*), the conscious feeling of the self. First purify your own feelings (*bhavashuddhi*); then the contemplation of the object of your love will become easy. The true meaning of purifying your feeling is to become as empty as the sky. To possess the All, it is first necessary to be empty, to be void. And in that void, your deep-rooted impressions (*samskaras*) will naturally arise in form. To give up everything in order to gain everything, this is the key to all practice of Yoga.

Chapter 11

Yoga without a Support

The Yoga of Sleep

I have said at the beginning of the Yoga of meditation (*dhyana*) that one must learn to distinguish between mental movement (*vritti*) and emotional mood (*bhava*). The mind's movements are scattered and disorganized; the emotional mood is even and one. Amid the dispersive movements, one kind of emotion or another is always present—it may be a feeling of pleasure or discomfort or fatigue. In the natural consciousness these feelings provide the background for the mind's activity; in the supranatural consciousness, the consciousness beyond the ordinary nature, pure feeling (*shuddha bhava*) is manifested; its essence is a spiritual clarity and ease.

And beyond this pure feeling, there is the Void (*shunya*). It is the Void that is the support of the single and even flow of perception. One can reach the Void through the stoppage of all mental activities (*vrittis*); one can reach it also through the purification and illumination of feeling (*bhava*); but until one reaches the Void, the realization of the goal is not complete. Where there is emptiness, everything overflows; this is the highest awareness.

The mind can become empty of activity in a natural way through fatigue or cloudiness of mind or even sleep; again, it can become empty in the waking state, as in the case of a child's mind. But in all these mental states, there still remains the seed of dispersion; therefore the naturally inactive mind is never permanent and cannot help in the ascension of consciousness. The dispersive activity of mind creates a kind of eddy, and while it stirs, the vast peace of the Ocean beyond cannot be felt. Such is the action of tamas, the obscuring or veiling power in mind. Thus the cessation of mental activity due to natural causes is not a yogic state of consciousness. For in the yogic state, in addition to an absence of mental activity, there is also an alert and luminous awareness (*bodha*), an awareness that is turned inward and concentrated on the Self (*atman*). To remain alert and conscious is a sign of the yogic mind.

Still, it is possible to utilize the natural absence of mental activity for the purpose of Yoga. Just as I am alert and conscious when the vibration of mental activity goes on in full vigor, so must I seek to remain conscious and alert when it slows down or stops. Unless clouds suddenly make the sky overcast, the light of day fades very slowly, till there is a meeting point where light and darkness meet; so it is with the light and darkness of the consciousness. Take, for example, the moment when waking and sleep meet each other. With a little effort this moment can be prolonged. At the time of sleep, the mind naturally tends toward cessation of activity; this tendency can be cultivated so that it comes very slowly, feeling its way. One should not snuff out the lamp all at once, but sink into sleep as the daylight vanishes into the bosom of the evening, as the child falls asleep on the breast of its mother.

No, this last simile is not yet complete. The child falls asleep, but the mother remains awake. The child may have a sort of trust that his mother stays awake, but he is not very aware of it. In yogic sleep (*yoganidra*), that awareness will be pronounced and clear.

Sleep is like the Yoga-heart of the Mother. In the depths of the night, the Earth lies asleep, but meanwhile the Sky (*akasha*) stays awake and looks on through the unblinking gaze of myriads of stars. That Sky is truly the heart of the Mother. To be asleep there means to be awake to the vast peace of the Sky. This awakening takes place very slowly, just as the moon rises slowly, diluting the darkness of evening with its spreading white light. The sleep of Yoga is like that.

Sleep does not mean an extinction or eclipse; it is not a blotting out in the Unknown. Sleep we know through the silence of wakefulness. We have only to invoke this wakeful silence and expand our consciousness into it, spreading it into the Yoga-heart of the Mother. In this way even sleep can be transformed.

The yogins speak of five kinds of sleep. The first three kinds—tamasic, rajasic, and sattvic—are natural in quality. Beyond them are two supranatural kinds—the sleep of the gopi and the sleep of Yoga. "My sleep never seems adequate; even after sleeping I feel sluggish and my mind is dull"—this is tamasic sleep. "My sleep is disturbed, my night is full of incoherent dreams, and when I wake up my mind is restless"—this is rajasic sleep. "My sleep has been total and dreamless, at least for awhile I am filled with deep contentment and waking up is like the light of dawn filling the sky"—this is sattvic sleep. The sattvic sleep is quite possible if only we invoke it by contemplating the Yoga-heart of the Mother.

"Sleep is to remain in the state of samadhi"—this is the formula for yogic practice. In meditation we forcibly try to stop the activity of the mind, but in sleep this stoppage occurs by itself, but because I cannot yet transform my sleep, my mind sinks into oblivion or gets excited by unwanted distractions. Yet the very aim of sleep is to find peace and to refresh and energize the mind by returning to the Origin, the Cause (*mahakarana*). The Origin is the Mother, She who, in the language of the Upanishads, is the Ruler of All (*sarveshvari*), the Womb of All (*sarvayoni*), and the Enjoyer of Bliss (*anandabhuk*).

Sleep is the invocation of this very Mother. It is also a Yoga, and with a bit of technique all the limbs of Yoga can be applied. First, lie down in the dead-body posture (*shavasana*), absolutely motionless. Then, through relaxation, spread out the body-consciousness like a rarefied gas. This is asana. Next, pay attention to the breathing for awhile, making it full and rhythmic. Then, in consonance with the breathing, do japa by continuously repeating the seed-mantra Hamsa, saying Ham while breathing out, Sa while breathing in. This is pranayama. At the same time picture yourself in the image of Narayana lying in eternal repose, and let the resulting mood spread in yourself. It is not upon your bed that you lie, but upon the infinite Causal Ocean of light. Upon this ocean your spinal column floats and it is charged with electricity. Now draw your whole consciousness into your heart; from there imagine your consciousness coursing upward, in an ineffable stream of sensation, to the throat center, the forehead center, and then through the crown of the head into the Void. Above, below, to the right and left there is only the vast emptiness of an unsupported infinite Sky. From it the Mother, in the form of Yoga-sleep, descends into your heart and then again flows heavenward into the consciousness above the head. This is pratyahara and dharana. By practicing this, it is possible to transform your sleep.

Out of the Unconscious, consciousness emerges; it is the consciousness of the Ineffable, the Unmanifest. A Upanishadic seer refers to it as *samprasada*, a limpid clearness as of pale moonlight. The Mother appears in the image of Balika, a little girl; one's sleep is full of the pure light of sattva. The moonlight deepens and is filled with an ecstasy of emotion; waves arise on the ocean of consciousness. The Mother now appears as Kishori, an adolescent girl; one's sleep is the sleep of the gopi.[1] The consciousness explodes, and the great sun is seen burning in the sky. The Mother is now seen as Savitri, a regal young woman; the sleep is the sleep of Yoga. Thus it is that "what is night for all creatures is day (the time of waking) for the yogin."

The whole of our day is busily spent on work. We say to our Mother: "O Mother, we have no time to invoke you. Where is the time to sit awhile and call you? This is why we do not remember you." But the Mother does not forget us. In the depths of every night She extinguishes our world of busy work and clamorous thought. In her deep compassion, she draws us into the fathomless depths of her Yoga-heart, into the pristine river of knowledge flowing back to its source. Even if I do not know, the Mother knows. Even if I can give her nothing else, if only I could give her my sleep. If only I could tell her, "In lying down, I lie at your feet; in sleeping I think only of you."

Note

1. The gopis are the cowherdesses of Vrindavana enamored of Krishna; they represent the soul's passionate attraction to the Divine.

Section II

BUDDHIYOGA

Chapter 12

BUDDHI AND BUDDHIYOGA

I

Buddhi, an important term of frequent occurrence in the Gita, does not occur in the earliest of the Upanishads. It is derived from a root which in the Vedas means "awakening, kindling, enlightenment," and which is invariably associated with Agni, the unaging (*ajara*) mystic Fire. Buddhi, though not precisely defined in the Gita, is still used there in this original sense of spiritual "awakening" or "illumination." It will be interesting to trace the significance of this concept from the earliest time, always keeping in mind that in India there has been an unbroken spiritual tradition from hoary antiquity up to the present day, and that though the outer garb of a concept has changed with the times, yielding to the demands of analytic understanding, its inner meaning as a concretely realizable mystic experience has always continued as a sutra or a shining strand of inner truth.

The mystic fire, as the Vedas say, is "the universal life, the immortal principle in mortals" (RV VI.4.2), "lying in us in so many wonderful ways to impel us to the journey" (RV I.31.2), "awaiting to be kindled from light to light by the wakeful men" (RV III.29.2). The root *budh* and its derivatives are used in the Vedas to speak of this "kindling" or "awakening," and Agni is distinctively called *usharbudha*, *usharbhut*, *jarabodha*, the ever-moving traveler that awakes with the dawn of spiritual consciousness and, kindling our waning energies, suffuses the symphony of our aspirations pining for the Vision (RV I.65.9; VI.4.2; I.27.10). In the Shankhyayana Brahmana, Agni is called *buddhimat*, where the word *buddhi* is perhaps used for the first time, of course bearing the usual meaning of "kindling."[1]

Psychologically speaking, the synonyms of *buddhi* in the Vedas are *dhi* with its derivative *dhiti* and its cognate *didhiti*. In the *Nighantu*, dhi is both spiritual knowledge (*prajna*) and spiritual activity (*karma*); dhiti is activity and the flames of the mystic fire figuratively called "fingers"; and didhiti is both these flames and the rays of illumination. Taken all together, they seem to depict a flaming aspiration and the internal illumination consequent upon it.

A very significant mantra of the Rigveda, occurring in a hymn of Savita, the luminous impeller of the aspirant, says: "They yoke the mind and they yoke the dhi—they, the tremulous, (aspiring) to the Tremulous One, the Ever-expanding, the Illuminator of the tremors of the Heart" (RV V.81.1). The express mention of yoga here with its two instrumentations, manas and dhi, following each other leaves no doubt about what the function of this dhi is.

This concept has been familiarized by the significant term of *nididhyasana* (striving for internal illumination) used particularly in the Brihadaranyaka Upanishad (II.4.4.5; IV.5.5.6), the radical meaning of which can be traced from a mantra in the Yajurveda (VI.20). As *dhyana* (a term used specifically in the Chandogya Upanishad), it is one of the constituents of Pantanjali's samyama and belongs to the fourth level of consciousness known as ekagrabhumi. In Buddhist psychology, the ninefold dhyanachittas also take their start from this bhumi beyond the pale of kamavachara plane. This equation of buddhi with dhi or dhyana (Mait Ar VII.7) illustrates one of the most fruitful of its spiritual functions.

Another term in the Vedas synonymous with *buddhi* is *manisha*. The *Nighantu* explains its derivative *manishi* as *medhavi*, meaning "a plunger, a penetrator." Yaska explains manisha as prajna or stuti, the esoteric significance of the latter being "an ecstatic attunement with the superconscious." Manisha thus connotes both the intellective and the emotive aspects of spiritual experience. Etymologically it is bi-radical like many of the vedic words, meaning "a mental upsurge." It is well known in the phrase *hrida manisha manasa* (Tait Ar X.1.13; Katha U II.3.9), which can be traced to the Rigveda itself, where as a means of abhiklripti or comprehensive realization its place between hrid and manas is extremely significant. It is an instrumentation subtler than the mind, but bordering on the heart (cognate with *shrad*), that shining core within the individual which contains "the luminous Void vaster than Heaven and Earth." From the Sankhya account of buddhi in all its implications, its identity with the vedic manisha becomes palpably apparent.

The nearest verbal similarity with *buddhi* is found in the vedic term *budhna* connoting both "fundus" and "illumination" or "the illumination of the depth," reminding us of a paraphrase of the concept in the familiar term *buddhi-guha*.

Another vedic term is *prabudh*, meaning "awakening"(YV IV.14); yet another form in the Brahmanas and the Upanishads is *pratibodha* and its cognates (Sat Br II.2.1.14; Ait Br II.11 ff.; Kena U II.4; Brh U I.4.10, IV.4.13).

The term clearly stands out in the Katha Upanishad (I.3.3), where it first occurs in the famous metaphor of the chariot and its driver, while the atman is the traveler. The chariot metaphor is well known in the Vedas, too; and there, though the word *sarathi* is not unknown, yet in every case the rathi or the divinity is himself the traveler. This distinction between the rathi and the sarathi in the Katha Upanishad makes a step toward the discrimination between buddhi and atman so familiar in classical Sankhya. Obviously buddhi is here the psychic principle in the individual, the controller of the mind and the senses; and in the hierarchy of spiritual experiences, it just precedes the cosmic illumination denoted by *mahan atma*. The emphasis is still on its character of spiritual instrumentation; it is the individual knowledge-self (*jnana atma*) in which the mind principle is to be merged, and at the same time it is the only means which by its ever-attenuated propulsion enables the aspirant to penetrate into the depths of the hidden Reality. Its psychological character is only once hinted at in describing the parama gati, where "the senses with the mind are at a standstill and the buddhi flutters not" (Katha U I.3.10, 12, 13).

The spiritual character of buddhi becomes further apparent in its identification with *vijnana* (Katha U I.3.6–9), a term occurring in the Atharvaveda, the Sankhyayana Brahmana, the Taittiriya Brahmana, and the oldest Upanishads and enunciated most clearly in the Taittiriya Upanishad.[2] As a stage of serial abhiklripti lying between manas and anandam, it answers to the intermediary instrumentation enumerated in the triad of manas, manisha, and hrid. In the Buddhist system, vijnana as the principle of consciousness forms the finest of the basic aggregates of the subjective organism, and through the evolution of the dhyana-consciousness passes into vijnananantya (infinite consciousness), the second of the formless planes. In one form of Mahayana mysticism, this vijnana, as pure consciousness, is the ultimate plane of Reality, where the polarity of consciousness being once dissolved into the Void is again established in the dharmadhatu (totality of existence). In man's spiritual journey to the ultimate Reality, vijnana (= *buddhi*) can aptly be described as the charioteer or the guide par excellence leading him "to the end of the Path wherein is That, the highest step of Vishnu."[3] Another equation in the Katha Upanishad, that of buddhi and sattva (essence), is extremely suggestive (Katha U II.3.7). The term *sattva* occurs only in the Tandya Brahmana (XV.12.2) as an arthavada of the Vamadevya Sama, where from a penetrative reading of the context, it seems to mean a "consummation of mystic experience." In the Chandogya Upanishad, it occurs in the term *sattvashuddhi* (the purification of the essence),[4] which brings upon the aspirant dhruva smriti—a stage where the spiritual upaya of memory by the intensification of consciousness crushes the time factor and in an integral sweep realizes eternity.[5] In the Maha Upanishad (V.25), sattvapatti is described as the fourth jnanabhumika coming after tanumanasa (attenuation of the mind), and is known as the first level of Brahma-realization, followed by three higher ones.[6] The conception of sattva as the luminous principle of prakriti is well known and needs no elaboration.

In the philosophy of the epics, which stands midway between the Sankhya yoga of the Upanishads and the classical Sankhya, buddhi is both a cosmological and a psychological principle. Describing the cosmos as brahmavriksha or brahma vana (a concept as old as the Rigveda, I.24.7), sprouting from the seed of avyakta, the epic makes the buddhi its trunk or the first evolute (Mbh XIV.35.20). From a psychical standpoint, buddhi is again the charioteer, as in the Katha Upanishad, with this difference, that the traveler is declared to be the bhutatma, corresponding roughly to the linga-sharira (Mbh XIV.51.4). This change in the position of the rathi and the sarathi we find in the Gita, too, where it is the Lord who is the charioteer of Arjuna. This elevation of the status of buddhi is dictated by a practical necessity, in preference to a theoretical enunciation of principles. The epic again makes the psychological position of buddhi very clear by defining it as vyavasayatmika or consisting of the discriminative and definitive function of reason, and distinguishing it from the analytic and discursive function of the mind (*mano vyakaranatmakam*) (Mbh XII.251.11; BG II.41, 44).

In mystic Buddhism, the esoteric aspect of buddhi is represented by bodhi or sambodhi, for the attainment of which a course of strenuous psychical training has been prescribed (Visuddhimagga 22.33 ff.). By attaining this bodhi, Siddhartha became Buddha, the enlightened one, the man of supreme intuition, though in his psychological makeup he was an analyst and a rationalist. From his time onward, and in spite of himself, the integral experience of mysticism and the analytical reason of philosophy began to drift apart, driving a wedge between the hitherto harmonious dual function of buddhi as a mystical intuition and enlightened rationality.

In the philosophical systems, the buddhi as a psychological principle par excellence has been interpreted in different ways. To the Mimamsakas, to whom the self (*atman*) is a dynamic principle incorporating the dual character of change and continuity, buddhi is identical with the self. To the Naiyayikas, it is a conscious principle distinct from mental instrumentation and covering the whole field of cognitive experience (Nyayasutra I.1.15). The Vaisheshikas, who subscribe to the same view, hold it to be an incorporeal but specific property of the self, capable of being introspectively cognized.[7] To the Sankhyas, it is a cardinal principle in the scheme of evolution—the first evolute from the evolvent Prakriti and having both a cosmic and a psychological aspect. Cosmically it is a great shining principle (*mahat*), reflecting the luminosity of the transcendental consciousness and necessarily embodying the dual principle of prana and prajna,[8] while psychologically, as described in the karikas, it combines in itself the faculties of intellection and determination, forming a composite of "intelligent will." It then manifests itself in two divergent sets of characteristics, the first set comprising the urge to the summum bonum (*dharma*), the faculty of subtle discrimination (*jnana*), the control and reorientation of the emotive explosions by dispassionateness (*vairagya*), and the acquisition and influx of supernormal powers (*aishvarya*). This upward function of buddhi is counterbalanced by another set of characteristics just the reverse of the above, following the downward evolutionary trend of lessening consciousness (Sankhyakarika 23). In its higher functioning, the approximation of buddhi to atman is so nearly complete as to require the most subtle power of discrimination to enable the aspirant to avoid a plunge into one of the abysses of the layas and cross over to the shores of the transcendent. The neo-Vedantists, however, have taken buddhi simply as a psychic instrumentation superior to mind and discrimination in character.

Assuming that all philosophies in their upward flight tend to the same goal and differ only in their outlook on derivative truths, we need glean from the various philosophical accounts only so many practical hints as will help us in our quest of the truth. From this standpoint, a philosophical concept as clothed in language becomes elastic in connotation, and admits of many subtle nuances always suggestive of the symphonious variations of the ultimate truth.

The following points emerge from the above considerations: (1) it has been universally admitted that buddhi, whether as a spiritual stage or an instrumentation, is something above the mental plane; (2) it has both a psychological and a cosmic aspect, the relation between the two in spiritual realization being that between a means and an end; (3) its intrinsic character is in the nature of an illumination granted by divine grace (BG X.10, 11), so aptly expressed by Sri Ramakrishna; when remonstrating against an intellectual speculation about spiritual experiences, he cried: "No, not that way! He makes you see in a blaze-up, you know!"

The above brief survey is intended as a preliminary to the understanding of the comprehensive way in which the term buddhi has been used in the Gita. Like many of its esoteric terms, buddhi has not been pinned down to any precise definition, but has been left as a plastic word suggestive of many colorful meanings, as is too common in mystic lore.

II

Buddhi as a specific category in an enumeration of the ultimate realities occurs twice in the Gita, occupying each time a significant position in the beginning of the second and third hexateuchs. In the first case, it is a cosmic principle, heading the eightfold division of the creative evolutionary nature of the Lord (*apara prakriti*), which expresses herself in the moving pageant of the manifest universe (*idam jagat*), and is sustained by His supreme nature (*para prakriti*)—the eternal and conscient life-principle emanating from Him and working dynamically upon and inside nature (BG VII.4, 5; XV.7). In the second case, it is a psychological principle forming one of the constituents of the fluxional embodiment of the psychic entity (*sharira*), which serves as the field of experience (*kshetra*) for the jiva and which is illumined by the light of the divine immanence.

In both cases, an emphasis has been laid on the experiential knowledge of the world of objective reality, starting from the basic material principles and culminating in the experience of the spirit transcending and yet impregnating all manifestations. The exact technique of the pursuit has not been detailed, but the stages in the spiritual ascent have been indicated by a serial enumeration of the principles of reality, according to the time-honored method of Sankhya philosophy. In this scheme, buddhi occupies as usual the place between the ego or the pseudo self and nature—the one forming the focus of the manifestation of the many, and the other pointing to the boundless horizon of the great Beyond. This peculiar position of the buddhi (even if we take it as upalabdhi or a simple factor of awareness in the psychical apparatus) enables it, by virtue of its natural freedom from egoistic preoccupations, at once to stamp out fluctuating experience of the concrete with the reassuring mark of the abstract reality, and by a reverse movement to prepare us gradually for the direct perception of the universal. In the evolution of the soul, buddhi thus becomes an essential vehicle (*sattva*)[9] for the development of the inner being and for the transmission of its acquired characteristics through the cycles of embodied existence (BG VI.43). As the first evolute, it necessarily contains within itself the potentialities of all further evolved principles involved in the downward trend of the evolutionary process. In this way, at any stage of the psychic development, it appears as the secret guiding power that determines our outlook on life, and through apparent anomalies adjusts it to the total plan of world-becoming.[10]

In this lower hemisphere of prakriti, where everything is oscillating between the buoyancy of illumination and the inertia of darkness, buddhi with its concomitant of dhriti or the fostering energy of tenacity is deployed into three types of personalities according to the three classical gunas. The sattvika type (BG XVIII.30, 33, 36, 37) is sustained by an uninterrupted sense of perfect equanimity and easy abandonment, which controls all the activities of mental and vital energies. This equipoise, guaranteeing a quiet mastery over the demands of our objective preoccupations, turns the mind inward and opens before us a wide vision of the subtle workings of the cosmic nature in us. The result is the dawning of a capacity of intense discernment, which can safely steer our course between the conflicts of our extrovertive and introvertive impulses and decide for us the problems of ethical conduct. Its best contribution toward our psychic development lies in creating a sense of inner liberation supported by a feeling of fearlessness which is not daunted by the prospective disturbance of one's status quo in any sphere of existence. This is attended with a chastening of the emotions, so that the heart's only response toward all stimuli is a quiet enjoyment of the upward stream of inner felicity started by the impulse of habitual introspection (*abhyasa*). Although the reorientation of the emotions is an irksome task at the beginning, as it means a death blow to one's cherished habits of stereotyped responses, its diligent pursuit will win back in the end our shining heritage of immortal bliss unmarred by any possible recurrence of the usual sense of frustration and pain. The process is helped by the development of a characteristic transparency (*prasada*)[11] in the soul-substance and the buddhi lighting them up with the light of the clear Void.

The second type of personality is the rajasa (BG XVIII.31, 34, 38), in which the driving force is a deep attachment to earthly ends and a passion for attaining some definitive objective dictated by a narrow vision of life. The aim of existence is determined by a hankering for accumulation of materials for the satisfaction of one's blind desires. The ethical sense is not entirely absent, but it is blurred by a confused perception of the ultimate values and so is content with an undiscerning compliance with the code of established morality. The outlook on life being essentially extroverted, the lack of the sense of inner liberation is never regretted. The emotional content of such a personality is derived from an easygoing pursuit of sensuous pleasures, regardless of its dire consequences on one's own inner growth.

The third type is the tamasa (BG XVIII.32, 35), characterized by a dullness of perception which cannot penetrate beyond the surface values of things and yet clings with the obstinate tenacity of an infatuated egoism to what might have otherwise been counted upon as a negation of all meaning in life—a nightmare existence of fear, grief, and gloom, from which the soul finds it hard to wake up. The intellectual horizon is narrowed by the gathering darkness of self-complacent ignorance, and the ethical vision is warped by an incurable perversity of nature born of a blinding egocentricism. The only delight that such a temperament knows is in leading a soporific existence of blundering indolence, oblivious throughout of any higher mission of the soul.

These three types, which are thus described in an ideal isolation, actually appear in the world in different degrees of intermingling and assortment, their specific labeling being determined by the preponderance of one or another of the gunas in the makeup of an organism. In nature, where external flux is the inherent law, the position is always a fluid one, because no organized being (*sattva*), whether it partakes of the earth-nature or the god-nature, is really immune from the undulating influence of the gunas (BG XVIII.40). To a superficial view, this scheme of things may appear entirely mechanical, lending no justification to human aspiration after the sublime heights. This would have been the case if apara prakriti had been the sole power of the ultimate Reality; but to it is linked the principles of soul-becoming as Supernature, the pivot on which turns the whole cosmic movement and which in its turn is moved by the Prime Mover according to the law of His divine wisdom (*maya*) (BG XVIII.61).

The above account of the buddhi in the Gita, especially in its psychological aspect, is largely descriptive in character and shorn of all metaphysical implications. The why of the evolution of the prakriti has been left out as an inscrutable mystery; an attempt has only been made to introduce into the motley confusion of its results a broad classification, in accordance with the accepted principles of guna-movements. But this has served the very useful purpose of awakening the dormant analytic reason in us, which as a potent function of the sattvikabuddhi releases the urge toward the practical realization of a theoretically sifted truth. This is the typical Sankhya method of discrimination, which is an essential preliminary to all solutions of the problems of existence. The sharp contrast between the sattvika and the other types of personalities is a silent pointer toward the ideal of the final culmination of the discipline of knowledge attainable by a purification of the buddhi together with the cult of self-control through dhriti (BG XVIII.50, 51). The relation between the buddhi as a psychological content of the individual kshetra and the cosmic aspect of the buddhi as a factor of the apara prakriti of the Lord is, however, not apparent at the first sight, though stress has been laid on the knowledge of both as an indispensable condition of attaining the supreme goal of existence (BG VII.10; XIII.5–6, 34). Evidently the knowledge of the cosmic buddhi cannot be gained by simply conceiving of it as a mathematical sum of the units of its individual manifestations, because the "matrix" producing a host of its own replicas, by its intrinsic nature of spontaneous productivity, must always contain an intellectually irreducible element of indeterminate potentiality. How to gain a direct experience of this buddhi and install oneself permanently on its plane, so that one may act in practical life from a poise beyond good and evil (BG II.50), is one of the cardinal problems of existence that has been propounded and solved by the Gita.

III

The problem makes its appearance at a moment when a crisis is imminent both in the moral and the material sphere. Whether the crisis is a historical fact, and the solution advanced by the teachings of the Gita in a spirit of such lofty idealism has subsequently found expression in the unimpeachable conduct of its hero, may still be the subject of a lively dispute. But the whole thing is to be judged not by modern historical methods preoccupied with the surface value of empirical facts alone, but by the old historical sense of the rishis, to whom the true function of history (*itihasa-purana*) is to amplify and illustrate the findings of the eternal spiritual truths (*vedartha*). History, according to them, should be selective in its procedure, and one of its chief characteristics should be to depict the innovations of universal thought cycles (*manvantara*) on the vast canvas of cataclysmic world process (*sarga* and *pratisarga*). Facts of personal life in this context assume a symbolic significance suggestive of the denouement of another vaster drama behind the surface, into which the spiritual sympathy of the present age too can be profitably ushered. This universalization of the personal factor, done with the consummate art of a rare poetic genius, has given the episode of the Gita a novel kind of historical veracity and has transfigured the crudities of material events into a spiritual drama of all times.

The moral crisis of Arjuna, the solution of which is avowedly the theme of the Lord's song, appears in the background of greater social crisis foreshadowed by the inevitability of a terrible fratricidal war. And an unexpected shock for the meekly pious is that the Lord himself sanctions the war: the Sermon on the Battlefield forms a strange contrast to the Sermon on the Mount. An attempt has often been made to tone down the grimness of this realistic background of the Gita either by ignoring wholesale the motive of its origination, or by giving an allegorical interpretation of this unpalatable business of war making. Of course, the suggestion that Kurukshetra is the symbolical venue of a spiritual contest between the powers of light and darkness cannot entirely be ruled out; first because there has been a long-standing vedic tradition to that effect,[12] and second because such an interpretation, as has already been said, does not outrage the historical sense specifically evolved in this land. But still, the exhortation to a righteous fight (*dharmya samgrama*) is so consistently interspersed throughout the Gita, and the Mimamsa canons of "setting forth (*upakrama*), repetition (*abhyasa*), and winding up (*upasamhara*)" fit in so aptly in this case, that any interpretation without a due regard to this vital point is bound to miss the integrity and the spiritual depth of the Lord's message. Political warfare has not hitherto been an everyday occurrence, and the average mind looks upon the Gita simply as a guide of spiritual liberation (*mokshashastra*), which it surely is and much more; hence it has been easy not to visualize the terrible agony through which the soul of an Arjuna has to pass when he is unwittingly going to be made the agent of a cataclysm of baffling significance. The demand that has been made on his unillumined buddh is really exorbitant and at the same time relentless in its insistence (BG III.2). The ideal of ahimsa in all its implications has not been lost sight of in the Gita; it has indeed been put forward as one of the essential conditions of knowledge (BG XIII.7). Arjuna has been calmly assured that he is fortunate enough to be born with a bent toward the divine aptitude (*daivisampad*), one of the chief contents of which is ahimsa; and for the very reason he is asked not to grieve (*ma shuchah*), because he has to fight to kill (BG XVI.2, 5). Surely this is a bewildering demand upon the common run of mental intelligence and we, who are seldom in the thick of a catastrophic convulsion, can conveniently ignore the "inexorable logic of facts," which a Savyasachi as the Lord's elect has to face. But in the modern world, with the vaunted annihilation of time and distance, the battle of Kurukshetra is going to be a normal affair, for how long none can tell; and with the propagation of democratic ideologies, the call to fight unrighteouness is tending to become universal. All the more reason that we wake up to the ancient Aryan ideal of integrating the spirit of brahma with that of kshatra and come to grips with reality in a spirit of sacrifice, clearing our buddhi from the accumulated confusion of ages brought about by lending too ready an ear to sophisticated utterances (BG II.52, 53).

The moral conflict that appears in Arjuna at a moment when things were taking a critical turn is as sudden as it is unwarranted by any antecedents. The storm has been brewing for a long time, and when all efforts at "persuasion" failed, "coercion" had become inevitable for upholding what was deemed a right cause. It was a known fact that the successful issue of the struggle depended largely on the valor of Arjuna; and his backing out at a critical juncture might very well blast the expectation of a warmonger, though it can as well be hailed as a case of "conversion" by a pietist. The only clue to his strange behavior is perhaps to be found in the reading of his character by Sri Krishna as one who is born with a bent toward daivisampad, which has been described in detail as an ideal of discipline leading to spiritual liberation (*vimoksha*). But the prescription of this ideal, as had already been noted, is specifically meant there as an incentive to the kshatra spirit, which should fearlessly and without nursing any personal sense of "grief" accept the challenge thrown out by the asura forces of creation. In the long and graphic description of the asura temperament that follows, desire, anger, and greed have been pointed out as its characteristic motives, and those who follow this demoniac bent have significantly been dubbed as persons of "scant illumination" (*alpabuddhi*),[13] possessing the rajasa type of buddhi mentioned later on. Kurukshetra is thus literally the eternal battleground of the two forces, daiva and asura, sattvika and rajasa; and the hero of this fight is "the fearless sattvika champion of truth burning with the fiery zeal" of a kshatriya.[14] A crisis may appear in his life, if the balance between the dynamisms of brahma and kshatra nature working in perfect unison in his character is disturbed either way. If the characteristic kshatra trait of ishvarabhava (spirit of self-assertive lordliness) devoid of dama (self-control) gains the upper hand, the hero will be yielding to the temptations of asura forces "ruthless in their workings and perniciously leading the world to havoc and ruin" (BG XVI.9). On the other hand, if the spirit of kshanti (forbearance) unduly preponderates in him over tejas at a critical moment, it may place him in a worse predicament of tamasa nature, ultimately inviting by his passivity the very dark forces which he had sought to defeat. The irony of the situation is that, while in the former case the consequences, being too patent and familiar to the mental intelligence, are immediately censured by it as due to the screening of the moral judgment by "delusion born of avidya," in the latter case "the delusion of vidya" becomes denser darkness through which the limited mental vision cannot look. It is this frustration of the mental intelligence groping in confusion at the dissolution of all its cherished values of life and crying for an illumination from a higher plane—the plane of buddhi—that is at the root of the moral and spiritual crisis of the hero of Kurukshetra.

IV

According to upanishadic nomenclature, Arjuna may be described as the type of an aspirant on the mental level of consciousness (*mano-maya kosha*). In puranic tradition, he is the typical man (*nara*), the hero[15] journeying toward the predestined status of the supreme man (*narottama*), the eternal consort of Narayana and, in an esoteric sense, the para prakriti in the making, of the Gita.[16] He is essentially the mental man, or as the Vaishnava would call it, the eternal energy of conscient individuation (*jiva-shakti*) standing on the borderland (*tatastha*) of the externalizing agency of the cosmic maya and the internalizing pull of the pure chit (*Chaitanya Charitamrita* I.2). In his psycho-spiritual makeup, he is the true disciple, opening himself up to the divine in complete self-surrender, in an agonizing hour of moral and spiritual conflict (BG II.7), which in all its forms is the conflict of the natural mind with a partial and distorted vision, doubting and arguing, and yet always pining for a solution to be vouchsafed by an illumination from a higher plane. This conflict, which has started in a highly sensitive mind from a causal preoccupation of the present moment, assumes the gigantic proportions of another Kurukshetra, in which the age-long accumulations of the unillumined or imperfectly illumined mind have been critically examined in the light of an impending revolution in the thought-cycle. And as a result, the whole field of consciousness has quite unostentatiously been raised to another level, where the conversion or transmutation becomes an achievement of the depth, leaving the apara prakriti apparently to take her habitual course, though to the illumined vision her total progression becomes charged with a new meaning. It is the spirit of a manavantara which has necessitated in the Gita the revision and enrichment of many old concepts: the individual spiritual achievements of the long past have been gleaned and assimilated, and by injecting a new life into the old forms, their total effect has been canalized into the momentum of a novel trend in universal evolution. This is the rationale of an incarnation (*avatara*), which is a compelling process in the cosmic unfolding, closely parallel to the familiar phenomenon of the descent of power from above (*shaktipata*) in the spiritual endeavor of the individual. In the spiritual history of mankind, this mighty gathering of forces, "not for destruction but for fulfillment," has not been a solitary event. The spirit of the Gita in its entirety has been lived again and again, generating a power of world-shaking intensity, an instance in the recent past being the unparalleled experimentation in the field of harmonic fusion of spiritual forces, carried out by the "man-God" of Dakshineshvara [Sri Ramakrishna].

The preparations for a Kurukshetra go on behind the scene long before its actual thundering occurrence, arranged by a mightier hand than we are ordinarily aware of. The immediate cause seems to lie in an attempt at vindicating some mentally conceived ideal of social justice, but in reality it is the pressure of a new idea to be born that works from behind, and its birth throes assume the character of a cataclysm sweeping away everything before it. The circumscribed vision of the mental man sees in the avalanche a clash of worldly interests determined by a personal outlook, though often dignified by the name of a national, moral, or even a spiritual cause. The mind, unable to penetrate behind the veil, cannot grasp the total plan of the divine providence and, in its characteristically one-sided view of things, finds it equally easy either to approve or to decry; like the Kantian antinomies, the arguments both for and against appear then to be logically valid. As long as this duality of mutual contradiction prevails, it is not possible for the mind to evolve an ethical ideal that will have any eternal value, unyielding to the challenge of temporal or environmental changes. In the last analysis, it may seem that the whole scheme of nature is amoral, because, as the orthodox Sankhyist would have it, Nature herself is inconscient and her only purposiveness (*pararthya*) lies in an indifferent provision of positive and negative experiences to the soul. But apart from this objective view of things, there is also possible an insight into a deeper subjective experience, which in the thick of the blind and maddening rush of events reveals to the heart the unfolding of a secret purpose that can be measured only in the terms of the silent joy of the spiritual blooming of the individual to which the whole cosmic process is made subservient. This spiritual intuition of the good, variously called lila, anandam, or the perfect self-poise of the liberated soul, is the ultimate basis of all ethical standards. But as is usually the case, this supernormal vision at one step further becomes warped by the partial vision of the tendentious mind and gives rise to the current norms of morality, which always contain a seed of violence to the real svabhava of the jiva. The mental limitation thus imposed on the integral perception of the spirit can be done away with only when we can live in the higher altitudes beyond mind in the stratosphere of the cosmic buddhi, where the conflict between the universal moral order (*rita*) and its perversions on the mental plane (*anrita*) can be so resolved as to secure for the action of the individual a sanction, not of the code of traditional morality but of the direct vision of the divine purpose behind it. It is the vision which reveals to the discerning spirit the mysterious ways of the divine action (*divya karma*) which are evolving the eternal good through apparent evils, the abiding values through the vicissitudes of circumstances, first in the crystal-clear inner vision of the realized man, and ultimately in the totality of the world movement which, however, always remains an enigma to the surface mind.

This want of an integral vision, which finds such a seemingly rational expression in Arjuna's impassioned pleading against war, has been rebuked by the Lord as an ignominous failure of the nerves which, far from ennobling the spirit, drags it down to the object level of the ignoble (BG II.2). His sentimental concern for the future weal of the social order He characterized as a cheap sample of faint-hearted impotence, his beautiful sermon on piety and renunciation He criticized as a travesty of wisdom (*prajnavada*), that is not even logically tenable (BG II.11). In his specious arguments against war, the very first reason advanced by Arjuna is: what pleasure or satisfaction (*sukha, priti*) is there in killing one's own kith and kin? (BG I.35, 36). But to make the pleasure principle, however refined or ennobled it may be, the guide in conduct of life is the ideal of the vital man; and hedonism has never been a universally accepted ethical standard. When the question turns on the evaluation of the merits of so-called violence and nonviolence, a subtle form of spiritually glossed pleasure principle may well lead astray the discerning intellect of the mentally wise. Of course, priti or the satisfaction of the heart is not in itself condemnable; but like all positive emotional contents of the mind, its value depends on the relative elevation of the consciousness.

In an unillumined mind, priti may become an extremely dangerous incentive. Although in Arjuna it did not appear in its lowest form of egocentricism, and even had the semblance of a self-abnegating altruism, yet its sphere was narrow. Expanding the ego, with which we are habitually associated, is but the first step toward an integral self-realization. It confers upon the soul the first measure of the titiksha,[17] which is the most potent lever in the process of soul elevation; but the power to suffer and suffer blindly will not carry us very far unless behind suffering there is the sanction of a higher illumination. Like priti, titiksha as a powerful volutional content of the mind depends on the guidance of the inner light for its fruitful functioning. Arjuna's solicitude for others and his willingness to suffer so that others may enjoy have given him the vision of, if not a higher then a wider aspect of the self—the self in the family (*kula*) and in the race (*jati*), whose accepted ideals he holds up as something having eternal values (*shashvata*) (BG I.42). This naturally defines the limits of the vision of a mental man; and we in the modern age, who feel pride in having outgrown the primeval tribal instinct or kula dharma, are still on a par with him in clinging to the fantasy of racial superiority or jatidharma. But the ego bound up with the family or the race, though it finds a wider objective field, still moves hampered by a preoccupation with a traditional past and a not-too-far-reaching vision of the future. Hence any code of conduct dictated by it can never have the self-poised catholicity of a universal outlook. If the individual soul cannot attain the all-encompassing status of the universal soul, its perception of the ethical ideal will always be dogmatic. To counteract this, it is necessary to widen the horizon of one's soul-being and make it coincide with the utmost limits of the world-being. Not the kula or jati alone, but the good of the loka, praja, or bhuta must be the criterion by which to judge one's actions, says the Lord.[18] And the concept of the universal good can find expression not in some mind-conceived planning, but in realizing in the individual being the total rhythm of the world-becoming by diving into the indiscernible depths of the spirit, "by consciously surrendering all activities to the Lord, and in complete conformity with the ideal of Buddhiyoga by being always conscious of Him alone" (BG XVIII.57).

V

This widening of the consciousness or the ideal of realizing the world in spirit is the objective aspect of the three-dimensional truth realization (Shvetashvatara Upanishad I.9.12), and must be prefaced by its subjective aspect of realizing the self in the spirit. This is the first step of the progressive cult of Buddhiyoga and in the Gita has been introduced by raising the pertinent problem of death, which in the human mind has always been the starting point of all spiritual inquiries. In philosophical analysis, the conceptual experience of death has been described as the inborn psychological reaction of fear of the prospect of self-annihilation irrationally persisting in all organisms (Yogasutrabhasya II.9). It is the all-pervading phenomenon, "the wide extended snare," as the Upanishad calls it, the root cause of which lies in the ego's obdurate preoccupation with the moment or abhinivesha, otherwise called andhatamisra or the blinding darkness of ignorance (Vachaspati on Sankyakarika 48). From this is derived the negative life impulses of shrinking at the prospect of the disturbance of one's status quo, which dogs at every step the march of the soul's progress, and even at the highest elevation of spiritual realization appears as the strange phenomenon of mokshabhiti before the last plunge into the abyss of the supreme Unmanifest (*avyakta*) is taken.[19]

In Arjuna's *vishadayoga* (the yoga of dejection), the lowest level to which spiritual degeneration can sink before it can start on its upward march,[20] his vicarious experience of the forces of death and devastation initiated the spiritual conflict. He himself was not afraid to die and even courted death to let others live; but he was afraid of inflicting death on others, though he had hitherto believed himself to have had moral justification for doing so. The problem, as it has already been remarked, introduces an antimony of reason, and imitating Pilate, we may very well inquire "What is death?" The answer comes significantly enough in the Gita in at least three places, from three metaphysical standpoints—the analytic standpoint of Sankhya (BG II.11–30), the practical standpoint of Yoga (BG VII.5–25), and the cosmic standpoint of what might generally be called the Vedanta (BG XI.25–32). In the first two cases the question has been dealt with as an incontrovertible and indispensable factor of subjective experience, which alone can prepare the buddhi for dispassionate and objective valuation of the great mystery and place one's conduct in a right location in the total scheme of things. The whole course of the teaching has again been so graduated in conformity with the progressive evolution of the consciousness as to enable it to become accustomed to the "logic of the infinite" loosely called by us the "inexorable logic of facts."

The discussion has begun by striking an intimately personal note. Apart from the haunting sense of abhinivesha mentioned above, death generally appears before us as the horror of actual or possible bereavement, giving rise to what Arjuna calls "an unquenchable grief, sapping away the vital forces." The antidote for this grief (*shoka*) and the consequent delusion (*moha*)[21] is to be found neither in customary doses of consolation nor in the normal healing property of time, which is only moha in another form; but the radical cure can come only when we ourselves have gone through the experience of death and seen beyond it. The eternal question about which "even the gods are of two minds" (Katha U I.1.xxii) poses itself before us: Is there a positive Beyond after the last plunge has been taken, and can it be a concrete experience in life? The answer has always been an emphatic "yes," and death, the supreme negation, has freely been equated with the ultimate basis of experience in its pristine purity—the colorless radiance of the self. The question of violence and nonviolence, which is only a retroflexion of the problem of death, can finally be decided at this empyrean height alone, and the way in which it has been taken up by the Gita is a direct challenge to our buddhi to tempt the abysmal depths of our being and see things for ourselves in the incandescent light of self-experience. Otherwise, the sanction, "You can kill because you kill the body and not the soul" can readily be dismissed as a transparent piece of sophistry, and the attempt to explain away allegorically the implications of a Kurukshetra as a palliation advanced by the impotent.

In applying sankhyabuddhi of the introspective and analytical process of illumination to the problem of death (BG II.11–30), the very first requisite is to transcend the sense of temporal limitation born of an exclusive preoccupation with the present, engendered by an accumulation of predetermined and habitual (*vyavasthita*) responses to one's environment (BG III.34). This narrowing of the time-vision, though necessary in the process of the soul's growth as a means of utilization and ripening (*vipaka*) of past energies, is nevertheless a force of inertia which makes one insusceptible to the innate rhythm of the universal life. The soul shrinks from the prospect of an abrupt change, though in its inmost being the hankering for change has always been there; and this is not strange, because change, another name of which is death, as the cardinal principle of the universal manifestation, combines in itself the dual process of dissolution and creation. The experience of change reflected on an enduring subject creates the abstraction of time-concept, which forms the substratum of our inwardly induced Becoming. To be in time and yet by a supreme effort of discrimination to live beyond it, enables us to catch the reflection of time-eternity, and this is the first step toward our realization of an unfettered Being. To the conceptive mind, the sense of time-eternity is a phenomenal creation of the speech habit devoid of all reality (Yogasutra I.5), but to the dhira[22] of discerning buddhi, it is the sensation of an unfathomable intensity of supreme concentration,[23] in which the moment, as the rock bottom of all direct perceptions, becomes without foregoing its unitary character at once the seed and the deployment of the totality of experience. It is this moment-eternity, if we can use such a term, which furnishes the wherewithal for realizing the self-Light, the ultimate point of intensive experience, on whose conceptual extension are arranged the events of the cosmic and the psychophysical order (BG II.12, 13). To this realization, death appears as a natural phase in a series of physical changes that should be equated, not with the process of the dissolution of the body but rather with the assumption of new vehicles by the spirit (*dehantaraprapti*).[24]

The above realization, in which death and life are felt as the systole and diastole of a universal force-rhythm, presupposes a discipline of habitual concentration which has been detailed elsewhere while explaining the yogic cult of death (BG VIII.5–28). The prerequisite of this discipline is the lifelong practice of titiksha,[25] which significantly enough forms the first practical instruction for spiritual guidance in the Gita. The inherent limitations of sense-contacts (*matrasparsha*), by which the mechanism of change is kept in perpetual activity in life, produce the fluctuating dualities of experience in the psychophysical organism that throw it into a state of irksome imbalance. The result is a slow but sure lessening of the illumination of consciousness, a gradual engulfment of the spirit by the creeping forces of inconscient matter, ending in the too-familiar phenomena of decay and death. To the illumined mind, this is the inscrutable mystery of the Unmanifest (*avyakta*), forming the two dark and unfathomable bounds encompassing the temporal phenomenon of limited manifestation (BG II.28). Notwithstanding the assumption that the end and the beginning of things are shrouded in mystery, the soul is secretly aware of the fact that this dark avyakta of negative content can be turned into the luminous avyakta brooding over it, in which the alternation of the cosmic Day and Night is absorbed in the positive and yet transcendent Light of timeless eternity (*parah sanatano bhavah*).[26] It is this avyakta which is dimly felt in the soul as the perpetual urge of self-exceeding, attended with the double movement of self-gathering and self-expansion; and this urge, although primarily expressing itself in a recoiling from pain, finally appears as a recoiling from the tedium of pleasure also. This is the genesis of the spiritual force of titiksha, which in its process of striking a balance, of self-poise (*shamatva*) in the tumult of the wavering experiences of dualities (*vyatha*), tends to reduce the consciousness to the naturalness of its pristine simplicity. Its last result is to make the time-sense homogeneous, where duration is measured not by the residuum left on the consciousness by the march of the objectively perceived event-series, but by the intensification of the subjective experience owing to the consciousness actively plumbing the depths of the self-absorbed being, and on the empirical level, this is reflected in the ever-present sense of immortality (*amritatva*) which has been acclaimed as the goal of all spiritual realization.

The problem of death is thus solved by what may analytically be called the linear experience of the time-real; and for an integral comprehension, it is to be supplemented by the extensional experience of the space-real, which has been symbolized by the vedantic conception of akasha.

VI

On an analysis of any moment of our empirical existence, we always find that our ego forms the center of a conceptual universe fluctuating in time, just as our physical bodies form the center of a sensible universe arranged around it in space. Between the two entities of a center and an environment, there is incessantly going on an interacting play of energies in which the one is always seeking to dominate the other and finally absorb it into its own homogeneity. This mutual struggle, which is the only sure sign of the action and existence of universal energy, is apparent to consciousness alone, which must be admitted as an irreducible factor of existence to make any form of experience possible; and experience is the ultimate standard of a materialistic, an idealist, or a nihilist. Even if we look upon consciousness as a luminous spearhead emerging in the process of material evolution, and do not bother about the degree of its latency in other levels of existence than our own, we must admit that in the human organism, as now constituted, it has acquired the distinctive character of turning round upon itself and making itself its own object. The spiritual benefit accruing to the organism from this development can never be overrated, because by engendering the two opposed and yet complimentary virtues of jugupsa (recoiling) and titiksha (calm endurance), it gives the organism an occasion for developing the soul-sense which becomes in course of time the most potent weapon for fighting against the encroachments of inconscient nature.

The forces of nature, whether from within or without, stimulate and stir a response in the soul, which utilizes the stimulus as opportunity for its self-expression; and for a time, it seems that soul and nature are working in harmony to ensure an ever-increasing fund of empirical values favorable to the inherent dynamism of the soul. But after a time, this harmony breaks down, as the law of progressive growth demands that, in a process, the supply of energy must be in quanta, punctuating its continuity with intermittent blanks which, however, serve as periods of rest or incubation. The breakdown comes as a form of exhaustion which is either natural or brought about by some unforeseen disturbance of balance. Whatever might be the cause, two results are possible: the soul-energy either succumbs to the lure of the shock and quietly subsides, or it reacts violently and fights hard to maintain its existence in spite of all odds.[27] It is this second possibility that starts the process of crystallization in the soul-essence which, through many vicissitudes, succeeds at last in organizing a distinctive ego-structure tending to become more and more introspective in character. An inner universe with the ego as the center is thus formed, which at first is but a reflection of the sensuous world, though essentially conceptual in its makeup. We ordinarily call this the mental plane, where the motivation is generally of vital origin, relieved by an infiltration of a dimmed illumination from the plane of intelligence above it. A preoccupation with things inwardly visualized makes the mind-sense more and more susceptible to the realities of another order—the order of conceptual existence (*bhava*) as distinguished from material existence (*bhuta*). So long as the hold of material realities on consciousness remains insistent, the mind has a tendency to treat these bhavas lightly, owing to their amorphous character. But dealing with abstractions is a prerogative of the human mind, and its power of rational destruction yields in the long run to its inherent power of spiritual construction. As a result, the amorphous abstractions become crystallized into concrete forms, and the vague generalizations are stamped with the assurance of particularized and tangible realities. In mystical parlance, this has been called the *bhavaloka* or the plane of conceptual existences, which form an intermediary between the world of impregnated matter and the world of pure spirit.

An ascent to this status of consciousness marks the triumph for the sattvikabuddhi over the bewildering confusion of the objective world, because in this state the rift between the ego and the nonego usually assumed by the normal consciousness is closed up by a direct perception of the sameness of the stuff from which they both have been created.[28] The positive gain for the consciousness from this is a realization of the simplicity and the all-pervasiveness of its essence, coupled with a unique manifestation of a deep sympathy capable of entering into the heart of all things. The meaning of existence then stands revealed in a simple harmony of an all-comprehensive unity in which there is no jarring note of a hitherto irreconcilable conflict and confusion of multifarious tendencies. The world there is, but is no longer a world marred by many scars or rent by many fissures; and the percipient of the world also no longer occupies a position of isolation from the rest—but the center somehow irradiates itself into the expanse of the circumference, and "the drop becomes the sea," as the mystics are wont to describe it in a language of inevitable paradox.

The psychological implication of such a realization is this. Just as before the calm dispassionate gaze of the witness-consciousness, the fleeting show of the inwardly objectified entities reveals an inner strand unifying the apparently disconnected moments into a linear continuity of pure time-experience, whose homogeneity at the same time reduces the percipient consciousness to the intensity of a luminous point, so the same calm abandon by a naturally initiated movement of expansion brings about the integral perception of a space-real,[29] the essence of which is the feeling of a vacuum, forming not only the substratum but also the impalpably subtle material of all formulations. The two movements, though at the beginning they may appear to follow a sequence, are really simultaneous and represent two aspects of an integral whole, in which there is a merger of what we empirically know as space and time. If, in consequence of a supreme abstraction, we take space as the static and time as the dynamic aspect of reality, then at this height we may term the former pure Existence (*sat*) and the latter its deployment as pure Existent (*bhava*) (BG II.16). The relationship between the two is that of an inalienable unity which runs throughout the whole gradient of their phenomenal manifestation. On the highest summit of generic conception, they are the immobile Existence and the Existent as we see here; on the plane of mobility they are the energizing of consciousness,[30] or the eternal bi-une of consciousness-energy evolving into the dual principles of purusha-prakriti, or the subject-object relation apparent on the plane of empirical consciousness. On the lowest plane, there is obviously an imbalance, a discord, and a confusion; but there is also in the soul an urge to retrace the steps and transcend them. As we rise higher, the differences are resolved, apparently by a shedding off, but really by a gathering-up and dissolution into the essence of a higher and harmonious whole, till at last we reach the supreme height of pure Existence whose sanction and seal support All.

The experience is stupendous and indescribable except by luminous hints, which can only serve as pointers to the aspiring soul. To the normal consciousness which subsists only by relational apprehension and cannot endure except by reacting on some preexisting data, pure Existence is a meaningless abstraction having no real content. Yet in its dealing with particulars, it secretly depends on a comprehension of the universals which, on a deeper scrutiny, seem to stand midway between the objective and the subjective poles of experience. Consciousness, which is accustomed to a forward movement in its relations with the objective world, can be trained to lean back more and more on the subjective aspect of its experience, on the intuitive comprehension of the meaning underlying it. The meaning may appear as a pure emotional content, free from habitual reactions of pleasure and pain or attraction and repulsion—a ripple on the serene bosom of existence. The meaning may grow, its element of emotion may deepen into an intensity, not of flutter but of a quiet repose initiated by a sense of an ineffable contact with the true Real (BG VI.27–28), which is felt as the common stuff of the experiencer and the experienced. Just as there is an indiscriminate identification with the subject, or rather of the pure and undifferentiated object-self with the subject-self; and this may lend to the consciousness either the character of atomicity, if the movement has originally been impelled by a process of exclusion, or the character of immensity, if there has been no mentally conceived reservation at the start of the movement. In either case we arrive at what might be called the status of pure consciousness, a conceptual projection from which may flood and permeate the whole gamut of existence (*idam sarvam*) and reveal to the spiritualized sense its inner essence of inalienable Identity. The last barrier then has been crossed, the last film has dropped from the spirit's vision; the great revelation may be formulated in the terms of the supreme law of spiritual intuition: Whatever is, is. It is the pure Existence, appearing as the dark Unmanifest (*avyakta*) at the two poles of all limited and fluctuating existences, which creates from its inexhaustible (*avyaya*) store of energy this unending panorama of its multiple self-formulations, and broods over them in its inscrutable mystery, permeating them with its essence of deathlessness (BG II.17).

Still, forms seem to appear from nowhere and then disappear into nowhere; but to whom? Only to the vision of the limited consciousness that depends on an array of feeble instrumentations for its perceptions and cannot penetrate into the beyond. Around every positive content of its experience, there is a mist of incomprehensibleness which tempts but never fully yields its secrets; and the mental consciousness is prone to equate the incomprehensible with the nonexistent. To it, the normal course of life appears as a mere spasm subsiding ultimately and inevitably into an all-engulfing death. Underlying the incessant flux of phenomenal existence, its imaginative reason can vaguely feel an enduring substratum, which to its objective vision must appear at most as an inconscient movement of energy; but to equate this substratum with an infinite consciousness seems to it to be an unwarranted assumption, because the meager measure of consciousness that the individual has is debarred from having any direct comprehension of an infinite Real which, by the very nature of real cognition, must also be the awareness of an infinite consciousness. Hence, as envisaged by the limited conscious being, the individual really dies; the notion of its survival after death is only a conjecture inspired by a fond hope of the continuation of the present existence; the only immortality that there is, is the objective immortality of the race or the flux of nature.

But the illumined reason knows that the fallacy of this dwarfed conception is rooted in the individual's preoccupation with the physically constituted structure of the ego, which is called the body. Even here, there is an inversion of perception because the objective reality of others' bodies is tacitly transferred to one's own case, so that while in reality every individual possesses only a subjective conception of the body, he readily confuses this with an objective reality derived analogically from the perception of others' bodies. The body-consciousness is thus turned irrationally into a body-object; and yet, at every turn of life, the individual rejects this suggestion in practical affairs, when, say, a surge of vital emotion makes him forget the body and identify with the emotion itself. It is therefore open to the individual whether he habituates himself to think in terms of subjective conception or objective perception. If he adopts the former course, which is really in line with his essentially constituted introspective nature, he will have in time pierced the first knot, "the knot of creative material energy," as the mystics call it (the *Brahma-granthi* in the Tantras), and find before him a hierarchy of ego-structures more and more refined, subtle, and expansive in character until finally he finds all egos as the reflection of one supreme Ego—"the Eternal, the Intensive, the All-pervasive, the Immobile, the Immutable, the Unmanifest beyond all thought and yet capable of being realized as This" (BG II.24–25). The path of the realization of immortality for the individual lies this way—through the exploration of one's subjective possibilities by a denial of the objective preoccupation. The law of sympathy which enables the individual to enter into a spiritual commerce with other beings, when expanded to its utmost capacity by a catharsis of the egoistic existence (*ahamkarito bhavah*) (BG XVIII.17), discovers for him the cosmic Ego, while the law of introspective self-absorption, worked to the extreme, launches him into the transcendent I-ness where everything is, and so death is not. Yet in that luminous Void, there are sparkles of change, the light-bubbles rising from and breaking into the incandescence of immutable That on the screen of whose self-extension they project themselves as the flux of phenomenal existences. But where are these phenomena, what are those changes? The former are but the polarization of the one into the other, of their mutual transfiguration. From whichever end we look, the substratum is eternal—eternal in its timelessness; and the flux is also eternal—eternal in its beating time to the dance of the Immobile. And covering both, Existence permeates All.

On this limitless canvas of the formless Vast, which is mentally incomprehensible and yet seizable by a luminous intuition (*buddhigrahya*), shimmering forms are delineated with conceptual contours that rise, intermingle, and pass away into other forms. The Many are there; yet they subsist not by their own right but by the sanction of the One whose self-figurations they are. Apparently there is a clash, a concussion when form grapples with form in the incessant flux of things to maintain their distinctive individualities, which ultimately derive their raison d'etre from the One individual comprising all. To read into this struggle the agency of an ugly and unjustifiable force of destruction alone is only a delusion of the ego that irrationally seeks to perpetuate the limited formulation of its existence, taking the part for the whole and yet knowing at heart that, to it at least, the meaning of existence is essentially bound up with the inevitability of change. For the growth of the phenomenal soul-being, Reality must express itself in a process, the conceptual continuity of which must be actually broken and linked up by intermittent gaps that apparently terminate but really continue the windings of the spiral of existence (BG II.18, 22). And yet in its core is established the self-gathered luminosity of a central being, the iridescence of whose all-comprising simultaneity is thus enrolled in the pageant of a temporal process. The two are the bi-une aspects of the same reality; and to cross over from the shadows of many deaths to the bright shores of immortality, the soul-being must learn to poise itself on this supreme status of transcendence-immanence beyond the wavering modes of phenomenal existence (*prakriti-sambhavah gunah*), where, let alone the events of physical birth and death, even the prospect of the cataclysm of cosmic creation and dissolution will leave it unshaken, because it would have entered into and become one with the nature of pure Being (BG II.20; also cf. XIV.2). Possessed and permeated by an indelible sense of immortality, because it has been focused upon and riveted to the perception of a basic *esse*, consciousness then becomes homogeneous with the obliteration of the distinction and interaction between the agent and the object, so that even in the conceptual projection of the phenomenal event-series, the mutuality of their relations is perceived as the self-activity of an indivisible existence;[31] and at the same time, the inwardly turned gaze of the witness calmly fixed on the self-vision of "an eternally inherent immutability knowing neither birth nor death" abrogates even the idea of an efficient mover of things (BG II.21).

Here is the supreme mystery of spiritual realization wherein the logical contradiction of nonbecoming and becoming is resolved into the ineffability of self-becoming, in which the consciousness of process and the consciousness of being are not polarized. If consciousness is the ultimate measure of all things and, in its approach to the utter comprehension of the self-identical Reality, it has the inherent tendency of bringing the two normally divergent poles of its operation into a state of final fusion, then psychologically speaking, the intensification and heightening of consciousness will naturally be attended with a process of translating the objectivity of things into the subjectivity of thoughts. The obvious consequence of this spiritualization of matter will be a gradual relieving of the dead weight of objectivity pressing upon consciousness, until at last the contacts of matter even in their most aggressive form will not be able to perturb the serenity of the spirit (BG II.23–24; cf. also VI.22; XVI.23). And this is not simply an experience of negative content initiated by the intensified force of titiksha; somehow, as the final point of tension is reached, a floodgate is somewhere thrown open and the resistance offered to the impact of matter melts into a suffusion of spiritual light in which all movements of matter are felt as the spirit's own modes. Consciousness then expands, so to say (if we are allowed to interpret its utter freedom in terms of spatial imagery), and becomes conterminous with Being, including in the boundlessness of its conceptual projection the totality of its self-becomings (*sarvani bhutani*), so that immutability through mutation, immortality through deaths, becomes the normal feature of the Featureless. This is the supreme wonder which is sometimes revealed to the eyes of someone or to the ears of another, while a third may even dare to speak of it in awesome speech, and yet none may have plumbed its fathomless depths (BG II.29).

Such, then, is the nature of the illumination arrived at by following the path of introspective analysis (*sankhyabuddhi*), in which the starting point is the cult of titiksha, which helps to converge the divergent movements of the soul-energy into a one-pointedness (*ekagrata*) leading to a state of supreme indifference (*upeksha*), devoid of all emotive disturbances; and normally this again either leads to or is accompanied by an intensification of the realization of a pure Existence forming the substratum, the constituent, and the dynamics of all existences. This background of supreme Reality has been called That (*tat*), when an emphasis has been laid on its universal aspect, or as a This (*ayam*), when it has been treated as the spotlight of the individual consciousness, which forms the self-illuminated focus of a cosmic vision. The phenomenal changes of which death is only a subjective form are to be evaluated from the standpoint of this ultimate Reality, whose illumination should suffuse all the facts as well as the acts of life. But the dizzy heights to which the cult of sankhyabuddhi points, if once attained, may make the return to the lower planes impossible, and the incentive to duty may die a natural death in a luminous inertness. As a countermeasure to this, sankhyabuddhi has been supplemented by what is called Buddhiyoga or the cult of practical illumination, which will turn Truth-realization into an integral whole by making the Reality real not only in abstraction but in concreteness, too.

VII

An integral communion with the supreme Reality and an assumption of the total nature of God is the summum bonum to which all human endeavors are secretly striving; and the sanction behind this lies not in a conventional superimposition of some timeworn and fossilized ethical or spiritual ideology, but in the inherent nature of consciousness that is marked by an indomitable urge toward expansion, freedom, and an enrichment of its potentialities. At one extreme of this realization is the Sankhya poise (though not in the traditional sense of the status of supreme indifference or tatasthya of the realized individual purusha, but in the sense of the utter and imperturbable freedom or svatantrya of the universal Purusha-Vishesha), in which the unrippling joy of transcendence illumines the limitless horizons of the pure consciousness; and at the other extreme in the yoga poise,[32] in which the same spirit of transcendence translates itself into the joy of cosmic experience sparkling with the scintillations of myriads of its self-figurations.

The God transcendent and the God immanent are both to be harmoniously realized in an integral experience; otherwise we run the risk of being content with "a defective computation," as Sri Ramakrishna pointed out—though the human mind is at liberty to choose either ideal at the expense of the other, the motive in each case being determined by the peculiarity of the spiritual constitution of the aspirant. It should be noted that this one-sided emphasis by the individual, if sincerely followed in response to the dictates of one's own inherent nature (*svabhava*), is not likely to be detrimental to one's spiritual career; nor does it run counter to the total scheme of things, because canalization of energies in one particular channel, whether in an individual or a race, in a particular age or clime, is an indispensable device of nature for the perfection of the several parts before they can be assembled into an integral whole. Since nature is always secretly conscious of the totality that has to be achieved, the antagonism that may arise in the process due to overemphasis is utilized by her, at least at higher levels of consciousness, not as an agent of mutual destruction but as a means of rounding off the angularities by mutual interaction and complementation. But still, the ideal to be followed in matters spiritual is to start with an intensive and comprehensive view of things, calling upon nature to bloom in a thousand-petaled affluence by letting the law of conscious harmony rather than the law of blind strife prevail.

Human life obviously starts in a cosmic field, where its presence as the culmination of an obscure and long-drawn-out evolutionary past and beginning of the progression of a dimly realized distant future is swayed by a host of divergent forces, creating a veritable chaos which it is its supreme business to turn into an ordered whole. The pattern of the order is supplied either by a none-too-illumined practical intelligence that glosses over its inheritance of a bundle of stereotyped tendencies with a modicum of ill-digested intuitions of the Real; or it springs from the depth of the Spirit, reflecting the true aim of the cosmic process that can only be realized by accommodating harmoniously all the factors of existence on the perceptual plane of a supreme consciousness whose homogeneity cannot be disturbed or adversely acted upon by the mutations in the objectivized world movement. The former calls upon the natural man to follow the beaten track of least resistance, though even in this case a good deal of strain is inevitable. But it involves a greater strain to move along the other course, which demands a rising up the stream to its very sources, so that its workings may be examined and controlled by a total view from the heights beyond. Both processes lead to what may be called the cosmicization of the spirit by urging on the consciousness to transcend the limitations imposed upon it either by external circumstances or by internal constitution.

Acceleration or shortening the process of time is a necessary factor in such endeavors; and this is a prerogative that can be utilized by the human consciousness perfectly on the subjective plane alone, because the movement on the objective plane is inevitably linked up with the march of time, whose pace can be quickened only up to a limited extent, but whose continuity cannot be changed into instantaneity without crushing the whole structure of existences dependent upon it. Acceleration is thus felt to be a real force on the conceptual plane where it appears as the urge (*samvega*) which drives the soul through the hierarchy of the spiritual realms shrouding in a luminous oblivion the things that have been left below. And this translates itself into para vairagya or the supreme detachment which has been equated with the ineffable status of the transcendent Purusha reflecting itself on the soul—the achieved condition of anavritti or the quiescence of nonrevolution.

This is one end of the process of cosmicization culminating in the realization of the transcendent Reality; at the other end lies the realization of the joy of the cosmic spirit embodied in the thrill of eternal Becoming, which on the ordinary level of consciousness finds expression in the cult of power and enjoyment (*bhogaishvarya*), with all the crudities incumbent on the natural limitations of the unregenerate spiritual vision. Just as an extreme emphasis is possible on the realization of the transcendent aspect, so it is possible to emphasize this, too, as both the cults of detachment and attachment ultimately rest on two original and mutually linked powers of the Absolute. To counteract the deficiency inherent in overemphasis by striking a balance between the two, not in a spirit of superficially induced compromise but with the illumined sense of a synthesis on a higher plane, is the eternal problem of the human spirit, to which a solution has been offered in the Gita in its formulation of the discipline.

VIII

Although the urge toward transcendence, which is but another name for the urge of self-exceeding inherent in human nature, is the keynote of all ideas of progress, we find it conditioned and confronted by an equally potent urge of self-assertion and self-fulfillment working within a circumscribed sphere. The ancients described this as the activity of the annada or "the eater of the food,"[33] taking the imagery from the field of the vital being intent upon the process of assimilation, which is its only means of releasing the higher potential involved in a lower form of energy. As thus constituted, this urge is an important factor that cannot be overlooked if we are to lay down a secure basis for an all-round and fruitful functioning of the spiritual endeavor, which is of course the only thing that counts in determining the ultimate meaning of life. To this end, an analysis of the vital urge as a counterpart of the spiritual is absolutely necessary, as this will reveal the nature of the field in which we have to work out our destiny, and of the forces that we have to reckon with in our march into the beyond.

To the normal man, the vital is the realm of the immediate—a form of energizing springing from some unknown source which hurls itself upon the tacitly assumed mass of objective realities and carries backward the force of their impacts to be translated into the colorful pattern of a phenomenal consciousness. The quivering energy inherent in it, which defies all ultimate analysis and must be accepted as an irreducible content of simple perception, is transferred by it to be the objective world, which it interprets as a vast conglomeration of fluctuating forces working with the multiplicity of materialized beings (*bhuta*) as their media. The subjective counterparts of these at the other end of the process are the spiritualized entities (*bhava*), which form the conceptually realized types or universals of the particularized beings. The energy linking the two has been variously described in different contexts as spanda (vibration), kshepa (projection), or shakti (potency)—its widest designation being karma (activity), which the Gita from a comprehensive point of view defines as the multipotent creative urge (*visarga*) giving rise to the conjoint principles of bhuta and bhava (BG VIII.3). The inclusion of bhava in the scheme of things makes the definition a fuller one, by refusing to excise arbitrarily the facts of subjectivity from a total view of the creational process.

But still, from a superficial and mechanical view of the origination of things (*arambhavada*), the principle of the atomic origination of the world may be extended to the domain of subjectivity, even—as has been done by some ancient and modern schools of thought—making the karmic operation appear as a meaningless spanda indifferent to the end to be achieved. But even then, the ancient idealists could not and did not do away with all meaning in subjective life, as their preoccupation with the cult of spiritual freedom invested the inner content of a being with the sense of a definite end to be achieved. The end might be a colorless Void—but still the cult of its achievement lent a deep moral significance to the entire life movement and meant a deepening and widening consciousness, which was a positive gain to the individual as well as the social being; while the wisdom of despair of the modern realist is nothing but a sign of spiritual bankruptcy or at best a self-complacent failure of nerve induced by a dogmatic refusal to accept or meet squarely all the facts of existence.

Of course, the ways of the mahat brahma, the matrix of the karmic energy, are as inscrutable as the poise of the supreme Purusha; but this welter of prakritic forces, which appear so only to the blurred vision of a feeble attempt at objectivization, acquire a meaning in jiva—perhaps warped at first and necessarily circumscribed by his undeveloped power of apperception. His karma, the store of vital energy with which he starts in life, spurs him to the realization of his own limited good and expresses itself primarily in a spirit of self-assertion and self-fulfillment. Leaving aside for the time being the question of moral evaluation, this much can be said: that the karma of the jiva introduces a new element—a tangible purpose, a force of conscious selectivity arranging the objective data into a specific order, which is the subjective addition to the mechanical movements of material nature. We generally find no difficulty in conceding that even the machine of nature works in accordance with a set of preestablished laws,[34] but then, the concept of a law is a purely subjective creation—a law is a law or an arrangement of facts in a particular way only to a perceiving consciousness which has behind its mode of perception the urge of a secret purpose compelling it to perceive things in the way it does. The inhering purpose working obscurely from behind in all subjective functionings can be pulled out and partially made an object of consciousness; and this will mean the canalization of the forces of subjectivity and helping the growth of individuation.

But a vast amount of purposiveness will still be left unaccounted for, appearing as an enigmatic play of forces to the perceiving consciousness, which will try to formulate it into laws, perhaps in obedience to the urge of the very purposiveness whose mysteries it seeks to unravel. Purpose, will, or desire (*kama*), by whatever name we may call it, thus appears to be an invariable concomitant of consciousness. Viewed in the context of the totality of things, will (which is the indispensable subjective version of what we call objective laws) seems to create and dominate phenomenal consciousness; while from the standpoint of the evolving individual, it is consciousness that appears to dominate will and use it as an instrument in its practical functioning. The close interrelation between the two presupposes the fact that both of them are but the dual aspects of the same reality appearing with a difference of emphasis on different levels of existence. Even if we take simple awareness as the essential characteristic of consciousness, as we are apt to do in an analytic definition of its phenomenal aspect or in an assessment of its transcendental value, still consciousness cannot be divorced from will; for even in transcendental consciousness the absorption of power into the immobility of the self only means an introvert direction of the will, which appears there as the intensive potency of self-sustenance of pure Existence.[35]

As for will, on the phenomenal level of individual existence it palpably appears as the direction of consciousness to an end; while in the total scheme of things it is our superstitious insistence on the limited ego as the only form of consciousness, which makes all things beyond its pale appear as inconscient and so their movement devoid of any teleological significance. But then the ego-ridden consciousness too is charged with a spirit of inquiry into or assimilation of the mobile facts of inconscient existence. As a result, it discovers therein laws or directions of energy in a field of ordered existence, which, as it has already been remarked, look very much like subjective formulations; and it cannot acquiesce in the admission of a conscious agent behind those directions, because it cannot go back upon its dogmatic exclusion of consciousness from everything other than itself. But the very spirit of assimilation suggested by the urge of inquiry or of knowing more and more about things keeps the door open between the realms of the conscient and the inconscient.[36] And if the investigation into the real nature of the objective world is aided not simply by an artificial extension of sense-perceptions and deductions of mental reason from these data alone but also by a refinement, and consequent amplification of the observing consciousness as well,[37] then the barrier between the conscient and the inconscient would not be so insuperable as it is now, and the admission of a cosmic consciousness as the agent of the play of a cosmic Will would appear to be a natural dedication, if not an obvious truth, following in the lines of a higher method of inquiry.

If, from the standpoint of highest abstraction, we understand by consciousness a comprehensive totality of self-awareness, we may define will as the urge of self-expression inherent in it. Analyzed from a lower perceptual level, in which an element of polarization has already been introduced into the unitary content of pure Being, the urge appears, as the ancient Vedanta called it, as the desire for self-multiplication which postulates a self-extension in space and a self-procession in time. To mental reason, which always poses a why against all statements of facts until it is wearied down to silence, this desire must appear as an enigma, the attempted solution of which ends in various speculations about the original motive of creation. The ancients did not try to give any reason for this primal desire but simply accepted it as a fact, equating it with the simple joy of life in its pristine purity. If the real as consciousness is an illumined Void (*akasha*), as will and power it is also the surge of life (*prana*) (Brahmasutra I.1.xxii read with I.1.xiii). We cannot explain by logical analysis the raison d'etre for this bi-une reality, but can only refer to the parallel phenomena in our own being, where consciousness and life (or its equivalent, power, desire, and will) appear as inseparable associates. Consciousness is not simply awareness of prearranged events but it is also an impulsion to growth, not only by widening the horizons of its awareness but also by deepening its intensity by an assimilation of an identification with whatever comes within its bounds.[38] This urge of expansion inherent in consciousness and inwardly felt as an insatiable aspiring toward the Light beyond (*svarjyotih*), the vedic seers called *brahma*—a term, though apparently connoting a subjective process, that cannot be arbitrarily divorced from the suggestion of the goal aimed at; as in all growths, the more so in spiritual growth, the different stages cannot be looked upon as mutually exclusive. So brahma, the Fire of aspiring consciousness in its progressive contact with the ever-expanding Vast (*brihat*), ultimately translates itself into Brahma, the ether of the realized poise of the Absolute—its will-to-become transformed into the mysterious potency of what the upanishadic philosophy calls *sarvatmabhava* or the ineffable experience of "All becoming the Self."

The will-to-become is thus the primal urge implanted in a conscious being carrying it through the vicissitudes of life endeavor, whose ultimate aim is to reach the supreme status where becoming and being coalesce. The process is characterized by two forms of activity—the incentive to assimilation (*samanayana*) and the incentive to projection or creation (*vishrishti*). The former typifies the law of vital hunger (*ashanaya*) ruled by death,[39] while the latter stands for the law of sacrifice (*yajna*) leading to immortality or the status of the Purusha whose incessant self-giving is upholding and promoting the eternal process of creation (RV X.90). In the evolutionary progression of nature, in which, in obedience to the dictates of mental reason, we arrange events in a logical sequence, the law of hunger seems to occupy a prior and predominant position; but from an integral view of things, it is the law of sacrifice that sustains and ultimately fulfills the law of hunger: the Purusha himself becomes the victim in the unending universal Sacrifice—it is an act of suffering as well as an act of grace. In the logical series of the evolutionary stages, hunger of the desire (*kama*) for assimilation appears on the vital level as the characteristic property of the jiva, by dint of which he transforms the energy of matter, from which he appears to have his being, into the energy of life and mind (Ch U VI.5.i). It is an inchoate form of the original urge of self-becoming which, in a field of multiple self-figuration, must necessarily be supported by a concentration of the ego-sense and hence also by a sense of exclusiveness appearing in the role of an annada.

But this is only a stage in transition: it is in the very nature of the evolutionary process that the perceptions of the vital must change into the perceptions of the mental or the spiritual. The ultimate aim of the desire for assimilation, when it has had its fill, is to prepare the ground for the fulfillment of the desire for creation; and herein the law of hunger is supplemented or replaced by the law of sacrifice. On the lowest level of the vital being, satisfied hunger takes upon the form of the procreative urge (*prajanah kandarpah*) (BG X.28): it creates bodies that can be created as fit vehicles for the reception and development of the consciousness of the Vast (*brahmi tanu*) (Manusamhita II.26–28). On a higher level it becomes desire in conformity with the Law (*dharmaviruddah kamah*) (BG VII.11), the creative urge refined and mentalized; and at last finding expression in the ideal of lokasamgraha or social service (BG III.20, 25), it creates ethical norms in tune with the indwelling spirit of sarvatmabhava, which are the highest forms of ideologies realizable by the mental being. On the highest level, when will and consciousness fuse into an integral whole, it becomes the desire of God to create man after His own image—the inextinguishable original urge which engages the Lord in "His never-ceasing labor of Love, though in none of the three worlds of being there was any want or expectation or compulsion to keep Him so engaged" (BG III.22). This is the culmination of the divine sacrifice—"the functionings of the Law that was before all" (RV X.90.xvi), which in the realized human consciousness appears as the consuming fire of Love that will not rest until it has caught the whole in its conflagration. From the heart of the divine Man goes out the call thrilled by the urge of a spiritualized creation: "Like waters running down an incline, like months losing themselves in the brightness of the year, let the seekers come into me from everywhere" (Tait U I.4.iii). And the great hunger is appeased when in its fullness it has transformed itself into the eternal creative fire of sacrifice.[40]

To evolve from the apparently mechanical karmic energy, a conscious will at first intent on a blind desire for self-fulfillment and self-aggrandizement, and then to turn it into the spirit of a never-ending sacrifice—this then seems to be the law of creation operating at successive levels of the evolutionary endeavor of nature. In a cryptic passage (BG III.14–15), the Gita speaks of this law as a grand cycle (*chakra*), of which the line of descent traces the realized status of the cosmic spirit and appears involved in the materialized being (*bhuta*), waiting to be evolved by a similar movement into the line of ascent—thus completing the cycle on the supreme plane of identity of the bhuta with brahma and akshara. There is the akshara, the Immutable transcending and yet covering All; it projects itself into Brahman, the matrix of all becomings, which from its very nature translates itself into the indeterminate totality of cosmic energy (*karma*). This energy impregnated by an original Idea (*bhava*), evolves into the spirit of the cosmic sacrifice (*yajna*) which brings down from the Unmanifest the shower of determinate cosmic powers (*parjanya*) congealing themselves into transformable matter (*anna*).[41] In this matter evolves the conscious being (*bhuta*) in whom lies concealed the whole potency of the brahma-akshara urge waiting to be realized in accordance with the rhythm of the original cosmic Law. The jivabrahma, caught in the whirlpool of unregenerate karmic energy at the initial stage, by a secret impulsion gradually transforms this into the radiant energy of sacrifice (*yajnatapas*), which releases the spiral of the upstreaming (*urdhavasrotas*) spiritual power, creating a new form of matter and a new type of being.[42]

In a deeper sense, it is repeating the same cosmic rhythm through the medium of the individual being, failing which human life becomes a meaningless adventure continuing in the narrow grooves of sensual pleasures alone (BG III.16). How to break the chains of unillumined karma (*karmabanda*) and mechanical round of existences (*janmabanda*) depending upon it, how to change the ignorant and halting life-movement into a luminous arrow's flight by a perpetual tapasya of self-giving—this, then is the problem, the solution of which is the crying need of every life.

IX

We have seen how the operation of karmic energy, apparently inconscient on the lowest level of existence, is interpreted by consciousness as laws, which, taken in the context of a total becoming, presuppose the working of a will—thus bringing the two poles of existence into a closer substantial contact. This will, secretly operative in the world of inconscient matter, appears as a blind will-to-be (*abhimana*) translating itself into the tenacious propensity of self-preservation (*abhinivesha*)—a basic fact which makes the determinateness of mechanical laws possible. On the level of life, where, using a vedic imagery, we may say that the enthralled consciousness is just peeping out from behind the veil;[43] the will-to-be, without forgoing its own nature, develops into the will-to-become, engendering in itself the impulses of self-fulfillment (*ashanaya*) and self-multiplication (*visrishti*). On the level of mind, which the Upanishads envisage as the sacrificer (*yajamana*) (Pr U IV.4) and the divine eye (*daivam chakshuh*) (Ch U VIII.12.v), the laws become more elastic, with a wider and subtler scope as they end to turn into self-laws (*svadha*), and consciousness tries to come to its own by wrestling itself free from the blindness of abhinivesha and the clamor of ashanaya. The lever which it uses to raise itself to a higher status is, as we have already seen, its power of turning upon itself as well as its power of projecting its contents on to a conceptual field. As the Rigveda says, "it can desist from ashanaya and yet can blaze forth in intense luminosity toward the feast of the sweet pippala" (RV I.164.xx). Following in the lines of the secret workings of nature, a wider view of life then opens out before the mind's eye and the will-to-become stands fulfilled in the eternal will-to-sacrifice, where the self-poise of the witness and the self-delight of the enjoyer blend into a supreme harmony.

This is a summary delineation of the process that is going on in nature and the goals toward which it is aiming. The conscious will must find its fulfillment in the consummation of the law of sacrifice; but before it can achieve its end it has to square its accounts with life, whose workings it has to rationalize. The life of man, as it stands, is in a sorry predicament inasmuch as it is pulled asunder by two opposing sets of forces. In one set, the original karmic energy emphasizes the animal (*pashu*) or the unregenerate vital impulses in man preoccupied with the fulfillment of his limited self-interests, wherein, as the Vedas say, like an asura he sacrifices not into the fire but into his own mouth the things that ought to have been offered to the divine; while, in another set, the same energy enkindles in him the flickering fire of mental illumination (*manushya*), demanding the sacrifice of the animal for the achievement of a greater good, which, if not inspired at the outset by a spiritual motive is at least necessitated by a too-human motive of upholding a social structure in which the individual may find an ample scope for his self-development.

Of course, the average human being starts his life with the first course of an unregenerate vital activity. That psychologically he is an extrovert is a matter of common observation; the hormic structure of his consciousness—the vital energy purposively directed toward a goal—presupposes the intuition of an objective field (*vishaya*) in which its potential energy may be released, and by an interaction of external and internal forces may gain in strength until it acquires the power of turning upon itself. This preoccupation with the objective field (*vishaya-dhyana*), so necessary for the evolution and establishment of the power of self-consciousness, starts, according to the Gita (BG II.62–63), a chain of reactions somewhat like the Buddhist chain of dependent origination, in which the hormic element of the consciousness is gradually strengthened and comes to the forefront until, after a last flare-up, it again subsides into its original potential stage—thus describing a cycle of vital activity in which it bypasses the urge of the other set of spiritual forces awaiting to be released into the stream of life. The objective preoccupation, which appears to be intuitive and almost irrational, has already a seed of selectivity implanted in it in the form of tendencies (*samskara*). The deepening of the samskaras by a secret urge of the individual nature (*svabhava*) grooves the conscious substance with tracks of particularized association (*sanga*), and at the same time tinges it with the colorful positive element of attachment (*raga*), which gathers strength to flare up into the flame of desire (*kama*), making the whole consciousness burn in a red-hot glow. The process which has been subconscious for so long now becomes fully conscious, and as it has all along been a process of intensification and canalization of energies in an objective field, it is naturally confronted by a host of adverse elements, to which it reacts by engendering the feeling of aversion (*dvesha*), which again ultimately finds expression in the outburst of anger (*krodha*).

Desire and anger, which the Gita elsewhere (BG III.36–37) describes as the root agent of all sinful activities and as the compulsive force of the rajasa element of nature paralyzing the will-to-the-good,[44] mark the psychological height to which unregenerate vital activity can rise; and their palatability lies in the intensification of consciousness and its attendant energism that they secure for the subject. But the flare is more than counterbalanced by the obscurity of delusion (*moha*) that follows, which is a natural consequence of the stricture of abhinivesha or the absorption of consciousness by the interest of the moment.[45] This moha, sustained by the blind tenacity of abhinivesha or tamasi dhriti (BG XVIII.35), creates a smoke screen, as it were, behind which the original conative urge seeks to find its fulfillment. To the normal jiva-consciousness dominated by the workings of the lower nature, the whole process appears to be a positive contribution to its fund of surface experience, although it really is not so. There may be an endless repetition of the cycle—the spent-up hormic energy apparently lapsing into the dullness of sammoha but really laying in the obscure depths of the consciousness the seeds of a future resurgence in the form of samskaras which, after a period of incubation, start anew the original round, beginning with the extrovert objective preoccupation. This is the ordinary course of our surface living in which the karmic energy, mechanically following a circular path, constitutes a veritable bondage (*bhanda*) for the secretly aspiring soul; and seen in the context of a cosmic view of things, this karmabandha appears to the discerning aspirant as the fearful possibility of janmabandha or the bondage of rebirth, in which even the prospect of the enjoyment of a sensuous heavenly bliss does not bring any solace to the reason—since neither in the extension nor in the intension of a sense-bound life is there a promise of that freedom, inherent in an untrammeled existence, which only a radical change of consciousness can bring.

X

The average man dominated by a desire-soul (*kamatma*) is of course blind to the fact that behind the clamor and confusion of his all-too-familiar objective existence, another secret destiny is silently working itself out; and perhaps it is the urge of a deeper Being that really finds expression in his skewed and irrational desires through the distorting medium of a lower level of existence. The postulate of a higher, subtler, and wider consciousness forming the substratum of the phenomenal being is not an unwarranted assumption, because even the sense-mind, which may dogmatically refuse to look beyond its bounds, is unable to carry on its normal functions without a modicum of lebensraum—which amounts to a tacit intuition of an infinity beyond the finite, an unmanifest beyond the manifest, or as the ancients would have put it, a vastness of the Void as the source of all thoughts and forms. The concept of a substratum is thus a subjective necessity in our dealing with any level of existence; and it will be in strict obedience to the normal laws of thought if we postulate such a substratum in the case of phenomenal consciousness, the proof of its objective reality lying, as in all cases of scientific inquiry, with the proper discipline and the skillful application of the requisite instruments. The substratum-consciousness is there, silent and secure in the depth of the being providing the life-movement with a telos, projecting the dream of an ideal on the mind's screen, supplying the deeper spiritual aspiration with the vision of a God. It is not as yet a palpably perceived reality, but its pressure on phenomenal consciousness or its insistent will-to-become cannot nevertheless be denied.

To describe its inextinguishable presence there, the ancients have used the term smriti (reminiscence or memory) whose connotation however hovers between the domains of the ideal and the real.[46] Smriti, as Patanjali would say,[47] is the conservation of the energy of a real perception with its perpetual tendency toward resurgence. On the ordinary level of consciousness bound up with the process of time, we have linked it up with the past and have assumed the necessity of a precarious spark of present association for its denotation; and even then we cannot explain why an association whose threads hang loose in innumerable directions should pick up a particular line of operation in exclusion to others. The suggestion, therefore, is that smriti may be looked upon not simply as a derivative function of the sense-mind but as an original power of the consciousness in which the awareness (*anubhava*) free from the limitations of time and space is not polarized into the duality of a subject and an object, but dwells upon itself pregnant with the untrammeled sense of eternality and infinity. It will be an ever-present power from above, whose pressure on phenomenal consciousness will, in accordance with the determination of the time-process, bifurcate itself into the dual functions of a memory of the past and an imagination of the future. But even then, it should be noted that the backward and forward movement of representative consciousness, which creates an almost unbridgeable gap between the past and future by driving them asunder to two distant poles, mostly represents the sensational part of the total content of an experience, leaving the attendant emotional portion in the background. This naturally makes the representation a colorless one, which could be animated only by reviving the missing emotional content (*rasa*).

But to revive an emotion is to relive the experience, and this may ultimately mean a drawing in and fusion of the particularized past and future into the fluidity of an everlasting present. In smriti as a mode of spiritual memory,[48] it is the emotional factor that predominates, transforming it in its final phase into the luminous sense of a timeless integral content. To the aspiring consciousness whose functionings have to be regarded as a process in time, smriti appears as the result of a penetration into the Beyond (*medha*) (BG X.34), but then the Beyond, which is a timeless entity, may charge the consciousness with the growing sense of an ever-present Real whose comprehension is interpreted in mystic experience as the recovery or recognition (*pratyabhijna*) not of an isolated fact of a temporal past but of an all-pervading essence in a timeless eternity. In the conception of an essence, the consciousness may well be absolved from the necessity of arranging its experiences in a temporal series; it may arrange the different shades-in-appearance as so many stresses, which being free from limitation in time may naturally possess a fluid existence of mutual interpenetration.

In the essence of a totality of aspiring consciousness, three such stresses may be formulated for practical purposes, that is, shraddha (faith), smriti, and prajna (final illumination)—the gaps being filled up by the dynamisms of virya (vigor) and samadhi (concentration) (Yogasutra I.20). In this scheme, smriti occupies an intermediate position in stress between shraddha and prajna (which in this context is the same as buddhi). Shraddha is an incipient stage of prajna, determining the being's intuitional outlook on life in accordance with the degree of development its essence (*sattva*) has undergone during the course of its spiritual evolution. Freed from all tamasika and rajasika predilections of a material and vital nature and even, like the shraddha of Nachiketa, overstepping the bounds of its sattvika preoccupation, it may grow to burn as the steady light of smriti and finally emerge as the all-encompassing illumination of sthithaprajna, sthirabuddhi, or sthitadhi. Its dynamism is inherent in the nature of man; and if on the superficial level of his life it appears preoccupied with a mechanical assimilation of the residues of past energies initiating a spiral movement of tardy and half-conscious development, in the depths it is secretly preparing to usher in at a crucial moment the lightning appearance of the glorious prospect of a fulfilled future—because it is the master of what has been and what is going to be (*ishano bhuta-bhavyasya*).

Such then is the nature of the secret spiritual unfoldment in man with which his sense-ridden life of desire is always coming in conflict. In the depths of his being, there is the vast serenity of a steadfast illumination (*sthirabuddhi*) (BG V.20); it is the silent witness whose secret consent initiates and fosters from a large vision the manifold workings of his soul, and its urge is dimly felt in his half-awakened surface-consciousness as the reminiscence of a pristine and supernal glory which in his daily conduct flashes out on the mental field the norms of a higher law (*dharma*) and is supported by an apparently irrational faith seeking to uphold his unillumined attempts at self-exceeding.

Into this inner process, still halting in its movements, the sense-life shoved by an unregenerate vital urge brings the tumult of impassioned desires, each clamoring and struggling for its pound of flesh; the organism receives a rude shock—its memory, the guardian of its conscience, is ruffled, blurred, and even effaced, blighting the promise of a nascent divine illumination and plunging the whole being into the darkness of spiritual death (BG II.63). The will-to-become, in its ignorant and mad endeavor of self-fulfillment, has missed its aim and after describing a circle has returned to the abyss of the Unmanifest from which it had sprung.

The movement is repeated again and again but not with the same end in view, as that would mean the too-restricted pattern of a mechanical material existence. As life grows, and parallel to its growth, the horizon of consciousness widens, the self-centered individual being feels the impact of the cosmic existence not as an ordered whole (*rita*) of divine harmony but as a confusion of complex forces pulling in different ways. The ever-growing richness of the field of experience lays upon the being the extremely difficult task of reducing its discordant elements into an all-comprehensive symphony. The task becomes almost insuperable by the fact that not only is there an endless variety of sense-objects in the world of appearance, stimulating a bewildering multiplicity of interests in the organism, but in its inner constitution, too, the being, as the Upanishads say, occupy simultaneously as different persons (*purusha*) different levels of existence which are arranged round a central core, in a tier commanding ever-widening horizons. The complexity of being owing to the interpretation of these multiple personalities is not resolved until the level of vijnana or pure buddhi has been reached. Mind, which appears to the ordinary consciousness as its highest synthesizing power, stands only at the beginning of a series of universalizing principles with a gradually wider and deeper content;[49] habitually dependent as it is on the sense-data for its functioning, it is more at home in a world of partially resolved multiplicity which it tries to, but cannot completely, arrange into an integral whole. Just as the indeterminate and discursive sense-operations are referred to it for a coherent interpretation, so its own experiences are made coherent by a reference to the ego-structure working from behind, whose exclusive individually again is put in a cosmic setting by the secret determination (*vyavasaya*) of buddhi or the illumination of the depth.

As a force of conscious determination, vyavasaya of course infiltrates into the level of mind and marks its experiences with the stamp of reality, but it lacks there the breadth and clarity of vision originally inherent in it. The one undivided (*avibhakta*) Real appears through the medium of the sense-mind as a divided Many, and to the perception of each of its modes vyavasaya lends its sanction, inducing a temporary focusing of the consciousness which, from the very nature of the thing, cannot develop into the poise of a comprehensive concentration (*samadhi*). In a general way, the reason for this may be sought in the character of our surface living, which contracts the Real at every step but has not sufficient force of penetration (*medha*) to enter into its essence. At the same time, there is lure of the Many, the insistent demand of life to drink deep at the multifluent fount of universal joy—creating for the sense-mind, sharing in the nature of the atomicity of the individual being,[50] the puzzling problem of grasping and assimilating the infinite with the necessarily limited means of the finite. The result is the endless ramification, on the mental plane, of the one buddhi into many buddhis (BG II.41), with the attendant frittering of its energy of vyavasaya, while life's insistence on the fulfillment of its rooted desires through the cult of power and enjoyment (*bhogaishvarya*) grows clamorous and blurs the spirit's vision (*chetas*) of the true aim of existence.

Along with this, the selective propensity of the individual being creates for it primarily on the vital plane the dualities (*dvandva*) of pleasure and pain, whose instinctive character is supplanted on the mental plane by the concepts of good and evil (*shubhashubha*), and on a further widening of the scope of consciousness by the moral concepts of right and wrong (*sukrita-duskrita*). The conception of an ethical norm is the highest point to which the mind, unaided by any higher spiritual principle, can reach. But as this may mean only a rarefication and not a complete purge of the sense of duality, it cannot be said that the mind has then contacted the Real in its entirety (BG II.50 read with V.15). Since the mind, as we have said, is a derivative and an instrumentation of the ego-sense, all mentally conceived standards are liable to be vitiated by the limitations inherent in the latter. If the end of all ethical conduct is a harmonious fulfillment of the will attended by a pure satisfaction of the emotions, the presence of the ego as the motive power behind it will naturally defeat this purpose. The dogmatic insistence of the ego upon the pattern of truth it has imagined and its determined refusal to look beyond (*nanyadasiti vadah, etavad iti nishchaya*) may carry out its will to its own satisfaction and may take pride in its having laid down a norm for all. But nevertheless it will only be an illusion of achievement which cannot persist against the Seer-will (*kavikratu*) that is secretly and surely fulfilling itself in the scheme of the world and utilizing even the errors of the ego for the realization of its total vision.

The ego or the pseudosoul is the highest synthesizing principle of our being that we are ordinarily conscious of. As it becomes the determinant factor in the manipulation of karmic energizings engendered by the original urge of will-to-become, it creates different ideologies or norms of conduct on different levels of consciousness. The first is of course the vitalistic ideology of the cult of power and enjoyment described by the Gita as the aptitude and achievement of the asuric temperament (*asuri sampad*). It ranges from the worship of crass materialism to a perversion of the kshatra ideal attended by all the evils born of blind egoism, greed, and infatuation, and the mockery of a nominal concession to the law of sacrifice (*namayajna*). Parallel to this, but apparently on a higher level, is the ideology of the cult of occultism (*vedavada*)—a travesty of the ancient spirit of sacrifice and a perversion of the brahma ideal, in which the motive is the same mad pursuit of power and enjoyment, the unhampered satisfaction of the volitional and the emotional urge, which is sought to be brought about by occult means of ritualistic excesses (BG II.42-44). Above this, and apparently as a countermove, is the ideology of the so-called cult of reason (*prajnavada*), in which there is an attempt at the reversal of the process of energism tending toward the status of an ultimate quiescence. Psychologically it corresponds to the human mind's natural power of introversion, in which lies the possibility of the consciousness being freed from the thralldom of a mechanical functioning. As such, it is a distinct gain and an indispensable aid toward spiritual development. But if introversion is induced as a form of jugupsa following upon some violent reaction to one's environment, it will have missed its aim. The cult of reason will then mean only a disguised form of the cult of ego, equally blind in its insistence as the vital urge and devoid of the illumination of a comprehensive vision.

XI

The gist of the matter then is this. Human nature, as we find it actually constituted, is dominated by a will-to-become whose final goal, however, does not appear in a clear light to the average consciousness. There is an urge toward self-exceeding which forms the keynote of all ideals of progression; but on the mental-vital plane, where the power of abstraction has not been sufficiently developed or is not commensurate with the power of projection, a certain amount of confusion seems to be the inevitable consequence of all human endeavors. Impelled by an inner drive toward domination and assimilation of the largest content of its objective field with the very limited means at its disposal, the mental-vital structure of the human organism usually loses its balance and succumbs to a chronic sense of indetermination which encroaches upon all its spheres of activities. Just as there is a chaotic imbalance in the domain of the emotion and the will, clouding the present issue with the clamorous demands of crude and unregenerate vital impulsions, so the horizons of the spiritual and the intellectual vision too appear blurred with the confusion created by religious cants and sophisticated ideologies. The general result of this turmoil is a sort of spiritual bankruptcy in which the lamp of faith burns low, turning the perspicuous intuition of the Beyond into a dull acquiescence in conventional truths, the memory becomes a mechanical device for endless repetitions of the vanities of superficial existence, and a clammy heaviness pressing down upon the consciousness damps all higher aspirations and bars the way to the illumination of a comprehensive concentration. If from this travail of nature anything emerges stark and strong, it is the Asura, the confrere of the Deva (Ch U I.2.i; VIII.7.ii; cf. BG XVI.6), who stalks the field towering in his self-gorging greed and self-assertive might, his false glitter (*virochana*) dazing the sight of "the many-too-many and the superfluous." The Asura is either frankly asuric in his professions, preaching a gospel of undiluted materialism; or he poses unwittingly as the champion of the deva-cult. In the latter case, he is either an occultist, prostituting the ideal of the sacrifice (*yajna*) in his attempt to compel the Powers to minister to his vile end of self-aggrandizement; or he is a follower in the path of askesis (*tapas*) which in his delusion he turns into a cult of senseless self-mortification or a passion for miracle mongering—all inspired by a perversity and obduracy of the spirit (*asadgraha*), whose only aim is an insane pursuit of self-glorification even if it means misery and devastation for others (BG XVI.9, 10, 14, 17; XVI.6).

This marks the high tide of the vitalistic achievement, which because it is devoid of the clarity of a comprehensive vision and serene illumination also creates for the average intellect a confusion of issues by parading a host of mutually contending dicta each asserting itself to be the only acceptable version of the true aim of existence and demanding the allegiance of reason to its particular dogma. The glamor of life lends a peculiar fascination to these specious philosophies, which blinds the human mind to the fact that all ideologies inspired by a positivistic outlook on existence, even though they might be supported by a bewildering array of plausible reasonings, are vitiated by what may be called an original defect of the lower nature, that is, an apparently insurmountable limitation of her evolutionary urge which compels all her progressive movements either to describe a circle or at best a spiral, dominated by a rhythm of ebb and flow. The crude impulse of life is translated into passion in the domain of consciousness and gathers strength as it madly rushes on, but is inevitably sent up and sinks back often to a lower level without wholly achieving all that has been dreamed by it. This frustration brings but small gain to the human society as a whole compared with the vast amount of energy that has been put forth. The cult of the occult, whether it takes on a scientific or a so-called pseudo-scientific coloring, because it underlines the sensate values of the human mind, confuses man with the promise of an idea of progress that is intrinsically false; and because its generalizations are fundamentally based on the evanescent and the specious, it can never achieve the ideal of the all-comprehensive simplicity of the eternal truths, and so leaves the intellect to lose its way in the maze of sophistications and speculative philosophies masquerading as newfound revelations. Religion then becomes a cloak for materialism, or materialism itself becomes a new form of religion, and rationality serves as a handmaid to crude vitalism. The malady is as old as civilization, and what the Gita describes in a phraseology suited to its particular social context is true to the conditions of the present day and will remain true for many days to come, until mankind is schooled by tribulations and sobered down to a saner and loftier outlook on the problems of life.

XII

As a remedy for this malady, the Gita from the very outset takes a most uncompromising attitude toward the whole problem. The background of a Kurukshetra, it points out, is formed not so much by material maladjustments as by the spiritual poverty of the individual and the social man.[51] To seek power and enjoyment and the gratification of the instinct of megalomania is but natural to the vital mind; but a crisis is precipitated when, for want of a true appraisal of spiritual values, the religious instinct of man can be to justify his own ends. The remedy lies not in turning society a-religious, as man has sometimes been constrained to think, but in taking a scientific view of the whole thing and curing the psychological maladjustments that have been responsible for the crisis. Any form of religion that emphasizes the positivistic outlook on life, be it aspirations worldly or otherworldly, must be severely corrected by what may be called a cult of negation, whose essential value is curative rather than destructive. It goes without saying that it means not the negation of life as such, but rather the broadening of its base by discarding its surface values. The justification for this negative attitude lies in the fact that all ideas of real progress, if it is not to be a tardy mechanical process of inconscient nature, must be based on the assumption of a psychological asset of the power of conscious projection which presupposes a power of withdrawal or gathering-in of the forces of being. The cognitive aspect of its process has been figuratively described by the upanishadic philosophy as "the inturned gaze of the seeker after immortality," while its cognitive aspect has been brought out by the well-known Sankhyan principle of discrimination which, by analyzing every complex of consciousness-movement into the polarity of subjectivity and objectivity, extricates, by a reversal of movement, the pure subject from the confusion of the subject-object whole of the natural being.

Now, this cult of introversion (*antaravrittata*) and discrimination (*viveka*), in spite of its negative emphasis, does not contemplate a philosophy of denial or nihilism unless we choose it to be so. Broadly speaking, its positive gain for the psychological being may be of a twofold nature. In the first place, it automatically induces a widening of the horizon of the inner vision, which enables the subject to place the contents of his complex experience in a well-ordered relational whole inspired by a spirit of scientific detachment; and this, as modern psychology had rediscovered for the edification of civilized society, means an introduction of the indispensable element of sanity into the pattern of human behavior. In the second place, it envisages the economizing of the thought-forces by training the mind to think in terms of universals rather than of particulars, which raises the whole process of thinking to a higher psychological level, where the mind in its function of ratiocination can proceed from the direct perception of a comprehensive truth to the legitimate deduction of its particularized applications. For the intellect, it means breathing in the free air of a few universal truths of intrinsic value which have been secured for it by throwing overboard the age-long accumulations of jumbles and noxious stuffs. As a philosophical discipline, it stands for an integral perception of a total whole whose characteristics it derives not so much from inductively processing the particulars of experience as from evolving from the depth of the being a new instrumentation for the direct perception of the universal reals. It is herein that the process of introversion as a novel method of psychological investigation becomes an indispensable necessity.

The practical beginnings of the cult of negation lie in a serious attempt to live beyond the preoccupations of the habitual and the commonplace, which are in most cases guided by motives of unregenerate vitalism. The natural man lives in a perpetual state of imbalance swayed by dualities (*dvandva*)[52] of sensational, emotional, volitional character, the root cause of which is in the inherently constricted sphere of his consciousness that can interpret all empirical contacts only in terms of an egoistic pursuit of a limited good. This is accentuated by the instinctive demands of the vital hunger which measures the fulfillment of life's purpose by the standard of the amelioration of sensuous living expressed in the widely propagated dictum: We must have and what we have we keep (*yogakshema*). It is of course a frank and brutal statement of the ageless cult of power and enjoyment, which in psychological parlance will mean the satisfaction of the urges of the emotion and the will, and is as such only a natural function of our consciousness. As original forces of the being, emotion and will cannot be condemned outright, for the simple reason that they have always prompted man to strive after the Beyond by dynamizing his perceptions and widening their scope.[53] The search for the Beyond in this sense can be construed as the attempt at unveiling the occult, which man has sought to do by manipulating either the psychic forces, as in some forms of religion, or the material forces, as in science. In both types of occultism, the idea of yogakshema has naturally loomed large in the unregenerate vital mind, giving rise to a number of complicated problems of individual and social being to which it has been impossible for the ego-ridden consciousness to offer a complete solution, even if that ego has been magnified and exalted to the position of the bearer of "a common will." There is an intimate relation between the habitual imbalance created by the dualities of surface living and the too-common hankering after yogakshema; it may be said that the former constitutes the psychological motive of the latter, and the two together form the source of all maladjustments from which human society is suffering. In recent times, the impulse of having and keeping has been dignified by the name of raising the standard of physical living, and in the context of a wide sociopolitical upheaval, it has got a certain amount of justification for its persistence for some time to come. But in the general clamor for rights, the sense of duty (*dharma*), which always carries with it the call for sacrifice (*yajna*) and can unhesitatingly be demanded of every individual as his most intimate and personal concern, has been allowed to wither away. Yet, it is the individual who can be looked upon as the real custodian of the social conscience, and it is in him that any attempt at leading society out of the common rut can be intensified. So the cult of negation becomes his own personal dharma, a lone adventure of the spirit whose intrinsic worth is the only appeal to him. To ask the society as a whole to live beyond the preoccupation of the moment will appear as a preposterous demand; to a certain extent it will agree to try to live beyond the dvandvas of passion and will, only to make decent social living possible; but to live beyond the idea of yogakshema is a horror to it, for has not experience taught it that it had to pay too dear a price for its emphasis on the cult of poverty and renunciation in the past?

Yet it is apparent to every thoughtful mind that an overemphasis on the positivistic outlook on life does not carry us very far, as the trend of world affairs for the last few decades has shown. Even if under completely changed circumstances cooperation and mutual aid take the place of struggle and competition, that is to say, even if it is possible to erect a utopian superstructure of social justice and security by an ideal humanization of the methods of yogakshema, still we will be confronted by two problems. First, unless there is a radical change in human nature and the asura in it is transmuted into the deva, coercion in one form or other will be necessary to maintain the high ideal of social efficiency: and where there is coercion, there always lurks the danger of frustration and retrogression. Second, if by some mysteriously happy means we succeed in maintaining our utopia by ensuring a complete and harmonious satisfaction of the possessive instinct in man, we must make an outlet for his creative instinct; or in other words, the vital hunger being appeased, the creative urge must be given a full play lest we allow the life-impulse to stagnate and so run the risk of courting atavism. But then, every form of creative activity presupposes, as the ancients would say, a modicum of tapas—a spirit of sacrifice (*yajna*) and in-gathering of forces (*nivritti*), which are essentially human characteristics that distinguish man from brutes. Thus even to make the ideal of yogakshema work with efficiency and security, we must at the last resort teach ourselves to live beyond the idea of yogakshema. And if, in the present context of human affairs, it is idle to expect a universal application of the principle of *nairyogakshema* (living above the hankering after and keeping), still it is incumbent on the few individuals of discernment and vision to keep its fire burning in their life with the firm conviction that the tapasya of these agnihotris for realizing the combined ideal of the true uplift (*abhyudaya*) and the highest good (*nihshreyasa*) of human society can never go in vain, since, in spite of the official condemnation of the cult of negation as a piece of outworn medievalism, it represents an original urge deep-rooted in human nature, which must obey its dictates to make all its ideas of progression truly fruitful.

But the cult of negation, as has already been hinted at, aims at something positive, and positive in the real sense of the term. This positive ideal that is to be sought by withdrawing ourselves from the preoccupation of dvandva and yogakshema has been described by the Gita as the status of an innate and immutable essentiality (*nityasattva*) and of selfhood (*atma*). From an analytic point of view, the former will represent the sole characteristic of what the Gita calls para prakriti, the matrix of pure indiviuality,[54] as distinguished from the modal formulations of the lower nature or apara prakriti; while the latter will of course stand for the conception of pure purusha—the principle of witness-consciousness in which the illumination of the cosmic and the transcendent is a normal potency. Coming to the ordinary level of empirical existence, if we seek to determine its values in terms of consciousness, we shall find that life has taken a decisive step in its evolutionary progress when it has changed consciousness into self-consciousness, and has thus secured a better change of gaining mastery over its environments by its capacity of translating objective facts into subjective values. This presupposes in the force of consciousness an inherent power of introversion and concentration, which though it does not acquire a distinctive prominence in our normal state of conscious living, yet forms its substratum and directive force, and at a certain stage of the evolution of the inner being can be made to follow its independent line of development. The culmination of introversion lies in a self-sufficiency of inner living (cf. BG III.17), which is in man the criterion of true spiritual growth; and in the attendant phenomenon of habitual concentration that a reversal of the force of being must bring about, the force of consciousness is intensified and a state of permanent wakefulness is attained which, though it may not have a content of distracting objectivity to maintain the conscious level, as in our normal waking state, is nevertheless flooded by an illumination penetrating into the essence of the subjective and the objective orders of Reals and disclosing their inalienable inner identity. Though described as a form of immediate perception, still the content of this experience is not simply a pure staticity, but is "a homogeneous thrill" of the silent symphony of a realized will and a spontaneous self-delight. The cult of negation, urged by an inner necessity of the evolving consciousness, seeks to divest it as much from the inertia of tamas as from the flutter of rajas natural to an extrovert existence, and points to this illumination of nityasattva lighting up the indeterminable

Void of the supreme Selfhood whose infinitude is at once the convergence and transcendence of all spiritual experience.

XIII

To live beyond the dualities of sensation, passion, and will in the calmness of an inner freedom and equanimity, and in one's external relations to keep oneself uncontaminated by the craving of acquisition and possession, or in a wider sense, to live beyond the fluctuating modulations of the lower nature which may encroach upon and exploit even the religious instinct in man; and as a positive complement of this cult of negation, to be poised in the inalienable dynamics of an essential illumination radiating from the shining core of the inner self—this then is the high ideal set before us, the realization of which is held out to be the unique factor conducive to the deliverance of the human soul from the "great fears" that beset it.

But the question may arise: Cannot the lure of the Beyond be an irresistible vortex engulfing the being and making a return to the surface impossible? Considered logically, are not the immobility of self-poise and the dynamism of essential illumination two contradictory concepts? A tradition has grown up through the ages that has answered the above questions in the affirmative, still taking its stand on the natural dichotomizing function of the mind, which must deal with a total reality by splitting it into two components of thesis and antithesis and then concentrating itself upon one of the two. An integral reality has thus been viewed under the dual aspects of passivity and activity, qualitative modulation and its absolute denial, unity and manifoldness, being and nonbeing. An acceptance of one aspect has commonly meant the rejection of the other, though integral realization repeatedly insisted upon the harmonious blending of all opposites in the totality of a comprehensive vision: the Potent and its potency, the Void and its manifestations in an infinite plentitude of forms and modes, are but the bi-une aspects of the one and same Real whose content can never be exhausted by any sort of affirmation or denial,[55] even the Nihilist losing himself in the supreme height of absolute negation has been constrained to affirm the identity of the Becoming (*bhava*) and the Void (*nirvana*) as the uttermost of his subjective experience. This supreme and comprehensive synthesis is supported not only by the metaphysical reason which, to give the complete account of existence, must subsume all modes of Reals under one Reality; but it is also proved in the characteristic status of the man of realization known in Indian mysticism as jivanmukti or the liberation of the living, in which there is a complete harmony between the status of the brahmic consciousness and its spontaneous energism (*brahma-karma-samadhi*) (BG IV.24). This synthesis is apparent even in our normal consciousness, whose functioning is, after all, a reflection of the consciousness of the Supreme and on whose modular renderings all systems of Indian philosophical thinking have been built. The human mind, whose incessant activity or restlessness has attained such notoriety among spiritual seekers, nevertheless contains at every moment of its functioning an element of witness-consciousness forming its background and directive force. The sense-mind, which like all other senses is an extremely sensitive instrument responding to the confused mass of external and internal stimuli, is only a part of the total psychical apparatus; Indian psychology speaks of buddhi, even in its fluctuating form of prakritic modulation, as forming its better part and supplying to the being a core of personality (*sattva*) which assumes the role of a director of the jiva-consciousness. A deepening of this force of personality, whose natural tendency is toward a calm deliberation born of a wideness of vision not generally vouchsafed to the sense-mind, means for the human organism a stable security of status for which a successful ordering of the empirical field is possible. And this is nothing but an avenue to the status of the integral brahma-consciousness, whose absolute immobility is the axle-point that communicates its inexhaustible energy to the eternal dynamism of the cosmic manifestations.

Though activity and passivity are thus harmoniously wedded together in an integral experience, we must be on guard on one important point. It has become fashionable of late to explain the message of the Gita as an exclusive call to activity, perhaps seasoned at times by a sprinkling of humanitarian motives, just as an emphasis has been laid upon it in the past as a gospel of purely personal liberation. Maybe we have caught the contagion from the feverishly dynamic character of the young West; and if the present worldwide commotion is but a prelude to the opening up of a new chapter in human civilization that bears a significance of wider application and deeper content, then this outburst of dynamism is justifiable as a means of letting loose many hitherto untapped and pent-up forces. But the dance of force must be the dance of Shiva and not the dance of a demonical host. Knowledge is power, but power does not necessarily mean knowledge; there is no gain to human progress in a dogmatic affirmation of a philosophy of power of activity, just as there is no illumination in the realism of the man in the street, even if that be raised to the rank of an academic system. Their only value lies in a protest against the inertia of living and thinking which the decadence of ages brings in; but the worth of their contribution to the assessment of the real values of being as a whole suffers by prejudice and a wrong emphasis on the aim of existence. The philosophy of karma cannot stand by itself, even if it be inspired by the best altruistic motive, unless it has struck roots in the soil of jnana, and its ideologies are derived from a direct perception of the ultimate Real. Since karma can be imitated, so its philosophy also can be widely propagated, though necessarily with uncertain results; but the cut of jnana is specifically an individual concern, and as yet we have not been able to discover any universal means for its communication except with the help of language, which is, however, not a perfect medium for the conveyance of the real meaning of a subjective experience—especially when that experience is above the threshold of normal experiences that have so far been possible to make socially intelligible. The only means of removing this bar (occult means being of course excepted), lies in perfecting the vyanjanashakti or the power of suggestivity of language, and this presupposes the creation of a charged atmosphere of the social mind whose hypersensitiveness might easily dispense with the dull and cumbrous means of mutual communication. But the social mind can be raised to such a pitch only by the agelong labors of individuals, of the chosen few whose lonely adventures into the Beyond bring not only the fulfillment of an indomitable longing for personal liberation but also a promise of the Kingdom of Heaven on Earth by an uplifting impact on the social mind (*atmano moksho jagaddhitancha*). India's preoccupation with the Beyond and its attendant cult of negation, which have almost assumed the character of a national trait, thus attain significance of worldwide application; and if today, in the same context, the call to karma as a means of a social cohesion and solidarity is growing increasingly insistent, the call to buddhi as a means of probing the depths of the inner being and discovering the true nature of the universal individual becomes no less insistent—unless we choose to delude ourselves with our imperfect and biased understanding of the grand message of the Gita. It is easy and even commendable to turn it into a gospel of disinterested social service; but that is only a means to an end—the end being, as the Gita succinctly puts it, the self-purification (*atmashuddhi*) of the aspirant after Yoga (BG V.11). Everywhere the emphasis lies on the achievement of the individual, even if that has ultimately to be changed into a socially useful commodity. Disinterestedness per se must have its point of origin in an intense interest in the harmonic expression of the pure Self; otherwise it runs every risk of being turned into a mechanical affair obeying the laws of crowd psychology, and thus being exploited by a social or political dictatorship whose morals are inspired by a passion of the moment or a superficial estimate of the values of human life.

XIV

In evolving a standard of conduct in which life activity will have a harmonious expression in a large rhythm of social well-being (*lokasamgraha*), the responsibility then primarily rests on the individual, the measure of the development of whose inner being will set the pace for the development of healthy social ideologies. Karma forms an integral part of total Being, just as buddhi does; but to save the former from the banalities to which it may sink from an uncritical attitude toward the aim of existence, we must have recourse to a higher source of illumination than what is guaranteed by the social conscience, which, after all, is never free from the undiscerning murkiness of the crowd-mind. A clear perception of the Light is always an exclusive privilege of the individual; it is really his consciousness which forms the focus from which a "private world" appears in normal course of things as a subjective-objective diffusion; and in social relations it is ultimately the interests of this private world which govern the individual's outlook on common life. The world of sensations and its reflection as the world of elemental passions are at present the only materials from which a real public world of general appeal can be built up; beyond this, the world of ideas and norms dealing with the universal aspect of things is a hazy affair, whose messages are imperfectly understood and tardily assimilated by the group-mind, which nevertheless exercises a profound influence in shaping the individual's philosophy of life. The liberation of the forces of the inner being and an uplifting of the social conscience by its imperceptible pressure is thus always a task imposed on the individual by the very nature of the evolution of the principles of consciousness in nature. In this light, the message of the Gita, even if the occasion for its dispensation rose in a social context and its emphasis on the concrete realization and universal application of an abstract idea never lagged, gradually becomes, as it proceeds, preoccupied with a grappling with the problems of an individual self-development. The urge to activity thus assumes the character not of an exhortation prompted by an acceptance of the common values of an undeveloped social conscience, but of a critical analysis of the deep impulses rooted in the individual's inner being.

Thus we see that the main problem of the individual in his attempt at realizing the poise of Buddhiyoga is the sublimation of his own karmic urge. Karma, as a rhythm of the Being in its functioning as a multipotent creative impulse (*visarga*) dominates the whole sphere of life, whether its energizings are directed toward the creation of values in terms of tangible actualities (*bhuta*) or nascent potentialities (*bhava*) (BG VIII.3). If the movement in the former is extrovert (*pravritti*), in the latter it is essentially introvert (*nivritti*); and the aim of life-consciousness will be a harmonization of the two, in which nivritti will of course preponderate as the inner dynamism supplying a right direction to the functions of pravritti. Pravritti has been described as natural to all beings (cf. Manusamhita V.56); and interpreted in terms of evolving consciousness, this means that its functions belong to the realm of cosmic nature, whose motivations have grown subconscious or unconscious in the individual in the course of the evolutionary process, and thus formed a soil of spiritually dead actualities from which the life of new potentialities has to sprout. The bearer of the new life-urge is the individual consciousness, whose essential function lies in canalizing the diffused energies of the subconscious and in supplying them with a meaning or aim. As concentrating consciousness grows in purposiveness and becomes meaningful, it creates values of ever-widening content as directives of karmic energies. But this movement, which means as much in-gathering as widening the field of the forces of consciousness as it rises to greater heights, gradually loses its hold on the particular and the concrete, and in a final straining dissolves in the quiescence (*akarma*) of the abstract and the universal, whose lure is as much fundamental as the lure of spontaneous diffusion. The aspirant must find a via media between the two; he must strike a balance between the actual and the ideal in his attempt at the realization of a total Being. Quiescence, like the prospective fact of death on the physical plane, or the mysterious background of the infinite Unmanifest in all intellectual adventures into the abstract, is perhaps the ultimate Reality, which is at once the basis (*pratishtha*) and transcendence (*atishtha*) of all movements, actual or conceptual; it is a substance in which "time must have a stop," and yet on which time leans for its being and dissolution. But the abyss of quiescence should not be tempted in a self-willed headlong rush (cf. BG XII.5); rather its potency, enlivened by the illumination of smriti, should charge the being with a deepening sense of an imperturbable poise in nityasattva, whence the rhythm of the karmic energy will appear not as a sturm und drang of unregenerate vitalism, but as a spontaneity of the blossoming of an inner essence—a dreamlike figuration of an illumined existence, where the stress of the Ideal-Real will change the momentum of the most intense activity into the serenity of a vast quiescence, which in itself will be pregnant with the throbbing potentiality of a creative energism (BG IV.18). This will be solving the mystery of karmic ways by entering into the total scheme of their energizings lightened up by the illumination of a consciousness poised beyond the mind (BG IV.17–18).

The first step toward this sublimation of the karmic urge lies in its rationalization. As pulsation of life, the scope of karma is of course commensurate with the totality of being; but its stress on consciousness gains as a direction of will or purpose begins to assert itself in it. The purpose is sometimes imposed from without, dictated by the group instinct or the social conscience, or sometimes it is derived from an inner urge of self-expression; and more often than not, it is an admixture of the two. In any case, the purposiveness of action, as common sense will say, has a greater chance of achieving its end if it follows a rational course. Reason, either from a sifting of past experiences or from an analytic imagination of future probabilities, can hope to predict results; and this adds a zest to purposiveness. But the difficulty is that in normal consciousness, reason cannot view things dispassionately; the predictable result is often not a strict logical deduction arrived at from a computation of all the factors concerned, but rather a suggestion of imaginative passion compelling reason to serve its cherished end. Impartial reason will say that as forces rise above the level of mechanical operation, the predictability of their specific results becomes uncertain; the motive (*hetu*) of activity should then lie not in some definite result (*phala*) aimed at (BG II.47) but rather in the deep-rooted urge sanctioned by the spirit of sacrifice (*yajnartham karma*) (BG III.9). Rationalization of karma will then mean its universalization, depending evidently not on some communal pattern of ethical conduct but on a perception of that luminous core of essentiality in being (*buddhi*) which truly universalizes the individual and secretly makes every one of his life movements a vibrant note of the grand symphony of All-existence.

Speaking in terms of mental reason, the means of attaining this high ideal lies in the cult of equanimity (*shamatva*)—a perfectly balanced response to all forms of dualities whether they appear in the sphere of sensation (*shitoshna*), emotion (*sukha-duhkha*), or will (*siddhya-siddhi*), or even in the ethical judgments of right and wrong (*sukrita-dushkrita*) and the still subtler rational ideologies of action and quiescence (*karma* and *akarma*). The course is, of course, a graduated one, and begins with the initial cult of titiksha and kshanti, which releases the power of conscious inhibition, going along with an introversion, concentration, and deepening of consciousness. The subtle aim of all this will be to deaden the force of emotive associations (*sanga*) of attachment made instinctive by the hormic structure of normal consciousness and ultimately to do away with it, so that the external stimuli coming from universal nature evoke only a pattern of pure perception minus the habitual reaction of an extremely personal coloring rising from the dualities of feeling-tone. This will be the poise of Yoga in its negative aspect,[56] an intensification of whose forces by a rarefaction of the perceptual field will lead to the status of quiescence, an indiscriminate predilection for which is expressly prohibited by the Gita.[57] Shamatva is to become a poise, a vantage-ground for the manipulation of prakritic forces,[58] its force of inhibition or negation is to be utilized as a corrective to the irrational ventures of the life urge, and this rational element in it can be maintained and developed if it is always in touch with the universalized and illumined consciousness (*buddhi*) forming its positive background.

This illumination is the invariable result of the focusing of consciousness, which presupposes a habitual in-gathering of its forces leading to a vacuity of thought processes.[59] Just as in correcting the psychological fallacy of hedonism we have to cease from the quest of pleasure in order to attain it, so here too, it is the inhibition or in-gathering of thought and will that releases an unsuspected fount of clarity and width of vision together with an effectual force of creative dynamism. As the illumination of the Void suffuses the horizons of the Being, a depth is touched and the whole secret of karmic energization is laid bare: an incisive discrimination (*viveka*) discerns two types of karma—one the lower (*avara*), belonging to the apara prakriti and so originating in the unregenerate vital urge of the Asura,[60] and the other the divine (*divya*), the dynamism of the Supreme's own nature (*sva prakriti*) manifesting a cosmic purpose through the spirit of the age (BG IV.7–9) and demanding the joyful surrender of the individual soul awakening to the total sense of the workings of the divine power (BG XI.33), which have opened out to its spiritualized vision (*divyam chakshuh*) in their stunningly awful sublimities. Viewed from this height, the pettiness of the karmic motive inspired by an ego-sponsored planning becomes only too apparent: what then becomes a paramount interest to the worker is not to be engrossed in the uncertain effectuation of some circumscribed vision, but to look up for guidance to a higher source of illumination beyond the gloaming of mental will and intelligence (BG II.49). The discrimination between right and wrong has then a higher sanction than that of the canons of standardized morality. It is not that all notions of morality are scattered to the winds, but rather that they are referred to the calm judgment of prajna, which is as distinct from the sophistications of mental reason (*prajnavada*) as fire from smoke, and which finds sanction for ethical conduct in the perception of the essentiality of things attained by a comprehensive concentration (*samadhi*). This dual rhythm of inward tension and outward projection then becomes the sole determinant of karma. In its inner staticity plumbing the depths and reaching to the heights in a single self-gathered movement of supreme absorption, and at the very instant bursting into an aurora of ideal creation illumining the farthest limits of conceptual extension, it is a representative of the Sankhya poise of buddhi described earlier; and its dynamic counterpart is the force (*bala*) which is intrinsic in forms of consciousness, and which creates or realizes the Ideal. As such, it is the supreme art (*kaushalam*) of life (BG II.50), which is itself nothing but an expression of "the multipotent creative urge (*visarga*) of the Supreme."

And far-reaching are the implications of this Yoga poise in practical life, inasmuch as it is a force of liberation bursting asunder all bondages—the bondage of karma as well as the bondage of janma (BG II.39, 51). Karma binds or, in other words, it arrests the progress of spiritual evolution in man when it does not follow the "straight movement" (*rijuniti* or *adhvara-gati* of the Vedas) induced by the law of sacrifice (BG III.9); it either, for want of vision, starts a circular movement of mechanical existence or, egged on by a vital urge of "scant illumination," describes a horizontal spiral of sharp ups and downs; its limitations become apparent in all sorts of karmic anomalies (*vikarma*), consisting of a criminal waste of energy due to blunders and detours, a haunting sense of frustration, and a mass of confused thinking that results from a clash of imperfectly conceived ideologies (BG III.9; cf. IV.17; II.40, 5, 53). And if theses qualitative limitations are given an unlimited lease of temporal duration in the individual being by the very possibility of an imperishableness of its spiritual core, then birth itself becomes a form of bondage perpetuating in its succession the ills (*amaya*) following in the wake of an unregenerate karmic impulsion. But Buddhiyoga, taking its stand on the immutable essentiality of Being, and acting not with the blind tenacity of a limited vision willing the effectuation of an egoistic motive, but from a spontaneity born of an impinging of the powers of the Vast realizing through the instrumentation of a universal individuality the undisturbed scheme of its seer-will, divinizes karma and divinizes birth—because it has known and imbibed the mystery of the law of divine Becoming (BG IV.6, 9). As karma then becomes to it the conscious rhythm of the creative urge moving in consonance with the cosmic law of sacrifice, so janma too becomes not an unconscious movement compelled by the lower prakritic forces, but a willed stress on the equipotential field of universal life; and in both there is the consummation of the aim of existence in an assumption of the total nature of God (BG IV.10).

XV

The whole significance of Buddhiyoga has thus been made clear; a vision rises of a calm and illuminating poise beyond the highest flights of mental reason, unperturbed by the dualities of sensation, emotion, and will—a luminosity of pure intelligence in the depths of the being, stabilized in an equable status of comprehensive concentration, in which the spiritual adventure has found a home by a harmonization from a transcendent plane of the apparently conflicting findings of intuitive reason, which now Self-light illumines into the constellation of an integral whole; and from this supreme poise, of the dynamism of an utter freedom pouring itself into the rhythm of the world-movement, and sustained by the perception of an immutable essentiality of things, creating from the raw activities of life a veritable piece of art. This is a picture suggested by pure reason, but the question remains: Can it not be made more definite to practical reason? Are there not some expression, some movement, some explicit indications of the status that may serve the aspirant as helpful guides?

The answer to this can be found in a psychological analysis of the different stages, starting from the normal consciousness and leading up to the high ideal envisaged. A course of action for the neophyte can come later on, after he has got a clear mental picture of the path to be covered and thoroughly assimilated the inner meaning of the whole venture. An ideal portrayal of a sthitaprajna in whom Buddhiyoga has achieved its end can thus be made—contrasting its poise to the movements of the normal consciousness, to which these contrasts become pointers of the desired goal to be attained by a method of catharsis or cult of negation. The scheme can be arranged logically for the purpose of a better comprehension, though in actual practice logical order is not always an indispensable necessity.

The crux of the matter of course lies in purging the mind of desires (*kama*)[61]—those turbid impetuosities of the emotion and the will—which are but confused and tortuous expressions of life's quest for self-delight—and training it by an introspective analysis and introvert movement to turn more and more to the things of the spirit, and at last be poised in that status of delight where the self is both its substratum and instrumentation.[62] In normal being, "where the apertures of senses have been bored outward by one's self-being and so one looks away from and not into one's soul"(Katha U II.1.i), the function of the sense-vitals (*indriya*) is to contact and manipulate the objective world in a groping, toddling, and hesitant manner. It is as yet nature's first experiments with life, in which vital energism has not yet attained the determinateness of a secure aim, and mind, the first synthesizing principle above the threshold of consciousness, is not yet the master but is compelled to give a mechanical assent (*anuvidhana*) to the demands of the sense-vitals (BG II.67). Life adds its flavor (*rasa*) to the whole and colors the habitual associations with a deep tinge of sensuous attachment answering to some secret purpose of nature's evolutionary endeavor, and on a higher level of being reinforced by mental energism, it bursts forth into the strong flame of desire. The movement is still confused, and the issues are not yet clear—even though the emerging ego-sense attempts to canalize energies and bring about a more compact synthesis—since it is as yet the vital that rules the day. The results are obvious: in life's grapple with the forces of objective realities, the inner structure is thrown into an imbalance by heterogeneous forces of a psycho-pathological character. Life in mind is not so healthy as life in matter, since nature's experimentations here are not yet complete and the adjustments are still a patchwork affair; even for the mentally wise, it is an impossible task to curb the overbearing impetus of unregenerate vitalism, which will carry the deliberating mind along its own reckless rush (BG II.56, 57, 60). A higher principle above the sense-dominated mind and ego—a principle large and deep enough to put the individual in right relations with the universe—must then be found that will harmonize the warring elements of the being and open up a new vista of the greater beyond.

According to a logical scheme, sadhana, of course, should begin with the practice of control over the sense-vitals. But in order that the cult of intelligent control (*samyama*) does not degenerate into a cult of senseless repression (*karshana*), the poise must be taken, as has already been remarked, at least on the mental plane, where it is possible to tap the subtler powers of the psyche for a rationalization of the whole process. What is aimed at is a complete control over the sense-vitals (BG II.61), not simply by a mechanical cutting off of the objects from the field of consciousness, which after all will leave life's zest for things untransmuted and only thrust it into the background of the mind (BG II.59; III.6), but by letting in the power and light of a higher principle—either by opening oneself up to the illumination of the depth or by entering into a communion with a supreme Personality,[63] which will mean a reorientation of the aesthetics of the life urge and its final absorption into the self-delight of the pure Being (BG II.59).

But this does not suggest a repudiation of the cult of negation, which certainly is a most powerful means of attaining the status of nityasattva, whence an enlightened and effective manipulation of prakritic forces is possible. There will be the urge in some souls to overstep the bounds, and as Jaigishavya says, "to enter by a supreme concentration into the ineffability of Quiescence."[64] Of course it is idle to speculate what exact measure the momentum of spiritual urge should or would take once it has crossed the threshold of normal consciousness; but there is no gainsaying the fact that in an adventure into the Beyond, the soul must be strung to the highest key and there must be a readiness to plunge into the abyss of immortal death without any mental reservation whatsoever. At the stage of recommitting the whole position, a predilection for nonreturn may be censured as a mental bias and as falling short of the ideal of integral realization; but its possibility, and even a sort of courting it in a spirit of calm nonchalance, can by no way be ruled out, since it will be initiated not by any mental predilection but by a pull of the divine will. So the ideal of Jaigishavya finds an echo in the Gita too in its simile of "a tortoise drawing in its limbs into the shell" (BG II.58); it guarantees "an utmost control over the sense-vitals," as Patanjali would say (Yogasutra II.55); in a poet's imagery, it is carrying the spirit of death into the spring-tide of life as the seal of immortality. It is, as Patanjali's psychology explains, "a complete detachment of the sense-vitals from their objects and their simulation of the self-form of the originating consciousness."[65] Yet it may not abrogate the most intense life activity; rather it will be there as the potency of Silence vibrating into the Word, the Void of Varuna irradiating into a multiform splendor by its divine maya. To the mental reason it is a paradox; but this paradox is resolved as the soul rises to the rarefied heights of pure Intelligence where the artist's poise on the razor's edge becomes a palpable fact of spiritual experience.[66]

The extreme tension of pratyahara thus marks the inner poise whose potency spontaneously translates itself into that lucent transparency of the soul-substance (*prasada*) which forms the very stuff of an integral experience rendered ineffable by the interpenetrating mutuality of subjective and objective existences (*samarasya*). The projection thus initiated is not the result of any blind vital urge, but just an opalescent irradiation of an inner light. The movement of the sense-vitals now follows the rhythm of an inner law and is no longer swayed by the dualities of attraction and repulsion, since the constrictions of the ego-sense are absent there, and the whole being has joyfully submitted to the guidance of a palpable Presence over-canopying it and charging its every grain with the secret sense of its seer-will (BG II.64). The characteristic of this prasada is a wide and deep sympathy capable of attuning itself with the self of things, so that a true understanding of their workings secures for the illumined intelligence a steady poise above the turbulent flow of life. And yet it is not a status of indifference, keeping aloof from all life-contacts; but since it is in communion (*yuktah*) with the integral Reality and has drunk deep at the fountain of the Void (otherwise the illumination consequent upon it will not have the certainty of an absolute manifestation), it has also been infused with the subtle potency of an ideational creativity (*bhavana*)—an inner movement initiated by the very contact of things, which probes into the depths of the being and in lightning flashes goes on discovering to the inner vision the mysteries of the Ideal-Real which constitute the soul of the objective realities, until in a supreme gravitation toward the inmost core of existence, it is gathered and poised in the unfathomable peace and ineffable bliss of the Immutable (BG II.66). And the force of vision is an act of creation in a double sense: subjectively, it brings about a supreme transformation of experiential values in the empirical self, changing it, as the vedic seers would say, into a madhvada or pippalada for whom the checkered pattern of existence has but the unique meaning of an undying beauty or unalloyed bliss; while objectively, by soul-contacts it will release by the impact of its seer-will the dormant potentialities of a realizable Idea in a being.[67]

With the onrush of the sense-vitals gathered in and the consequent dawning of golden light bathing the whole being in an unruffled peace, there blossoms a simple joy when the assertive and the possessive clamors of the ego have been hushed into the quiescence of an all-pervading Void; and with a keen feeling of the subtle thrill of an inner dynamism imperceptibly projecting itself into the outer world, the self-poised soul of a yogi lives ever-wakeful in a world of undimmed illumination whose mystery descends as a pall of night on the eyes of mundane beings, although through their nightmare existence the steadfast gaze of the silent seer (*pashyan munih*) penetrates into the vision of a limitless Beyond (BG II.69). His soul is like a vast ocean of light, serene and imperturbable in its ineffable self-poise, wherein shimmering dreams of life's desires rising from the luminous depths of a far-off cosmic mist seem to float on, bubble, and blissfully melt away into the profundity of a nameless peace. No chasing of the phantoms of desire, no clamor for possessive rights, no tyrannous self-assertion of purblind egotism—the yogi moves along the path of life poised in an inner calm which "silently brings the glad message of a new spring to souls of men."

Such is the brahmic status, the status of supreme all-pervading integral consciousness to which the cult of buddhiyoga leads, securing for the soul an inextinguishable illumination which never allows one's footsteps to falter on the walk of life, and in its final movement crowns life's endeavor with the supreme achievement of the deathless Void (BG II.72).

XVI

And so we come to our journey's end. The cult of Buddhiyoga, as we have seen, provides us with that rational procedure of self-exceeding which forms the keynote of all human aspirations, whether they point to above or below. Its rationale is to be found in the logical scheme of Sankhyan principles, where buddhi, which forms the core of man's nature, occupies a peculiar position that marks the farthest limit to which the concept of an upward march of evolutionary nature can rise. Man takes his stand on the threshold of those synthesizing principles enumerated under the last pentad of Sankhyan categories, wherein a gradual deepening and organizing of the principle of consciousness becomes notably apparent. Below him are the world of concrete and abstract objective reals of materialized entities, and the world of affected and effective sense-vitals dominated by the vital urge; characteristically in him are the principles of mind and ego, imperfectly illumined by the principle of intelligence (*buddhi*) which forms the core of his personality and shines with the distant promise of a universalized individuality; and above him, overtopping the highest flights of his pure intelligence are the infinitudes of the Unmanifest and the Ineffable. What he can hope for and attain by a comprehensively rational manipulation of the forces of his being is to be poised in that Illumination which forms a connecting link between his worlds of the Real and the Ideal. Obviously what he must exceed are the blind lure of matter born of mechanical association, the turbulent surging of the vital defeating its own purpose by a lack of illumination, the vacillations of the mental pulled in different ways by imperfectly organized forces of his nature, and the insistent demand of his ego bent on realizing the ideal of its circumscribed vision. The first emphasis is always on the individual, who must penetrate into the depths of his own being before he can hope to have a glimpse of the secrets of the world-being or an intuition of the pure Being whose Void sets the stage for the drama of the world and the soul. The psychological method for this self-finding is in the cult of comprehensive concentration (*samadhi*) inaugurated by the discipline of titiksha and shamatva, and supported by an inalienable sense of the all-pervading essentiality of Being which deepens into the status of brahmic consciousness integrating all movements of life into a rhythmic expression of the divine will. It is an adventure beyond the mind and all its formulations, a diffusion of the ego-structure into the living sense of a universality, a suffusion by the great Illumination (*mahas*) which commands at once the depth, the width, and the height of the potentialities of the Being in its triple status of the soul, the world, and the Absolute.

But the question still remains: is not Buddhiyoga a supremely idealistic venture? Are its implications compatible with the actual workings of the grim forces of nature (*ghora karma*), with the blood-bespotted realism of a battlefield? Religiosity seeks either to ignore the question or to tone down the rigor of its demands; intellectualism dismisses it with a smile of incredulity, and regards the whole setting of the Sermon as an ill-grafted foisting of overzealous sectarianism. And this is not to be wondered at: illumination and action become incompatible when we artificially divide the total activities of man into spiritual and secular; but this is certainly against the true spirit of Indian culture. From times immemorial India has been seeking to harmonize into an integral experience the apparently diverse ideals of brahma and kshatra, of sankhya and yoga, of mokshadharma and rajadharma, or speaking in terms of mystical philosophy, of akasha and prana, of spirit and life. And with a true intuition, she has sought to make spirit the guide of life, since it is in spirit in its widest sense that life has its chance of progression and fulfillment. Even when as a realist we imagine "thinking to some purpose" to be the directive of life activities, we make thereby a concession to spirit, since purposeful thinking cannot be readily and ultimately fruitful unless there is an element of universalization in it; and this will of course mean a prelude to spiritualization. So, by laying an emphasis on spirit, what India aimed at was a direct hit on the solution of the problem of life. She never denied the rights of economics (*varta*) and politics (*danda*) to be considered as permanent factors of life; but she equally insisted that rational thinking (*anvikshiki*) culminating in spiritual realization (*trayi*) also be regarded as things of everlasting value. Today the same eternal problem stares us in the face. As life's clamors and demands have been growing bewildering, we are living under the persistent shadow of Kurukshetra; and the old trick of escapism will not avail. What are we to do? That the clumsy manipulations of varta and danda which have precipitated two world wars will not save us, is crystal clear. Is it not then high time that we look up to some greater source of illumination, not in a spirit of easy acquiescence but with the determined vigor of a hero who will see things for himself? "*Buddhau sharanam anviccha*—seek your refuge in Buddhi, the Illumination of the Beyond," rings the commandment of the Lord down the passage of time; and perhaps mankind has never been more in need of it than today.

Notes

1. Shan Br I.4; for verbal similarities also cf. Shat Br VI.8.2.6; VI.8.1.6; Tait Br I.3.1.3.

2. Atharvaveda VII.13.3; XV.2.5. (In the latter mantra, vijnana is very significantly described as the vasas of the Vratya); Shat Br III.3.4.11; VIII.7.2.10; X. 3.5.13, where it is used in the sense of "esoteric knowledge"; Tait Br III.1.1, where it is said to be the second of the shuklapaksha (cf. BG VIII.24); Tait U II.5.1; III.5.1.

3. Katha U I.3.9; read with this the injunction of the Gita in II.49.

4. Ch U VII.26.2; in BG XVI.1; sattvasamshuddhi is one of the daivisampads leading to vimoksha.

5. Yogasutra I.20; a special technique has been detailed in the Satipatthana Sutta: Digha Nikaya II.9; Majjhima Nikaya, I.1.10.

6. Katha U II.3.7, where sattva is followed by three other stages.

7. Padartha Dharma Samgraha, pp. 34, 38, 39.

8. Friedrich Otto Schrader, *Introduction to the Pancaratra and the Ahirbudhnya Samhita* (Madras: Adyar Library, 1916), pp. 72 ff.

9. Sattva has been widely used as a psychic entity forming the core of personality.

10. BG XVII.3, where sattva is equated with buddhi.

11. BG II, 64, 65. The idea of prasada is applied in Buddhist philosophy to explain the origination of the senses from matter (Visuddhimagga 14, 73); cf. dhatuprasada in the Katha Upanishad, leading to the experience of the illimitable resplendence of the Self (I.2.20); samprasada or the light of the clear Void

described in the Chandogya Upanishad (VIII.6.3; VII.11.1), and the Brihadarnyaka Upanishad (IV.3.15).

12. *Kurukshetra* has been variously described as "the sacrifical ground for the gods" (Shat Br XIV.1.1–2; Tait Ar V.11), "the altar of the Lord of Creation coextensive with earth nature" (Tan Br XXV.13.3), and the holy land where grew the mystic nyagrodha tree, the first of its kind (Ait Br VII.30). The Rigveda speaks of Indra "killing the ninety-nine Vritras with the bone of Horse's Head which had been stowed away in the mountains and was found by him at Sharyanavat" (I.84.13–14). The Shatyayana Brahmana in this context (quoted by Sayana) speaks mysteriously of this sharyanavat as a "lake quivering at the bottom end of Kurukshetra." In the vedic tradition, Kurukshetra is thus a double source of the brahma and kshatra spirit.

13. BG XVI.4, 17–19, 21. The passages read like an accurate and minute description of the hydra-headed fascist tendencies springing up at home and abroad.

14. Abhaya, sattvasamshuddhi, tejas, and dhriti are included in the daivisampad (BG XVI.1, 3); cf. XVIII.43, where intrepidity together with tejas and dhriti have been described as the natural expression of a kshatra temperament; daivisampad combines in itself both the brahma and the kshatra ideals. Cf. BG XVIII.43–44 with XVI.1–3.

15. This is the accepted meaning of the vedic term which has been applied both to Man and God; Yaska also explains it as connoting "rhythmic activity" (Nirukta VI.1.2); Nighantu lists it also among the synonyms of ashva, the symbol of spiritual vigor.

16. This is the eternal relation between the Divine Teacher and the human disciple. A very significant phrase occurs in the Gita XI.44, priyah priyayah, where the madhurarati of the Vaishnavas is foreshadowed.

17. Etymologically conveys the sense of a "sharpening of the energy of consciousness"; cf. BG II.14.

18. *Loka*, *praja*, and *bhuta* are the three vedic words meaning in a general way the totality of creation. Etymologically loka would mean "levels of consciousness" (derived from the root *luc* "to shine"); praja would symbolize the "dynamic march of life," and bhuta "the final phase of Becoming," culminating in the materialization of the spirit. These shades of meaning have not been carefully preserved in the Gita, though in some passages a distinction has been made between loka and praja.

19. Mandukyakarika III.39; also BG XII.5.

20. Vishadayoga seems to be a graphic and poetic version of the tenet of duhkha, the first arya satya.

21. *Shoka* and *moha* are the two upanishadic terms typifying the rajasa and tamasa temperaments.

22. *Dhira* is the great vedic term for the highest type of aspirant, one who has ascended to the dyusthana or the plane of unitary aditya-consciousness.

23. Hence the common equation, Death = Kala or the Time-spirit.

24. BG II.13. Buddhist philosophy, from the standpoint of eternal flux, has completely discarded the idea of death and has substituted for it the notion of "birth in another plane" (see the theory of chuti, Visuddhimagga XIV.123–124).

25. Also called the *vibhuti of kshama* in BG X.34, where taken in the reverse order it is the first of the series of spiritual powers developed in the aspirant.

26. BG VIII.18–21; cf. Shvetashvatara Upanishad IV.18.

27. A Sankhyist would speak here either of tamasa inertia or rajasa activity accompanied by a sattvika vision gaining ascendancy in the psychophysical organism.

28. In the Upanishads an analogy has been drawn between this and the dream-state of ordinary consciousness, and Patanjali has recommended it as a means of realizing the *nirodhayoga* (Yogasutra I.38).

29. In the Upanishads, akasha is the first evolute from Atman (Tait U II.1.3), it is the originator of name and form (Ch U VIII.14.1), and for the purpose of meditation it has been described as the cosmic aspect of Brahman, while mind is the individual aspect and an equation between the two has been hinted at (Ch U III.18.1). In Buddhist mysticism the infinity of akasha forms the first plane of the formless meditations.

30. In the upanishadic philosophy, this is known as *tapas*; cf. Mundaka Upanishad, I.1.viii–ix, where the *jnanamayam tapas* is said to be the origin of all things.

31. BG II.10. The instance cited in the original in this context is, of course, that of the "slayer and the slain." There is a record of at least two parallel experiences in the life of Sri Ramakrishna. Once, seeing a dragonfly being tortured by a small boy, his first reaction was a feeling of excruciating pain, which was suddenly changed into a sense of elation as the luminous vision of the self-activity of the Lord was revealed to him. On another occasion he saw that "all three were the same substance—the victim, the block, and the executioners!"

32. Aishvara Yoga (BG XI.8), which is a multiple self-becoming (*vibhuti*) founded on self-poise (*yoga*). Cf. BG X.18.

33. Cf. Samaveda VI.1.9; Atharvaveda XV.14.

34. Prathamani dharmani of the Vedas, which on a deeper scrutiny turn out to be "spiritual laws selective in character" (*daivya vratani*).

35. This is described in the tantric philosophy as the mimesha movement of shakti by which she remains absorbed in the eternal self-poise of the Benign (*Sadashiva*).

36. It is interesting to note that the neo-Vedantic theory of knowledge explains perception as essentially a process of identification of the subject-consciousness with the object-consciousness. The theory is suggestive of a progressive intensity of assimilation as consciousness rises to higher levels.

37. Hence a Naiyayika insists on the purification of the means of knowledge to enable it to have a clear comprehension of the object to be known (*manadhina meyashuddhih*). The dictum is confined not to the process of phenomenal knowledge alone, but extends to the method of the knowledge of the Real also.

38. This stands out clearly on the level of vijnana-consciousness, the pure dream-state of the Upanishads, where the seer "sees All because he sees as All" (Pr U IV.5).

39. Brih U I.2.1. In the Rigveda, this is amati or self-ruining poverty of the spirit, the root of "sin" (Ait Br II.2 on Rigveda III.8.2).

40. This starts a line of spiritual descent (*vidya-sambandhakritavamsha*) with acharya as father and Savitri as mother (Manusamhita II.148).

41. Brahma is also interpreted as vak. The whole scheme of descent will then suggest the progressive actualization of the five principles of creation. The evolution of jiva-consciousness also follows an identical line—it is an actualization of its potentialities.

42. This is the whole sense of the vedic sacrifice. The typical objects of desire expressed by the triad of anna, pashu, and praja crowned by a fourth, that is, svar or the Light-word, carry the esoteric significance of the three primal urges of evolutionary nature pointing to a fourth status (*turiyam*). The cult of sacrifice brings about either an extension or a sublimation of these powers.

43. This is the meaning of the vedic symbol of pashu derived from a root carrying a double import.

44. The vedic philosophy traces the origin of sin to the asuric impulse expressing itself either in the sense of duality (Ch U I.2.1–7) or in vital hunger (Ait Br II.2). Cf. BG III.13.

45. Kama, krodha, and moha of the Gita correspond to Patanjali's three forms of constricted functioning of consciousness (*klesha-vritti*) appearing on the empirical field and called by him raga, dvesha, and abhinivesha, respectively.

46. According to the Nyaya system, which takes a matter-of-fact view of things, smriti is an unreal form of experience. Patanjali, in explaining the psychology of the Sankhya system, admits this as a form of constructed consciousness but also speaks of aklishta or unfettered smriti as an upaya of samadhi (Yogasutra I.5, 6, 20). This is supported by the Vedanta system of thought also (cf. Pr U IV.5; Ch U VII.26.2). For an antagonism between moha and smriti, see BG XVIII.73; for its place in the scheme of the development of spiritual powers, see BG X.34.

47. Yogasutra I.11. The sutra of course defines *klishta smriti* as an experience in time, but the same may also be construed to mean the timeless experience of aklishta smriti, if we transfer the agent of the anubhava (experience) from a phenomenal self to a real self.

48. The dhruva smriti of the Upanishad. The epithet dhruva means not only the force of conservation as it appears from the standpoint of the aspirant in time but also the recovery of an eternal projection as it is experienced in timelessness.

49. The last pentad of the Sankhya principles, which Vedanta will explain as forming the stages of spiritual evolution of the being.

50. Nyaya, from a realistic standpoint, speaks of this as the characteristic of the sense-mind.

51. Cf. BG IV.7: *dharmasya glanih, adhyutthanam adharmasya.*

52. Spoken of in the Gita as shitoshna, sukha-duhkha, and iccha-dvesha, all based on matrasparsha (II.14; VII.27). To these may be added the dualities caused at a higher level by the moral conflict of sukrita-dushkrita (II.50).

53. The urge really comes from the Supreme Person (*parah purushah*) enshrined in our corporeal being as bhokta maheshvara, in whom power and enjoyment have found their supreme fulfillment. But in the spiritual evolution of the jiva, this status represents the last of a series, that is, upadrashta, anumanta, and bharta (BG XIII.22). Real power and enjoyment can come to the individual only when the successive steps beginning from the status of Witness-consciousness (*upadrashta*) have been realized.

54. Nityasattva is also known as shuddhasattva, or as the Yoga system puts it, sattvaprakasha, the specific attribute of God which is the source of its divine knowledge and activity (cf. Tattvavaisharadi on Yogasutrabhasya I.24).

55. So Sri Ramakrishna would often say in answer to the dispute about the nature of the ultimate Reality: "But He is with form, as also without form; and who knows what else He is?"

56. BG II.48. This is preliminary to Patanjali's nirodhayoga initiated by vairagya (Yogasutra I.12, cf. BG VI.35) which is essentially the same as asangatva. What Patanjali aims at is a complete liquidation of the disturbing forces of will and emotion (*vaitrishnya*) so that an exclusive concentration (*samadhi*) may lead to a status of selfhood (*svarupavasthanam*) analogous to a status of the Void (*svarupashunyata*). If the rhythm of vyutthana (rising to the surface) spontaneously following this is not forcibly checked (as is done by some Buddhist cults) it will lead to what the Gita elsewhere speaks of as "the conquest of the forces of creation" (V.19). This becomes normal by following the method of viveka (analytic discrimination) suggested by Kapila, where the field of consciousness is allowed to widen and subtilize itself according to the laws of a higher nature responsive to the intensification of staticity of purusha. Obviously the Gita does not stop at nirodhayoga (whose essence it of course assimilates in its cult of

yogabuddhi), but goes a step forward and speaks of the very same yoga as an art (*Kaushalam*). Cf. BG II.48 read with II.50.

57. BG II.47. Consciousness must always be a free agent, not lending itself to any form of mechanization.

58. Even in normal consciousness, this becomes evident in scientific investigation and artistic creation, where a certain amount of samatva reflecting the impersonal witness-consciousness is indispensable at all times.

59. BG VI.25. Patanjali will call this the creation of *nirodhasamskara*, which may become a normal background of the phenomenal mind, whose motivations will then rise not from below, i.e., from the vital plane, but from a higher source above the mind. Ordinarily we would call this the function of intuition or the flash of inspiration.

60. BG II.49. This avara karma, even when it is dignified by the name of yajna, is denounced in the Upanishads too (Mundaka I.2.6), where it is said that though there is a truth in "mantra-inspired karma" (I.2.1) pointing to a sunlit path leading to the One (I.2.5), yet men miss its significance by their blinding attachment and their dogmatic refusal to look beyond (I.2.8-9).

61. BG II.55. The Gita speaks of three planes of desire, the plane of sense-vitals, of mind, and of buddhi (III.40). The intermediate plane of mind is here put first, disregarding the logical order from considerations of practical necessity, since it best suits the aspirant to take up a middle position from which he can look above and have a better control of the lower forces. This is of course in accordance with the time-honored practice of "following the middle path."

62. BG II.55. From desire to self-delight (*atmatushti*), the stages passed by the soul have their counterparts in the stages of normal consciousness in awakening, dream and sleep. If we take awakening as the standard for measuring consciousness, then in desire we awaken to a world dominated by sensations where ideas, though they form the most powerful instrumentation for all kinds of progress, are nevertheless not there in their own rights; in dream, we begin to awake to a world of Ideas, which is still dominated by the crudities of sensations, but where the stuff of consciousness can be so processed as to reflect the world of pure ideas; in sleep we awake to the plane variously called the Matrix, the Cause, the Unmanifest—its psychic counterpart being called Bliss. In our normal being, rooted in sensation, there appears a gradual lessening of the stress of consciousness as we follow the inward track. But the reverse also can be the case. Attention is consciousness, says normal psychology; but then it is attention extrovert. What if it is attention introvert? With full awakening we shall then trace back the path which normal consciousness has mechanically trod before and pass on, as the vedic seer has said, "from light to higher Light and on to the highest Light." The reality of mystic experience is thus grounded in a process of normal consciousness to which sensationalism so fervently clings, and it is in its reprocessing that the secret of rational mysticism lies. The Upanishads, in numerous places, speak of the dream and sleep state, whose mystical significance is often ignored, and they are freely equated with states of normal consciousness. In fact, it is one of the major discoveries of the science of mysticism that India has made

in the past and which has been one of the basic factors in her investigations in supernormal psychology (cf. Yogasutra I.38).

63. BG II.61. *Yuktah asita mataparah*. This is the first and apparently a casual mention of divinity as the aim of existence. Though a complete surrender to the supreme Purusha is the goal toward which the evolution of jivaprakriti is moving, yet the emphasis is still on the principle of buddhi to enable the individual to attain to the full stature before a true surrender and the consequent attainment of divyabhava is possible.

64. Quoted with approbation by the scholiast on Yogasutra II.55, where several other views are also discussed.

65. Yogasutra II.54. This explains why and how *rasopyasya param drishtva nivartate* (BG II.59).

66. It is well known how the simile of the tortoise, with all its implications of integral realization, came true in Sri Ramakrishna's life.

67. The former is specifically the bhavana of jiva, his inward movement toward self-poise, and the latter is the bhavana of Shiva, the bhutama bhutabhavana of the Gita, in which is expressed his effective dynamism of spiritual metamorphosis. In the realized soul as Guru, the two combine, and their combined activity becomes most apparent in soul-contacts as grace or transmission of power.

Chapter 13

Spiritual Values

Introduction: The Role of Inwardization of Consciousness

Theology speaks of man as a spirit who has been born into flesh; but there is obviously a prelude to a real spiritual life. Every religion distinguishes between the natural and the spiritual man: to be born spiritually is an event in life which is consecrated by a sacrament either social or individual. In the Arya society, there was the social sacrament of upanayana, which admitted the child formally into the spiritual heritage of the community, and there was the individual sacrament of diksha for the adult to launch him into his personal spiritual endeavor. But in spite of this formal recognition, the whole is a process of inner continuity, like the growth of a seed. To clarify an idea, formality proceeds with discrimination and so draws a line between the spiritual man and the natural man, between spiritual values and life-values. But if life is nothing but the blooming of the inner spirit, too much importance need not be laid upon this artificial division. A free interaction between the two sets of values is absolutely necessary. There must be a congenial social environment which will so mold the life values as to enable them better to reflect the spirit; and there must also be the intensive training of the spirit so that it can take up and change the life values into something rich and new. Forms can be used only as means for broadening the outlook on life, so that in the end life and the spirit become conterminous.

An instance of this may be found in the change of value that the concept of karma has undergone in the Vedas and the Gita. While the word *karma* is almost exclusively used in the Vedas to mean a conformity to a type of action which is considered spiritual, the Gita has widened its scope to spiritualize every form of activity, including even the unconscious physiological movements of life. This has meant not only a heightening but also a deepening and broadening of consciousness; and, of course, this is the whole aim of spirituality. It cannot be divorced from life's great aim—the aim of growth. In short, spirituality may be spoken of as life's conscious endeavor to grow by harmonious assimilation. It is at once an intensification of consciousness which marks the inner enterprise and a harmonization with the environment which determines life's aesthetic and moral values.

The enterprise is, of course, difficult; but it is also universal. We are spiritualizing every moment of our life either knowingly or unknowingly. The unconscious endeavor, whether sustained by social forces or by an inchoate inner urge, is, as we have seen, a prelude to the conscious one; and the whole process is based on a dynamism of consciousness seeking for clarity. A sort of clarity comes when the sensate values of an animal life develop into the ideal values of a human understanding. The power to deal with ideas independently of the sense-data is an achievement of consciousness which marks the beginning of the life of spirit. Sensations are clear and particular for all, even for animals. But are representations also equally clear? To the animal, obviously they are not. In man, they gain universality but lose in clarity, as the Naiyayika observes. Their universality, or the power of the human consciousness to frame universals, enables man consciously to order his experiences and so to discover laws of nature and make regulations for his own conduct. This gives him a power to control things and derive a maximum of satisfaction by a repetition of the sense experiences. And it helps to create an inner world which has yet to depend on the outer world for the values it derives. But in the long run, the arrangement is found not to be satisfactory. The particular, which becomes a guarantee for truth, still belongs to the sensuous world. And the crux of the problem is, to speak paradoxically, how to particularize the universal on the ideal plane. This is the pivot on which turns the whole of man's spiritual endeavor: to change the world of senses into the world of ideas so that consciousness may be dynamically free in its self-enjoyment.

The first inevitable step leading to this is inwardization of consciousness. The upanshadic seer laid down the law very clearly: "Self-existence has bored outlets for projecting itself into the phenomenal world; and human consciousness follows the same impulse. The result is a dissipation and deadening of the conscious energy. To keep its fire ever burning, the process has to be reversed." If put in an abstract form, the demand for introversion appears fantastic and even alarming to the normal mind. But the urge for looking into one's own self is a necessary stage in the evolution of consciousness. Even for practical purposes, the object to be handled must be rendered clear and its possible functions anticipated. And this cannot be done within the thought process itself. In other words, one has to think before deliberately guiding his action; and thought can rise only when the automatism of action has been suspended. One has to hold the breath, take in the situation, and make the plunge.

So even in practical life, a temporary suspension of activity cannot be avoided because it is absolutely necessary for a clarity of consciousness. But a clear consciousness will judge not only the outer world but simultaneously the inner being also, though in this case the judgment is generally a reflection of the clarity of perception and is overlaid with a feeling of confidence. To have control over things, at which the practical judgment aims, one must have control over thoughts. A mastery outside thus inevitably creates a personality inside; and personality is a spiritual value that is indispensable for a successful life.

Value as Pure Existence

A peculiar characteristic of human thought is that in its attempt to reduce the concrete into the abstract for a better grasp of things, it becomes in the course of time preoccupied with the abstract for its own sake. Pure science and metaphysics as great ventures of the human spirit have been born in this way. If positivism and empiricism have been eager to exploit these achievements in the abstract, they show only one trend of the movement of consciousness; the countermovement is equally strong and equally natural.

When a man is preoccupied with the development of personality, which his self-esteem will compel him to do, he cannot but be carried away by the lure of the abstract. It is simply a question of spiritual dynamism. If the law of conservation of energy is true in the spiritual field also (considering for the time being the individual as a closed system), energy withdrawn from the outer field will very naturally gain in strength in its inward rush and, measured quantitatively, what has been lost in extension will be recovered in intension. Intension in its final phase may completely denude the field, so that consciousness might be left without an object to deal with. If induced abruptly or by some external cause, the denudation might not mean so much. But if it is cultivated deliberately, it will lead to a perception of pure existence (*sat*), where the polarity of the subject and the object has been fused in a rarefied feeling of innate identity. And this perception is a fundamental spiritual value.

The experience where qualities born of the polarity of consciousness cease, not by abrogation but by mutual absorption (*samarasya*), is of course beyond the depth of the normal consciousness, which can subsist only by a split in the unity necessitated by its preoccupation with particulars. Yet this experience in a nascent form stands behind all other experiences, not only as the call of quiescence in all rhythms of life and mind but also as the creative matrix that throws out new forms when old ones are exhausted. In an individual, and even in a race, the quiescence motive may become dominant for a certain period. To look askance at it as escapism is wholly to misunderstand the rhythm of nature; it is better to take it as a prelude to a creative urge. If in an individual a force seems to be lost by a plunge into its own self, it must reappear somewhere or sometime if a free play of conscious energy is allowed. Relying upon this law, we may take introflection (*nivritti*) of consciousness as a spiritual value of supreme importance which can be very profitably utilized even for enhancing the life values created in the normal way. The indwelling consciousness appears to be passive, but it is really not so. It creates an inner tension which outwardly simulates the inertia of dead matter, but is nevertheless a living force with a definite feeling-content. The value of an absolute perception is to be judged by the energy it releases into the feeling and the will: it may be the unmoved mover of things in the spontaneity of a total rhythm both inside and outside. The practical philosophy of dispassionate and disinterested action even while moving with the cosmic current of forces with a clear sense of the ultimate end (as it has been preached and illustrated in the Gita) is one of its first fruits on the plane of will. On the plane of feeling, the Bhagavatas have notably built upon this foundation the structure of the multicolored ecstasy of divine Love, which has sublimated some of the fundamental emotions of the social being.

In actual practice, quiescence may well become a vantage ground for attacking the problems of life. "The energy of experience moves in quanta and one has to fix one's consciousness on the intermediate void," said a Shaiva philosopher. The technique will be to counterpoise every positive output of energy with a negative weight that leans backward into a nothingness; and this cannot be done unless a split has been brought about in the normally conjoint action of feeling and will. Consciousness then takes a direction without swerving, but is sustained in its course not by an anticipation and hence a conceptive experience of its emotional contents, but on the contrary by its alertness, which will constantly check and change these emotional by-products into a force dissolving in neutrality. Certainly, this will not be apathy, which, having a positive content, is bound to have a reaction; it will rather be the deadening of all shocks by offering no inner resistance. It will not be inactivity, because the will is there; only the will, even while taking a linear direction, will not be oblivious of support of the unbounded space that surrounds it. The movement of will will be an event in time, but it will carry in each of its pulsating moments the gradual unfolding of a seed-impulse inspired by the stability of a total vision. If will in this way is welded with vision, it gives an original perspective of reality which has been so luminously described by the vedic seers as kavi-kratu, the creative vision of the divine Fire. A spiritual space-time corresponding to the upanishadic concept of akasha-prana then becomes the measure of existence. We move and yet we move not; for all movement is simply the deployment of what was already contained in the seed, which in its self-sufficiency can remain gathered in itself if it chooses. If evaluation is made in terms of the ultimate satisfaction that things bring to thought, then a seed-thought, which in every moment of its development can intensify all its energies into a perception of its original existence, need not evolve at all. And yet it evolves; and this is maya, which is certainly not the sensuous valuation called "illusion," but a meaningful mystery beyond the intellect. Maya is the divine will—the core of a coil expanding into space and creating time to mark the process. And as such, it creates the dynamic spiritual values projected from the staticity of pure existence.

Metaphysical Implications of Pure Existence

Two sections of world existence, one in space and another in time, determine two concepts of spiritual values—the static and the dynamic. Upanishadic thought reduces all ultimates of consciousness into the two interdependent forms of akasha and prana—the consciousness of extension and of dynamism. Logically they might represent two poles; but in feeling—in life itself—extension naturally sprouts into becoming. Being is then the distant prospect of a horizon, which might be the view of a moment inclusive of all existences. "The Void makes room for All," significantly remarks the Vedantist. But is the All a nirriti, a chaos? The concept, which is self-contradictory, is just possible because it hints at the beginning of a process. The vedic seer stood before the abyss and described it as the indescribable where all description can only be negative; and hence it can only be a reverse process of darkness deepening into darkness (*tama asit tamasa gudham*). But evidently, the process cannot be continued ad infinitum. Somewhere the discerning consciousness (for, even in the abysmal depths of darkness there is the unwinking Eye that looks calmly on) strikes a rock bottom, and the formless through self-consciousness sends a thrill of forms that ripples toward expression: the darkness melts into light and a world is revealed. The sleeper awakens, the unborn is born: and in his perception rita or order has come into the chaos of nirriti.

But was not rita itself a preexistent idea, a significant form of truth? Can truth as existence (*satyam*) and truth as order (*ritam*) be really separated? Is this order a static perception in space or a dynamic feeling in time? Or does it comprise both in a bi-une aspect of reality? Convincing answers to these questions can be given only from the standpoint of the individual consciousness, which forms a center around which all existences are ordered. But the individual itself is a moving entity (*samsari*). Its experiences, which must always be ordered experiences to meet the demands of life, describe a spiral which has a tendency to widen its convolutions as it rises in the scale of being. Several cross-sections may be taken of the spiral ascent at different levels. Each section will then represent to the consciousness an apparently closed universe ordered according to a definite pattern. Stationed on each of these levels, the individual may think that he has come to his journey's end. But it is only an apparent end. There is the mysterious urge of the mystic Fire (*preti-ishani*) impelling onward to a goal that is only dimly perceived. "It is the growing perception of the Vast and the attendant spiritual vigor, with sprinklings of death in between, that sustain existence," said a upanishadic seer. In the end, life wins when it resolves into the luminous death of immortality. The Unmanifest has again returned to the Unmanifest, describing the iridescent rainbow of manifest existence. The sun rose from darkness and returned to its home (*astam*) of the unknown Light. If the beginning was the Unmanifest as nonexistence (*asat*) when viewed retrospectively by the individual consciousness, the end must also be an unmanifest existence (*sat*) viewed prospectively: the order or rita stands between the two poles. It is the law of dynamic existence unfolding itself in the rhythm of life's seasons (*ritu*), attuned to the march of the one cosmic Light, as the vedic seers saw it.

The end as quiescence is inevitable: but it can either be the quiescence of darkness or of light. The predilection for light will determine the norms of life, which perhaps will only be relative values according to one's vision of the ordered universe. But the lure of the absolute, which will mean the widest convolution of the spiral where existence might burst its bounds into non-existence, is still there. It is the purely static spiritual value—the value which space as unencumbered and unlimited extension of pure thought connotes. But its staticity may not include dynamism, because "it gives room to all." The labor of life to bring out order from chaos by arranging the movements of will and the colors of feeling into a harmonious whole around a core of integral simple perception (*sahaja*) finds its consummation in a form of existence in which akasha and prana appear not as polarities but as a complete fusion.

And this forms the metaphysical background of the concept of existence as a spiritual value. It had to be dealt with somewhat fully, because it is the pivot on which all other values turn, and its influence on the spiritual evolution of India has been a source of mystification to the modern mind when it has come to appraise her age-long outlook on the aim of existence (*purushartha*).

Derivative Values: Personality, Joy, Will, Knowledge, and Dynamism

The inwardization of consciousness is essentially a phenomenon of life. It is a process of absorption and assimilation of experience helping the growth of a personality—a spiritual personality which rises above the mind, but instead of rejecting it might use it as a pliant instrument of the spirit. The focusing of consciousness by inwardization creates the real individual—the radiant ego, the pippalada of the Vedas, who can transmute the varieties of experiences into the stuff of the spirit. The individual stands between the two vastnesses of objectivity and subjectivity, of the particular and the universal. The object strikes to awaken a reaction; this is the general pattern of the working of the natural forces. But if the shock is absorbed at least partially, it can be made to spread like flood water in the background of the consciousness; and a repetition of the experiment will waken and strengthen a luminous sense of the universal, which will make room for all the particulars and let them arrange themselves in a world of harmony without any intervention from the lower ego. The individual in this way becomes universalized and discovers the basic unity and identity of all ego structures. The perception automatically translated into feeling becomes the understanding sympathy that can create an artistic vision of life by dispassionately entering into all its movements. It is thus that the individual is transformed into a Person (*purusha*)—a universal form of Being gathering in itself, as the vedic seer says, "all that has been and all that is going to be." The creation of this personality is a supreme spiritual value born of the quiescence of transcendence.

The inwardization and the consequent intensification of consciousness need not create a blank at the outset, unless the tendency to blankness is deliberately induced or has been inherent in nature. Consciousness, as the vedic seer imagined it, is like the marine fire conceived in and nourished by the waters of life. As long as the life-urge continues, it is essentially a creative force which uses its whole field of its experiences. My world and I must become one; there must be nothing unknown, impervious, or unassimilable in what excites my interest. Consciousness as a life force is "an eater of food (*annada*)," says the Veda. The process of assimilation is a struggle for overcoming resistance. In ignorance it is pain, but in knowledge it is energizing, automatically manifesting itself in radiation (*tapas*). What has been conquered and consumed must be given out as higher values. This taking in and giving out which seems to be the systole and diastole of the process of creation is an active feeling of quiescent joy (*ananda*).

Joy, quietly abiding in a perfect equipoise and in an unhampered sense of illumination where knowing can be freely equated with becoming, is the third great spiritual value which dawns toward the end of the venture into the Beyond. The value can be both static and dynamic; and the surest means of fixing it in consciousness is to lay stress on its static aspect. The poise in the pure being and the ever-alertness of the spirit radiating itself in simple awareness, without initiating any movement in the field of experience, creates a reserve of power which might well be inexhaustible. The feeling of power in restraint is the quietude of joy which can clearly see truth and unerringly direct its dynamism. The calm witness is not uncreative; only he has a complete vision of the end in the beginning and so his creation is not a painful struggle in the unknown but a carefree deployment of the seed-impulse. The joy of arriving is already contained in the immobility; and so the movement becomes a play of consciousness where determination is perfectly balanced by the prolificness of chance.

Life seeks expression. Even an inner integration in which power is crystallized into a point apparently immobile and adamantine throbs with an energy that creates vibrations on different planes of consciousness. The immobility which results from the finesse of movements drawing themselves to the inner core may be described with upanishadic seers as the movement of life into its ultimate of the luminous Void—a supreme movement (*paragatih*) whose measure is eternity. It is a fact of life, because it is a fact of consciousness. Its expression is in radiation, in creative joy—the joy that thrills, flashes, bursts into ideal rhythms, and finally materializes in forms. Creative joy liberates, because it depends for its creation on nothing extraneous. It is the projection of a self-vision, first in the luminosity of an ethereal perception which automatically proceeds toward a polarity simply because space has been possible for the manipulation of forms. Since the process is not an absolutely new beginning but an enigmatic cycle where time can curl into a point, materials which have been discarded during the movement of integration can be taken up again to infuse them with a deeper meaning. The spirit that soared to the heavens returns to the earth and changes its face. Where there was a clash, joy in its infinite toleration creates a harmony of lights and shades. And then the pure perception of a totality by its ingathered force touches in the heart of existence the mainspring of all creative spirals. The total perception discovers the unique meaning—the cosmic Will which like a seed has thrown roots down and branches up. The discovery of the cosmic Will and its assimilation in the individual will-to-be, not in its groping futility but in its lucid sense of mastery over chaotic movements, is a new spiritual value starting a dynamic series that forms the natural complement of the static trinity of existence, personality, and joy.

The rest of the process is simple. Once will has been mastered and poised in the integrity of a total vision, the unity of purpose spontaneously arranges the multiplicity of materials, linking each of their varied movements to the causal urge. And this relation we call knowledge (*jnana*), viewed not as a passion but as a creative operation. This dynamic knowledge is the second in the triad of the spiritual values born of power.

The third, spiritual activity (*kriya*) is a value which is the natural consummation of all that has gone before. It is inevitably bound up with the process of time, which may move either slowly or quickly according to some occult determinism. The indeterminability of the pace of time creates a host of problems for both the inner and the outer world. The timeless vision appears anemic to the sceptic, and the martyrdom of faith seems to be a sheer waste of misdirected energy. Yet all acts are acts of faith. The urge to act is meaningless without a vision. The vision that rose in the one Self as a retrogressive movement of consciousness now hurls itself back on the field of the many. The forms slowly evolving there have to be quickened; but how? A grim battle ensues, sanctioned by the impetus of the divine Will. The travail of Mother Earth is reflected back from the face of the Void as great compassion (*maha-*

karuna). The omniscience that guides to freedom (the supreme attribute of Godhead conceived by the rationalist) lets its mantle fall on the soul of the one liberated in life (*jivanmukta*). The upward curve of power has come back to its point of origin. The circle has been completed; and in its center throbs the meteroric soil of a Shankara tearing the veils of maya, or shines the sahaja bliss of a Kabir plying the weaver's shuttle.

Have the life values found their consummation in this? Yes. Says the Upanishad: "Of all those who have known the Vast, worthiest is he who delights in the Self, sports with souls and wields a silent dynamism of the seer-will."

Chapter 14

The Spiritual Quest

The world of spirit is as real as the world of the senses; and mysteries abound in both. The adventures of the human mind in both theses realms are equally justifiable, because their ultimate aim is the creation of some abiding values that will widen and enrich the consciousness—the last irreducible factor in the scale of being. What is occult must be laid bare; and its forces must be mastered and made to yield to the growth of the being as a whole. Here science and religion meet as on a common ground: a leap into the beyond, whether it be with the aid of an imaginative flight of hypothesis or with the aid of a living faith sustained by an inchoate perception of some emerging truth, is the motive force in both. And both aim at converting knowledge into a currency of practical utility which will lead to a harmonious growth of the collective life.

But in the recent past, there has been a tendency to create a cleavage between the science of matter and the science of spirit. Sophistication takes one as the quest of some objectively real truth, while it looks upon the other as running after something subjective and ideal, if not in the last analysis an illusion. The modern mind prides itself on its scientific attitude, which seeks to build the structure of truth on the sensible and the obvious (*drishta*, *laukika*) belonging to a public world. But surely this cannot take us far, because the field of experience is not confined to sensible facts alone. As the human mind can soar into the world of universals, so it can also pass judgments of values—aesthetic and ethical. These visions and judgments, though rising from a private and subjective source in the individual, tend to grow into a public order of things as the law of sympathy finds a wider and wider scope; at last it leads to the concept of a unitive human life—the purusha of the vedic vision.

From a free play of this urge of unitive growth and expansion in the human consciousness rise the spiritual values which are nearer to life, and thus in a sense more primary and comprehensive than other creations of inner values. The obvious then deepens into the occult (*adrishta, alaukika*), and perception utilizes not a discursive reason but an integrative intuition to decipher its meaning. The movement is inward, and yet not divorced from peripheral contacts. In fact, the vedic seers frankly equated the spiritual urge with a sublimated life-urge, setting for its goal a complete mastery over the forces of decay (*jara*) and death (*mrityu*). This motive has persisted throughout the ages in various forms. Sometimes it has appeared highly rationalized and almost overshooting itself, as we see in the Buddhist venture and the like; but it has also been more attuned to the demands of nature, as can be seen in the appendage of occult practices in the yogic and the tantric cults. Naturally, ethicism has come to the forefront in the one and aestheticism in the other, though the healthy instinct of the collective consciousness has always attempted at a harmonious blending of the two, and so keeping the ideal of the spiritual achievement nearer to its vedic original.

If the root-impulses are taken into consideration, science and religion do not seem to vary much in their objectives. If the aim of science is to create such all-round life values as will ensure the fullest self-expression of the individual in a social group, this has no less been the aim of religion, too. The methods of attaining this aim will be fundamentally related to the same spirit of enquiry, powers of reasoning, and utilitarian motive common to the human mind, but they will be worked out in apparently different fields with different assumptions. If science lays stress on tangible data, the spiritual quest is more concerned with an array of subjective phenomena which seem to elude the senses. In both, the mind is confronted with some indubitable facts of experience behind which it perceives the existence of some occult forces whose working it tries to seize and manipulate.

Whether these forces are to be regarded as material (*bhutashakti*) or spiritual (*devashakti*) is an issue that may mean much to a modern mind, because its intellectual predilections have created a rift between spirit and matter. But it was not so with the ancient vedic seers. A pristine purity of consciousness allowed them to see reality as a whole: and in the scale of matter, force, and spirit they could discern only a process of gradual illumination occurring in some ineffable neutral Being of universal extension and infinite potentiality. It is this integral vision on which rests the whole scheme of vedic gods (*devah*) and worlds (*urvih, loka*), wherein matter was as easily spiritualized as spirit was materialized.

This can be seen in the use of the word *atman*, which occurs so freely in the vedic literature. Indologists have variously interpreted it as body, breath, or spirit, and have seen in it a gradual evolution of religious thought from a crass materialistic bias to some probable heights of spiritual abstraction. But this is a logical analysis of a total psychic experience in which the polarity of subjectivity and objectivity is not yet apparent. The experience is characterized more by feeling than by thought; it is the intimate feeling of selfhood that is freely projected into different planes of existence which are never regarded as mutually exclusive or as having no interrelation or interaction between them. Indeed, the atman is an integral whole of body-life-spirit—a triune entity whose constituents can be separated only in thought but not in feeling. Feeling records the operation of what may be called a law of density and rarefication which determines whether one is moving up or down the scale of mutual transformation of spirit and matter. In no period of this process can the triunity be broken into three wholly disparate elements, for the simple reason that, while thought is analytic, feeling is unitive; and in spiritual experience it is ultimately the feeling (*anubhava*, lit. "a becoming in accordance with something") that counts more than the thought.

To recognize the supremacy of feeling in this respect may appear unpalatable to intellectualism, which looks upon the former as something crude, hazy, and erratic. But it cannot be denied that it is only feeling at its sublime height that can infuse the sense of a living realism into the abstractions of a schematizing intellect; it alone can make reality whole again by bridging the gap which the logical mind has created between subject and object, between spirit and matter. Feeling is simple and primary, while thought is elaborate and evolved. But the things of the spirit also are simple and retain their freshness and creative energy while they still rise unalloyed from the depths of the being. Their elaboration by the architectonic methods of the thinking mind is not a gain in terms of evolution. Indeed, the current evolutionary canon may prove here to be a signal failure: when a man evolves intellectually, it does not mean that he is on the road to higher spiritual evolution as well. The great mistake of modern scholarship is to apply its intellectual standards in judging things that spring from sources other than the intellect.

And so, to assign a higher place to revelation as a source of true knowledge than to externalized sense-perception and reasoning, as is done by spiritual philosophy everywhere, is not to cherish a dogma. It is an extension of the field of perception by bringing about a radical change in its mode. This change is effected by seizing upon the natural power of universalization in the human mind and intensifying it by the yogic method to such an extent as to make its abstractions appear in concrete forms. It, however, does not mean a hallucinatory return to the senses, but a discovery of another world of reality where the instrumentation of sense-perception (*jnana*) is changed into that of idea-perception (*vijnana*). It is an experience with the whole being—a total and living experience with a stamp of universality, which makes it analogous to the feeling-experience of the normal mind. But we must bear in mind that the feeling-tone of vijnana is not of the nature of a murky emotional disturbance, but of a serene illumination and of an ineffable joy whose creations depict reality in meaningful forms of massed ideation.

It is a mistake to suppose that these things can be understood and rationally interpreted by an application of the laws of biological evolution. In evolution of forms, we can have a series starting from the simple and the homogeneous, and proceeding through a laborious and complicated process, we come to the complex and the heterogeneous. The last gives us some discrete sensate values. These can be clearly grasped by the mind and again pieced together to form a hazy notion of some universal concept or idea. But we may suppose (and this will need nothing more than a change of perspective) that this idea, which is reconstructed by the reasoning of the sense-mind, was the original driving force behind the evolution of forms. We may go further and claim that a direct perception of this idea through a supersensuous intuition translating itself into ideative sensations is not an impossibility. And then we have another way of looking at existence—the anticipatory way. It will be a moving not from the known to the unknown, from creation to its source, from a sensible nature to an imagined God, but seeing God face to face as the inmost meaning of the self, and deducing nature from Him.

This vision is a total experience whose extent or intensity is beyond the computation of any graded scale. The school of thought which looks upon religion as wholly a social product and, in deference to objective methods, attempts to link its development to the progress of social evolution can only give a superficial account of the collective and the average. But it cannot explain the appearance of outstanding individuals, nor can it plumb the depth of their experiences. Spiritual giants have appeared in every age and every land, even in circumstances most unfavorable to spiritual growth. And this points not to the strictly measurable culmination of some laborious ascent of evolutionary nature from below, but the descent of the spirit from above in a cataract.

The phenomenon can be best explained on the Sankhya conception of purusha and prakriti—purusha the timeless, the immobile, the seer, and yet an ingathered totality, and prakriti its dynamism of will in time. The life-urge rushes on, driven by some hidden force that pushes it from below or pulls it from above; but after reaching a point it subsides into quiescence, which to awareness means a fusion of the Plenum and the Void. In itself, this quiescence is simple, colorless, and indeterminate; it is the final abstraction of pure consciousness. It is the dead end of all spiritual endeavors, of all adventures into the Beyond. Its value cannot be measured: it is at once the zero and the infinity. Values ascribed to it (as is generally done in academic philosophies trying to create a hierarchy in the Void) are simply projections of the values that have been created on this side of the line by measuring the intensity of the prakritic drive and mapping the extent of the phenomenal existence it has covered or conquered. The sole positive value that can be given to this quiescence of simple consciousness (and, even then, this value can be made explicit only with a backward reference to the strain to which prakriti has put herself to reach the point of self-annihilation) is a feeling of relaxation and expansion, a sense of serene poise in the Void. And it may mean a Plenum which, like the consummation of death, may burst in all its glory at any point of the prakritic evolution.

The vedic seers expressed this by the imagery of *div*, the luminous expanse, and of *vyoman*, the security of the Vast; their psychological counterparts were given by such terms as *Brahman* and *brihat*, meaning the ever-growing vastness of consciousness. The imagery of *akasha*, which has been such a fruitful source of inspiration in mythology, is an exact symbol of the deepest spiritual experiences. And the ideas derived from it have dominated all subsequent speculations in philosophy about the ultimate nature of reality. The soteriological outlook of the Indian mind, whether in the orthodox or the protestant schools of thought, has its source in this vedic conception of the luminous Void. If we come to consider the problem of the origin of the religious instinct, this concept can be shown to underlie all shades of spiritual endeavors and achievements in man. Their aim is everywhere to reach an ecstatic condition to which he is driven by an inherent urge of going beyond himself—an urge which for him is a biological and a psychological necessity.

Paradoxically speaking, ecstasy may be called a simulation of sleep in order to see more clearly, a simulation of death in order to live more intensely.

It is the secret method of conscious nature for pushing ahead in her evolutionary endeavor, which must henceforth be carried on along spiritual lines in the broadest sense of the term. The central fact of this ecstatic condition is a clear sense of the Void, whose ultimate value, as we have seen, lies in the irreducibility of simple and absolute consciousness. As such, it is beyond the scheme of prakritic evolution. It is the neutral light which illumines all the workings of prakriti, and the illumination can rise into awareness at any stage. If self-consciousness is the decisive factor which differentiates man from animals and is the definite mark of a saltus in nature's evolutionary process, then all the deeper instincts which are distinctly human must have their roots in the idea of the self; but there, by idea we do not mean any logical abstraction made by the analytic function of later thought, but an empirical seed-content embodying a direct feeling-awareness. The seed has life and it sprouts into power.

Religious instinct, then, is not so much the product of an impact of the objective world upon an inchoate psychic structure as the dynamic expression of the idea of the self as it lives and grows. The vedic seers symbolized this as the spark of Fire "lying in so many ways at the root of life" (*shayuh katidha chid ayave*), and spoke of the flowering of the spiritual consciousness as the "awakening" of the Fire. The self awakes and expands: the Fire is born and it consumes and assimilates its source, and spreads, burning whatever comes in its way until all is Fire.

There could be no better portrayal of the origin, growth, and end of the religious aspiration than the vedic imagery. In reality, the spiritual quest is a phenomenon of universal Life whose origin is bound to appear to the individual as surrounded in a mystery. But its kinship is nonetheless felt to be palpably real, beyond the bounds of time, in the sheen of the quickened moment which reflects eternity. It is not only an awareness but also a power. In its creative vision, the barriers between matter and spirit break down, and the will in the individual becomes the magic wand of the divine Magi awakening the slumbering dreams in the cosmic depths. And then, the quest of the spirit discovers a perfect equipoise of kaivalya and siddhi in the nudity of the living Void.

Chapter 15

NEW HOPES

In one of his recent books (*New Hopes for a Changing World*, 1951), Bertrand Russell has surveyed the present world situation in his usual lucid, well-reasoned, and engaging style. Like ancient Rationalists of India, he has followed the therapeutic method of practical philosophy: he has observed the symptoms of illness, has diagnosed it, held out hope for an ideal state of well-being, and suggested a method of cure. The parallelism of his thought with that of the old Rationalists is in some way striking enough to provoke a critical estimate of the values of the two systems. We may takes Russell's view as representative of the Western mind's conception of the aim of existence and call his ideal world the neo-Rationalist's utopia, reflecting the dominating trend of Rational Realism in modern philosophy. Kapila, who is at the head of the Indian Rationalists, had suggested no utopia, and modern Realism might look upon him as an escapist. But he has also offered to humanity a way of thinking and a pattern of living which might be named Spiritual Realism to distinguish it from the Rational Realism of the West. Whether this brand of Realism is rational or irrational remains to be seen. We may concede that both Kapila and Russell are Realists in two spheres of philosophical living which might not, after all, contradict each other, although modern Realism is naturally suspicious of anything that smacks of the spiritual.

The neo-Rationalist's philosophy of life starts with an analysis of the conflicts in which human beings have always been involved. They are the conflicts of (1) man and nature, (2) man and man, and finally (3) man and himself. All conflicts in a sentient being are followed by a heroic struggle to overcome them and, in case of a victory, may end in the emergence of a value of life higher than what it started with. The Sankhyist took up the same problem, but described it in terms not of conflict but of pain. According to him, pain is a fact of life (which obviously results from a state of conflict), and its causes may lie (1) within one's own physical and mental self, (2) outside one's physical organism but still within the domain of living beings, or (3) in physical nature beyond the control of human agencies and so providential in their working.

We find a close resemblance between the analysis of the problem in the two systems, but in the suggestion of a solution they have not emphasized the same points, since their outlooks are fundamentally different. The objective method of removing the pain of conflict by apparent natural means, which is also the age-long collective method, has not been found sufficient for the purpose by the Sankhyist, although he does not deny its efficacy up to a certain point. There are three defects, he says, in the objective method: it does not provide a radical cure of pain, it cannot guarantee an independent source of happiness, and finally, being confined to the mental plane, it leaves dormant the seeds of envy and hence of greed and unrest. And so he stands for the subjective method and prescribes the practice of critical discrimination and emotional detachment as the radical cure for all ills. Like the neo-Rationalist, he also speaks of fortitude as a prime virtue of the inner being, but unlike him, he changes its negative implication into a positive means of deepening and stabilizing the force of consciousness. The move is, of course, toward inwardization, which is, however, not a pleasant prospect to the extrovert. But if pain is a phenomenon of consciousness, it is quite logical to seek for the means of its eradication in the principle of consciousness itself. If flowing in and flowing out are the two natural rhythms of the consciousness-force, one need not be afraid of losing the world by a little practice of conscious inwardization according to a perfectly rational and scientific method. On the contrary, it will just bring in the desired balance between the inner and the outer life, the absence of which, in the long run, causes all the ills to which we are being subjected.

But the objective method still endures and will endure for all time as an expression of the natural impulsion of the creative forces. Its prestige has been enhanced by the labors of man during the last few centuries. Science has worked wonders and hopes to work more. It has met the challenge of nature in many fields and put in man an unquenchable faith in his abilities. It has brought nearer to realization the prospect of One World knit in a comprehensive economic and political system. The scientific attitude of mind and its propagation through facile means of communication are going to stamp the whole world with a uniformity of culture. The spiritualist's dream of a brotherhood of humanity is going to be a tangible actuality in the near future. And, yet, within less than two generations two world wars have been fought, and the nightmare of a third, even more drastic than its predecessors, is haunting the mind of civilized man. Evidently, everything has not been going well. Old Kapila might have the grim satisfaction of knowing that the solution of the positivist has not gone to the root of the problem and his own solution might still have some chance.

The whole of the civilized world, in spite of its splendid achievements, lives under a constant shadow of fear. Fear is there because real unity has not been achieved; and unity cannot come unless there is a broadness of vision, a clarity of understanding, and a willingness to help and not to hinder. Though the superstitious fear of nature is being dispelled by the spread of scientific knowledge, the social and moral causes of fear still persist. We are not afraid of nature since we are learning her secrets; but we have not learned the secrets of the cosmic life or probed the depths of the inner spirit. So we are mortally afraid of our fellow beings, because a blind rush for material acquisition has increased our greed and envy; and we are equally afraid of ourselves, because the uncontrolled lust of our nature is intensifying our sense of guilt. Civilization is morally and spiritually starving in the midst of material plenty, and the prospect of a happy world is receding before the onset of aggressive nationalism.

The neo-Rationalist is perfectly right when he says that "the real obstacles to worldwide social cohesion are in the individual souls." A happy world, constituted by a coalition of independent and yet freely cooperating units, cannot be built up unless there is a dominating influence of sane, tolerant, and intrinsically happy individuals. The whole problem then boils down to the training of the individual, keeping an eye to the development of those essential characteristics of his being which are in tune with the process of spontaneous expansiveness inherent in human consciousness.

The neo-Rationalistic comes forward with a scheme of education, beginning from childhood, as a necessary prelude to the establishment of his utopia. The factors emphasized in it are: a congenial environment created by a happy and understanding family life, an attempt to cure "provincialism in space and time" by judicious teaching of history and internationalism, a creation of opportunity for the development of the artistic tendencies, and a careful guiding of the will toward some useful creative activity. The aim is to let life grow spontaneously. Spontaneity is the greatest virtue in children, and we should try to maintain and foster it by all means. "The good life is a happy life. . . . The happy man can live the life of impulse like a child." Indeed, all our hopes of the future lie in the preservation of this amiable virtue of spontaneity in all stages of life.

All true. And yet, we know, spontaneity is killed so soon in practical life. It is a fragile blossom that can hardly endure the rude blasts of life. Children are spontaneous only in an ideal surrounding we have been able to create for them. Suppose we have been able to create ideal surroundings for the adult world too, by an accumulation and equitable distribution of material goods, a low birthrate, a democratic or communistic pattern of government, a high grade of mental culture fostered by a scientific habit of mind, and enough leisure to enjoy all good things of life—all commendable Western values, serving as excellent materials for a Rationalist's utopia—but are we sure we shall be able to retain "the spontaneity, the expansiveness, and the joy in living" of a child? Can these virtues be sustained by a handling of environmental forces alone, without the aid of a cult of deliberate inwardization?

The spontaneity of a child may, after all, be a surface value. To carry this spontaneity into the complexity of a grown-up life is not so easy, as everyone may know from experience. Psychologically speaking, spontaneity is akin to simplicity and relaxation, and can hardly grow where complexity and tension prevail. A society built up only on the impulsive and acquisitive tendencies will not provide ideal surroundings for preserving spontaneity, even if we substitute cooperation for competition as its motive force. The reason is not far to seek. The world is growing fast, and problems are multiplying. If we are determined to maintain progress on the impulsive side of life, we have to create a pull in the opposite direction to counterbalance the headlong rush of the natural propensities to avoid an inevitable crash. On the moral plane, to keep intact the full value of things that we have earned (*yogakshema*), we have to supplant the law of desire by the law of sacrifice. Retracing a step further, we have even to cultivate the negative virtues of self-control and passivity, leading to a denudation of the field of consciousness, just to create a reserve of power within to absorb the shocks without. The serenity of comprehensive contemplation, which alone can disentangle complexities in the cognitive field, must be reflected on the active life also to relieve the tension created by the whirl of environmental forces. And to ensure this, we have to add another item to the Rationalist's scheme of education—that of the cult of intensive spirituality.

In the neo-Rationalist's utopia, spirituality, in its ordinary sense, hardly counts. There is no place for God there; but this need not be grudged. In India, where every system of philosophy is based upon some inner realization and prescribes an appropriate way of life, the concept of a personal God was not found absolutely necessary for spiritual progress. If spirituality is not a dogma to be cherished but rather an experience to be lived, it must be primarily subjective in character and must rest upon independent inner growth and expansion of consciousness. The soul or personality grows into the universe and expands into an impersonal Godhead—this has been the rationalistic formula of spiritual realization in India. The neo-Rationalist concedes to this in a manner when he asks the individual "to open the windows of the ego as wide as possible," thinks that "Plotinus was right in urging the contemplation of eternal things," and admires Spinoza, who "would have us live not in the minute, the day, the year, or the epoch but in eternity." But presumably these will remain only as pious hopes unless a definite discipline is prescribed for the realization of the spiritual values.

Here the Spiritual Realism of the East can step in and fill up the gap left by the Rational Realism of the West. The individual must, of course, be the starting point for creating a happy world, and utmost emphasis laid on education in any scheme of social reconstruction. But broad-based education should develop the whole being of a man and not leave any part of it neglected. Rational Realism, being positivistic in character, will be occupied with physical, intellectual, aesthetic, and moral education of the individual. It will not be concerned with the problem of spiritual education and may hope that with the advancement of scientific rationalism, religion will die a natural death. But an antagonism between faith and reason is not inevitable. The religious instinct can be rationalized and the spiritual problem can be approached as scientifically as any other problem. The Sankhyists did this and gave to the world a system of Spiritual Realism, supported by a detailed technique in the form of the yogic cult. It produced at least one of the world religions (Buddhism), which, with its trenchant rationalism and spiritual positivism, is perhaps going to lay the foundation of the universal science-religion of the future. The Sankhya doctrine of Subjectivism reduces all objective phenomena into psychic values and thence by a cathartic method reaches the absolutism of the pure consciousness, which "looks on, sanctions, sustains, and enjoys" all prakritic movements, controlling them by its sheer negative weight. It is just what is needed at the present juncture.

The problem of the world crisis has to be approached dispassionately, without any rationalistic bias. There is no question of shunning the responsibilities of the world. But then, if we have accepted and met the challenge of outer nature, we have equally to meet the demands of the inner spirit. The mad rush of the collective consciousness, driven by unregenerate impulses, has to be checked. The yogic method of comprehensive self-culture, which has stood the test of time and been scientifically formulated, should be made a necessary part of all educational programs. The spirit as pure consciousness and the psychic core of the being must be accepted as real realities and their secrets mastered, just as those of the outer world. Spiritual Realism must be given as high a place as Rational Realism in the scheme of life unless we allow our new hopes for building a happy world to be belied by a willful blindness to an integral vision of reality.

Chapter 16

Sri Aurobindo and the Mystery of Death

The news of the passing away of Sri Aurobindo had put at first many of his disciples in an embarrassing position before the problem of death. But his death can also be looked upon as the first sacrifice for a noble cause. Sri Aurobindo in one of his letters speaks of the conquest of death as a problem which can be solved by the Supermind alone, but in which way he does not say. His own death, which cannot be characterized as a normal phenomenon, will appear to many as a masterpiece of supreme art.

Death is natural; and so is grief for the departed. For one who has been born, death is the inevitable end, points out the Gita with philosophical unconcern. If birth and death are the two ends of the life processes, the position of the Gita is unassailable. If the body has been born, it must die.

And yet man has always hankered after immortality. The explicit ideal of the vedic spiritual realization has been the conquest of decay and death. The theme has recurred again and again throughout the whole of India's spiritual history, and ways and means have been sought to give it a practical shape.

The mind naturally asks: What lies at the root of this persistent idea? An animal has no prevision and hence no thought of death; it is simply overtaken by it and quietly submits. A man can feel death before it actually comes, and so tries to avoid it. This instinctive avoidance of death in its crudest form has been described by the yogin as *abhinivesha*, which he explains as soul's inertia, its fervent clinging to the status quo. It is the worst form of delusion, he says. And yet it is this avoidance of death, pictured as its conquest by the spirit, that has been the age-long quest of human spirituality. Does it not sound like a paradox?

We find a solution if we state the problem in other terms. Death is a form of quiescence: dreamless sleep (*sushupti*), death (*mrityu*), and dissolution (*pralaya*). The first is an actual experience, and the other two conceptual, but nevertheless real. We are not afraid of the quiescence of sleep, because we believe it to be a rhythm in an incessant activity. Sleep might very well turn into death, but we feel it will not. There is a hope of resurrection. The experience of life, which can be the only meaning of sentient existence, overflows the blank of the daily death.

Consciousness persists in life through both its periodic activity and quiescence. The process is physical; but it can be easily extended into a metaphysical concept by introversive thought. To the three forms of natural quiescence can be added a fourth, the quiescence of samadhi. An indrawing and consequent intensification of consciousness, which characterizes all forms of samadhi, can release its power of transcending all changes. The transcendence might become a living experience, which would induce an indelible feeling of timelessness. In this feeling all experiences become homogeneous and hence colorless. But his homogeneity can very well become the background of manifold heterogeneous experiences. All stimuli from the external world will then draw out from the depths of the being the monochromatic reaction of a pure conscious existence—the sole manifestation of the purusha absorbing and transmuting the shocks of prakriti into his self-light. And the basis of the idea of the immortality of the spirit will be in the experience of an abstract and colorless void. The realization of a living death will then be the guarantee for the deathlessness of the spirit. A paradox again!

But "the essential immortality of the Spirit" is confronted by the phenomenon of eternal change in nature. The metaphysical idea underlying this is very simple. Viewed conceptually, there is the eternal Void of akasha with the eternal play of prana on its bosom. The two ideas do not clash, because it is the basic structure of our consciousness also: we can calmly look at the dance of our own thoughts. The vedic seer has added a rider to the formula: the Void transcends (*atitishthati*) life. In other words, to be eternally in death will mean giving a free scope to the eternal play of life.

The idea in its setting of universal timelessness is no doubt true. But the problem and a travail of the spirit ensue when we connect it with the process of time. The universal spirit endures with universal nature, let us concede, as a realizable idea. But the realization comes at one pole—the pole of the spirit, and not at the pole of nature. Of the three quiescences of nature, individual consciousness can overflow the first—the quiescence of sleep. But can it overflow the other two? Can eternality be a real experience in time? Rationality based on normal consciousness will very naturally doubt it. Consciousness appears to it to be a by-product of material processes. The living body emits consciousness; when the body disintegrates, consciousness is extinguished. The survival of the soul cannot be scientifically proved. The concept of immortality is an unjustifiable hypothesis born of our power of projecting the consciousness into the future. So argues the materialist.

But the validity of this argument is not absolute. Consciousness does not simply flow out; it can gather itself in, withdraw from its phenomenal play and yet retain a sense of value in intensity. The intensity reveals another form of time—a concentration of duration without losing the potentiality of projection. A moment may contain eternity, not in an infinitely drawn out chain of process but in an extreme consolidation of an ultimate and homogeneous meaning. The Upanishads admirably describe this by the term *vijnana-ghana*. There the two concepts apparently involve a contradiction. Universality inheres in idea, and consolidation in sensation; there is juxtaposition between the two, but no fusion. But in yogic consciousness the formless universality of the real Idea can absolutely contain the whole gamut of consolidation in a uniquely realizable potentiality. In simple words, the One, the Many, and Power (*shakti*) vibrating between them may form a unitary and comprehensive experience. The concept nearest to this in normal life is that of personality, which when intensified and universalized becomes the metaphysical concept of Atman.

The Atman, like a spider, spins out the web of experience and gathers it in. The first drawing-in we see in sleep, where the mental function is withdrawn, but not the vital or the material. The experience is of a quiescence—a kind of normal seed-consciousness, as the Upanishads describe it so often. A deeper quiescence would come when both the mental and the vital functions are withdrawn. This will be what is known as death. But to the normal consciousness, death is not the same kind of experience as sleep; it is rather the end of all experience. This might be true if we associate experience always with activity and heterogeneity, but not with passivity and homogeneity. If, however, quiescence becomes a yogic consciousness of natural samadhi (*sahajsamadhi* of Kabir), the negative value that we attach to sleep and death might turn into some supernormally experienced positive value. Nidra samadhi-sthitih—sleep as a poise of samadhi—is not a very uncommon experience with the yogins.

A plunge into the inner depths in a wakeful sleep may open a vista of eternality that can be projected both backward and forward. The experience will apparently belong to a measurable duration of normal time, but its meaning will be immeasurable in extension and infinite in formulation. A single experience of this kind will convince the mind of the immortality of the soul. Normally such an experience will come at the point of liberation from the terrestrial chain of existence. If the witnessing self looks backward, the theory of rebirth as taught by Indian spiritual science will be the logical outcome. If it is a vision of the future, it will correspond to the idea of eternal life in heaven. A confusion has been created in some religious beliefs by an attempt to make a universal application of this vision to the after-death existence of souls of different grades of maturity. The Indian idea of rebirth explaining the backward projection, and the idea of liberation by stages (*kramamukti*) describing the forward projection, give a complete logical picture of the whole movement of spiritual evolution.

This vision of eternality, when translated in terms of temporal movement, gives the idea of "the psychic survival of death," which is the second of the triple immortality envisaged by Sri Aurobindo. To the illumined it is a dogma, which up to a certain stage has not much influence on a man's spiritual evolution. But if spiritual consciousness is essentially an indrawing of the conscious force liberating an awareness of growing intensity whose impact unfolds new worlds of experience, the vision of eternality becomes a power and an instrument in the hands of the yogin. At the initial stage, the awareness of immortality which sunders "the veil of temporal ignorance" makes death a conscious event in life. At a higher level, it becomes a willed event; and the phenomenon is not wholly rare in spiritual history. A more complete mastery over nature will be a conscious and willed birth—the idea underlying the theory of incarnation. All this will mean an effective realization of immortality in a process of time, which in a liberated soul will give, at any given point, a total vision of reality, not necessarily in an omniscience of events, but of truths.

The third form of quiescence, the quiescence of dissolution, need not be considered here, because in Sri Aurobindo's vision the emphasis has always been on life and creation, though an integral vision cannot draw an artificial line of separation between being and nonbeing.

The crux of the problem of immortality lies in the third type of immortality that rose in the spiritual vision of Sri Aurobindo, and which has been called physical immortality—"the conquest of the material inconscience and ignorance even in the very foundation of the reign of matter." This idea supported by the very clear and logical thinking of Sri Aurobindo centers around the idea of transformation.

The human mind has divided the unity of existence into a duality of spirit and matter. The relation between the two can be most clearly and directly seen in one's own being, where a lump of matter has become endowed with life and consciousness. Consciousness as simple awareness and even as active but unmentalized consciousness does not reach a crucial point until it has become the witness consciousness. In this form, an ideal division is made in the body of consciousness itself, and the possibility of a consciousness independently centered within its own being is created. Just as a multiplication of impacts from without clarifies and consolidates an objective idea, so inward impacts can build a solid structure of soul-consciousness, which might appear to transcend and remain aloof from its peripheral phenomena. This detachment of the spirit in its self-formative period is reflected in the mind as duality of spirit and matter. But in reality, it is one substance that can be interpreted in various terms in accordance with the graded experiences of different densities. Viewed from the bottom, consciousness has emerged from evolving matter. If we maintain the notion of duality, we may say there is an interaction between the two. A better way of putting things would be to advance the upanishadic theory of the transparency of the substratum (*dhatuprasada*), leading to the luminous expansiveness of the soul-structure. Or, to take a vedic imagery, consciousness, like fire, may be said to have entered into matter to transform it into its own substance. The upanishadic seer will say, "The elements composing the material structure of the body have a gradation of densities, and each has an absolute property which can be released by yogic consciousness. If these yogic properties emerge, the physical body becomes permeated with yogic fire and no longer knows disease, decay, or death."

From the sensuous view of things, in which the idea appears as a half-real appendage, this might seem improbable. But if the viewpoint is reversed, if the idea that is evoked by the sense-contact is looked upon as real reality, and if the will seeks to manipulate these realities on this new basis, a novel order of things might be born. Disease, decay, and death might be attacked, as perhaps had been done by the Buddha, with the spiritual forces. One cures the diseased mind and thus cures the diseased body: modern therapeutics knows something of the trick. The conquest of decay and death on the same lines might be looked upon as a case of extension of what has already been achieved. At least the adventure is worthwhile.

But the conquest of death is a problem that can be solved on a cosmic level alone. There must be a complete reversal of the present plan of life-evolution on earth before this can be achieved. Sri Aurobindo saw this and launched into the bold adventure of tackling the cosmic forces. He has been ridiculed and abused for this and often branded as a heretic. "It is against God's plan," they said. "No, it is just making way for the inevitable and fulfilling His plan," was his reply to the charge.

There is no denying the fact that Sri Aurobindo is the first sacrifice in a noble cause. His death very forcefully reminds one of the saying of the rishi of the Purushasuktam: "The gods, as they spread the web of sacrifice, tied the Purusha Himself to the post as the victim." And if death, as the upanishadic seers speak of it, is the concentration of a final illumination of the heart, Sri Aurobindo's death has been like an explosion illuminating the horizon of the distant future, and its impact on the living has been and will be far-reaching in its results.

Glossary

The following glossary of Sanskrit words is based on the glossary in Sri Anirvan's collection of essays, *Buddhiyoga of the Gita and Other Essays* (New Delhi, 1983). It therefore contains not only terms found in the present text but also many other Sanskrit words that have an important place in the whole body of the Indian spiritual tradition. Note on pronunciation: *jna* is pronounced *gya*. Thus *jnana* is pronounced *gyana*.

abhaya: Fearlessness; √bhī—to fear.

abhiklripti (abhiklṛpti): Comprehensive realization; √klṛp—to make, frame.

abhimana (abhimāna): Blind will to be, erroneous conception regarding one's self; √man—to think, imagine.

abhinivesha (abhiniveśa): Soul's inertia, its fervent clinging to the status quo, instinctive avoidance of death, the worst form of delusion; √viś—to penetrate, pervade, be absorbed into, ni—deeply.

abhyasa (abhyāsa): Repetition, constant practice.

abhyudaya: Uplift, prosperity; aya (√i)—going, ud—up.

acharya (ācārya): Teacher, guru, spritual guide, teaching ācāra or rules.

adevah (adevāh): Men who denied the gods.

adhibhutam (adhibhūtam): Phenomenal reality as manifested in phenomenal existences.

adhidaivatam: Reality as abiding in spirit.

adhikara (adhikāra): Competence.

adhiyajna (adhiyajña): Relating to sacrifice.

adhvara gati: Straight movement; √dhvṛ—to bend, to move in a zigzag way.

adhyatma (adhyātma): Reality as intuited in the self, spiritual.

Aditi: Virgin-Mother of gods and men; Indivisible Infinity; √di—to cut, divide.

aditya (āditya): Sun.

adrishta (adṛṣṭa): Occult.

agni: The mystic Fire, the immortal principle in mortals, leading them forward; √ni—to lead, agra—forward.

ahamkarito bhavah (ahamkārito bhāvaḥ): Egoistic existence; aham—I, √bhū—to be.

ahimsa (ahiṃsā): Nonviolence; √hiṃs—to harm, injure, kill.

aishvarya (aiśvarya): Mastery of supernormal power; √īś—to be master of.

aitihya: Tradition.

ajara: Unaging; √jṛ—to wear out, grow old.

akarma: Inaction, quiescence.

akasha (ākāśa): Luminous void, space; √kāś—to shine, ā—pervasion, extension.

aklishta smriti (akliṣṭa smṛti): Unfettered memory.

akshara (akṣara): The Immutable; √kṣar—to flow, wave, perish.

alaukika: Occult.

alpabuddhi: A person of scanty intelligence.

amati: Self-ruining poverty of the spirit. (This is the meaning when the word is accented on the first syllable. When on the second, it means splendor.)

amaya (āmaya): Disease, ills.

amrita (amṛta): Immortality.

amritatva (āmṛtatva): Immortality.

ananda (ānanda): Bliss, quiescent joy.

anantam: Infinity; anta—end.

anarya (anārya): Not of the arya.

anavritti (anāvṛtti): Freedom from repetition (rebirth).

andha-tamisra (andha-tāmisra): Blinding darkness (of ignorance).

anibadha (anibādha): Unboundedness.

anna: Matter, food.

annada (annāda): The Spirit, eater of food.

anrita (anṛta): Perversion of rita, chaos, discord.

antaravrittata (antarāvṛttatā): Cult of introversion.

anu (aṇu): Atom, atomic.

anubhava: Awareness, experience; √bhū—to become, anu—along.

anumanta (anumantā): Permitter, one who sanctions.

anuvidhana (anuvidhāna): A mechanical assent.

anvikshiki (anvīkṣikī): Rational thinking, metaphysics; anu-√īkṣ—to see, think.

anyad antaram: The inner other.

aparaprakriti (aparāprakṛti): The lower nature, creative evolutionary nature of the Lord.

apaurusheyatva (apauruṣeyatva): Nonhuman (nonpersonal) origination; puruṣa—person.

apavarga: Renunciation leading to final beatitude; √vṛj—turn, apa—away.

apta (āpta): Authoritative person.

arambhavada (ārambhavāda): The principle of the origination of things.

arthanitya: Eternal in spirit (meaning).

arthavada (arthavāda): Explanation of the meaning of any precept, eulogium.

arya (ārya): Noble, cultured; √ṛ—to go.

arya-satya (ārya-satya): (Four) noble truths of Buddhism.

asadgraha: Obduracy of the spirit.

asana (āsana): Disciplined posture, as in yoga.

ashanaya (aśanāyā): Impulses of self-fulfilment, vital humger; √aś—to eat.

asangatva (asaṇgatva): Nonattachment.

asat: Non-existence, the zero.

ashrama (aśrama): One of the four stages of a brahmin's life; a guru's household.

ashva (aśva): Horse, symbol of spiritual vigor.

ashvattha (aśvattha): Mystic tree with roots above and branches below representing the universe; commonly the holy fig tree.

ashvin (aśvin): Vedic twin gods.

asta: Home.

astika (āstika): One who believes in the existence of God and another world, etc.; asti—there is or exists.

astikyabuddhi (āstikyabuddhi): The buddhi of an astika, the intuition of the existence beyond.

asura: Demon, demoniac force, opposed to deva.

asura (āsura): Dark, demoniac, hostile.

asurah (asurāḥ): Men of asuraic temperament.

asutripah (āsutṛpaḥ): Men whose only (√tṛp) delight, is in the good things (asu).

atishtha (atiṣṭhā): Transcendence; √ati—beyond, √stha—existence.

atitishthati (atitiṣṭhati): Transcends.

atman (ātman): Self; an integral dynamic whole of body-life-spirit; √at—to go.

atmano moksho jagad-dhitan cha (ātmano mokṣo jagad-dhitañ ca): Self-liberation and philanthropy.

atmashuddi (ātmaśuddhi): Self-purification.

atmatushti (ātma-tuṣṭi): Self-delight.

Aum (also *Oṃ*): The sacred syllable, the supreme mantra, the seed and source of all wisdom.

avara: Lower.

avatara (avatāra): Incarnation.

avesha (āveśa): Possession by the divine; √viś—to enter.

avibhakta: Undivided.

avidhya (avidyā): Ignorance.

avyakta: The unmanifest, a synonym for Prakriti.

avyaya: Inexhaustible.

ayam: This (creation), manifest existence.

bahudha (bahudhā): As many.

bala: Force.

bandha: Bondage.

bhagavata (bhāgavata): Follower of Vishnu (Bhagavan)-cult.

bhakta: Devotion; participant in bhakti.

bhakti: "Devout sharing"; devotional worship.

bharta (bhartā): Supporter; √bhṛ—to support.

bhava (bhāva): Spiritual entities, an original idea, conceptual existence, the becoming, nascent potentialities.

bhavaloka (bhāvaloka): Plane of conceptual existence.

bhavana (bhāvanā): The subtle potency of an ideational creativity.

bhoga: Enjoyment; √bhuj—to enjoy.

bhogaishvarya (bhogaiśvarya): Power and enjoyment.

bhokta maheshvara (bhoktā maheśvara): The Supreme (mahā) Lord (īśvara) in us who enjoys.

bhumi (bhūmi): Level of consciousness.

bhuta (bhūta): The final phase of becoming, physical being, conscious being, tangible actualities; √bhu—to be, become.

bhutama (bhūtāmā): Subtle body, individual soul, soul of all beings.

bhutashakti (bhūtaśakti): Material forces.

bhuvana: The world, the dynamization of existence as phenomenal appearances.

bija (bīja): Seed-form.

bodhi: Perfect knowledge or wisdom, illumined intellect (in Buddhism and Jainism).

brahma: Expanding consciousness of the Vast, the all-pervading matrix of creation, the pure Existence-Consciousness-Bliss, the power of knowledge, the transcendent, etc.; √bṛh—to expand.

brahma-karma-samadhi (brahma-karma-samādhi): A complete harmony between brahma-consciousness and its spontaneous energism.

brahmagranthi: The knot of Brahma, i.e., creative material energy.

brahma-mimamsa (brahma-mīmāṁsā): Authoritative dissertation on spiritual knowledge.

Brahmanaspati (Brahmaṇaspati): Vedic god, Lord of Vak (Word).

brahmavada (brahmavāda): The philosophy postulating brahman as the highest and all-pervading entity.

brahmavana: Cosmos conceived as a forest.

brahmavriksha (brahmavṛkṣa): Cosmos conceived as a tree.

brahmi tanu (brāhmī tanu): Body (fit to realize the brahma-consciousness; √tanu—body.

brahmodya: Dissertations about brahma.

Brihaspati (Bṛhaspati): Vedic god, lord of the Vast Word.

brihat (bṛhat): Ever-expanding Vast; √brih—to expand.

brihati (bṛhatī): Rhythm of brihat.

brihat jyotih (bṛhat jyotiḥ): Ever-expanding vastness of Light.

buddha: The enlightened one.

buddhau sharanam anvicha (buddhau śaraṇam anviccha): Seek your refuge in buddhi.

buddhi: Intelligence, spiritual awakening or illumination; √budh—to kindle, to wake up, be awake, arise, know, a perception of the luminous core of being, universalized and illumined consciousness.

buddhigrahya (buddhigrāhya): Seizable by buddhi; √grah—to seize.

buddhiguha (buddhiguhā): The innermost hidden depths of buddhi; √guh—to hide.

buddhimat: The kindler—an adjective of Agni.

buddhiyoga: Communion with the Supreme through buddhi; √yuj—to join.

budhna: Bottom, depth, illumination, illumination of the depth.

chakra (cakra): Cycle, wheel.

chetas (cetas): Vision, consciousness; √cit—to perceive.

chandas: Rhythm.

chela (cela): Disciple of a guru.

chid ayave (cid āyave): (kati-dhā) At the root of life (āyu).

chit (cit): Consciousness.

chitti (citti): Planes of perception.

chyuti (cyuti): (Theory of) flux; √cyu—to move, fall, perish.

daiva: Divine.

daivam chakshuh (daivaṃ cakṣuḥ): The divine eye.

daivi sampad (daivī sampad): Divine aptitude and achievement.

daivya vratam (daivyā vratāṁ): Selective divine laws; √vṛ—to choose.

dama: Self-control; √dam—to control.

danda (daṇḍa): Politics.

darshana (darśana): Seeing; vision of God or His representative.

dashavara parishad (daśāvarā pariṣad): Council of at least ten members; avara—at least, daśa—ten.

dehantara-prapti (dehāntara-prāpti): Assumption of new bodies, re-incarnation.

deva (pl. devāḥ): Gods, luminous ones; √div—to shine.

devanid (pl. devanidaḥ): Deniers of gods; √nind—to censure.

devashakti (devaśakti): Spiritual force.

devatati (devatāti): Expansion into god-consciousness; √tan—to spread. *See* sarvatati.

devavada (devavāda): Theory of God and gods.

devayu: Person yearning for deva.

dharma: Law, the fundamental law of being, eternal laws, law upholding life; √dhṛ—to hold, preserve, maintain.

dharmadhatu (dharmadhātu): The basic element of creation.

dharma-mimamsa (dharma-mīmāṃsā): Dissertation on dharma (duty, law, sacrifice), name of Jaimini's purva-mimamsa.

dharmaviruddah kamah (dharmāviruddhaḥ kāmaḥ): Desire in conformity with dharma.

dharmya samgrama (dharmya saṃgrama): Fight for the cause of dharma, righteous battle.

dhatuprasada (dhātuprasāda): Transparency of the substratum, purity of the basic elements (dhātu) of body-mind.

dhi (dhī): Spiritual knowledge and spiritual action.

dhira (dhīra): Steadfast, equipoised, balanced, highest type of aspirant who has ascended the plane of aditya-consciousness.

dhiti (dhīti): Activity, flames of the mystic Fire.

dhriti (dhṛti): The energy of tenacity; √dhṛ—to hold.

dhruva smriti (dhruvā smṛti): Timeless memory.

dhyana (dhyāna): Meditation; √dhyai—to meditate, one of the constituents of Patanjali's samyama, belongs to the fourth level of consciousness known as ekagrabhumi.

dhyana-chitta (dhyāna-citta): (Ninefold) states of consciousness in meditation.

didhiti (dīdhiti): Flames and rays of illumination.

diksha (dīkṣā): Initiation in spiritual life; √dah—to burn.

div: The luminous expanse; √div—to shine.

divya: Divine.

divyabhava (divyabhāva): Divine state.

divya karma: Divine action.

divyam chakshuh (divyaṃ cakṣuḥ): The divine eye, spiritualized vision.

dravya-yajna (dravya-yajña): Sacrifice by offering material things, realization through rituals.

drishta (dṛṣṭa): Visible, sensible; √dṛś—to see.

duhkha (duḥkha): Sorrow, misery.

dvandva: Dualities (of pleasure and pain, etc.); dvi—two.

dvesha (dveṣa): Aversion; √dviṣ—to hate.

dyusthana (dyusthāna): Plane of unitary aditya-consciousness.

ehipashyika (ehipaśyika): One who comes and sees for oneself; ehi—come, paśya—see.

ekagrabhumi (ekāgrabhūmi): Fourth of the five levels of consciousness, viz., mūdha (ignorant), kṣipta (restless), vikṣipta (distracted), ekāgra (concentrated), and niruddha (restricted, absorbed).

ekagrata (ekāgratā): One-pointedness, concentration.

ekam sat (ekaṃ sat): The One Existence.

ekam tat (ekaṃ tat): That One, the Ineffable.

etavad iti nishchaya (etāvad iti niścaya): Determined refusal to look beyond; etāvad—thus far and no farther.

Gayatri (Gāyatrī): A particular vedic meter; the mantra RV 3. 62.10 in that meter. *See* Savitri.

ghora karma: Workings of the grim forces of Nature.

gopi (gopī): Cowherd woman; village girl, devotee of Krishna.

gotra: Lineage through the male line.

guna (guṇa): Threefold qualities of individual and cosmic nature, viz., sattva, rajas, and tamas.

guru: Spiritual guide, teacher; √gur—to raise, lift up.

hetu: Cause, motive; √hi—to impel.

hetuka: Logician.

hetu shastra (hetu śāstra): The science of dialectics.

hrid (hṛd): Heart, the luminous seat of mystic realization.

hrida manisha manasa (hṛdā manīṣā manasā): By heart, by intellect and emotion, by mind.

hridat ashta (hṛdat aṣṭa): Fashioned by the heart; √takṣ—to chisel, fashion.

hridayya akuti (hṛdayyā ākūti): Yearning of the heart.

ichcha (ichchā): Desire.

idam jagat: This moving-world, manifest universe; √gam—to go.

idam sarvam: All this, the whole gamut of existence.

indriya: Sense-organ.

Ishano bhuta-bhavyasa (Iśāno bhūta-bhavyasya): Lord of what has been and what shall be.

ishtadevata (iṣṭadevata): Chosen image of the divine.

Ishvara (Īśvara): Lord, God.

Ishvara-bhava (Īśvara-bhāva): Lordliness.

itihasa-purana (itihāsa-purāṇa): History, amplifying and illustrating eternal truths.

jalpa: Polemics, maze of speculation; √jalp—to prattle.

jalpi: Same as jalpa.

janma-bandha: Bondage of rebirth.

jara (jarā): Decay, the process of aging. *See* ajara.

jarabodhi (jarābodha): Application of Agni, who kindles our waning energies; √budh—kindles.

jati (jāti): Race.

jatidharma (jātidharma): Racial instinct, custom, tradition.

jijnasa (jijñāsā): Spirit of inquiry; √jñā—to know.

jiva (jīva): Individual soul.

jivanmukta (jīvanmukta): Liberated in life.

jivanmukti (jīvanmukti): Liberation in life.

jivaprakriti (jīvaprakṛti): Individual nature.

jivashakti (jīvaśakti): Energy of conscient individuation (jīva).

jnana (jñāna): Knowledge, faculty of subtle discrimation, sense-perception; √jñā—to know.

jnana-atma (jñāna-ātmā): The individual knowledge-self.

jnanabhumika (jñānabhūmikā): (Sevenfold) levels of knowledge.

jnanakanda (jñānakāṇḍa): The section of the Veda dealing with knowledge, i.e., Upanishads.

jnanamayam tapah (jñānamayaṃ tapaḥ): Askesis through knowledge.

jnanayana (jñānayāña): Sacrifice and realization through knowledge.

jugupsa (jugupsā): Aversion, recoiling-shrinking; √gup—to hide.

kaivalya: Perfect isolation, beatitude; kevala—alone

kala (kāla): Time-spirit, Death.

kama (kāma): Desire.

kamatma (kāmātmā): Desire-soul.

kamavachara (kāmāvacara): (Sixfold) spheres or worlds of desire (in Buddhism), also called devaloka.

kamayani (kāmāyanī): Daughter of Desire (Primal Creative Urge), adjective of shraddha.

karma: Action, cosmic energy, spiritual activity, the store of vital energy with which one starts in life; √kṛ—to do, act.

karma-bandha: The chain of unillumined actions.

karmakanda (karmakāṇḍa): The section of the Veda dealing with rituals.

karma-mimamsa (karma-mīmāṃsā): Dissertation on rituals, same as dharma-mimamsa.

karmasampatti: Effective realization of an end.

karshana (karṣaṇa): Senseless repression; √kṛṣ—to torture.

kaushalam (kauśalam): Art, skill.

kavikratu: Seer-Will, epithet of Agni.

kavya (kāvya): Poetry, the yearning of a poetic soul; √kū—to cry out.

kirtan: Sacred chant.

kleshavritti (kleśavṛtti): Constricted functioning of consciousness.

klishtasmriti (kliṣṭasmṛti): Fettered memory, an experience in time. *See* aklishta-smriti.

kramamukti: Liberation by stages.

kratu: Creative will; √kṛ—to act.

kriya (krīyā): Action, spiritual activity; √kṛ—to act.

krodha: Anger.

kshama (kṣamā): Forbearance; √kṣam—to endure.

kshatra (kṣatra): Spiritual vigor, the urge to conquer new realms by self-exertion.

kshanti (kṣānti): Same as kshama.

kshatriya (kṣatriya): A man of the warrior caste.

kshepa (kṣepa): Projection; √kṣip—to throw.

kshetra (kṣetra): Field of experience.

kula: Family, caste, tribe, etc.

kuladharma: Family customs, primeval tribal instrinct.

lila (līlā): The state of desireless ease and play.

linga-sharira (liṇga-śarīra): Subtle body.

loka: Levels of consciousness, planes of Reality, worlds; √luc—to shine.

loka-samgraha (loka-saṃgraha): Social service, social well-being.

madhura rati (madhurā rati): Love between the lover and the beloved, the fifth and the highest kind of love toward the divine, the other four being śānta, dāsya, sakhya, and vātsalya.

madhvada: Enjoyer of bliss, getting joy in all experiences of life; √ad—to eat, madhu—honey. *See* pippalada.

mahakaruna (mahākaruṇā): Great Compassion.

mahan atma (mahān ātmā): The Great Self.

mahas: The Great Illumination; √mah connotes greatness, strength, and light.

mahat: The Great Shining Principle reflecting the luminosity of the transcendental consciousness, universalization, the first evolute of Prakriti.

mahat brahma: The matrix of the karmic energy, the creative aspect of brahma.

manadhina meyashuddhih (mānādhīnā meyaśuddhiḥ): Clear conception (śuddi) of the object-to-be-known (meya) depends (adhīna) on the purification (śuddi) of the means of knowledge (māna).

manana: Thinking, reflection, meditation; √man—to think.

manas: Mind.

manisha (manīṣā): Higher intelligence, synonymous with buddhi, connotes both the intellective and emotive aspects of spiritual experience, mental upsurge; √maṇ—to think, √īs—to go, or √iṣ—to pour out, stream out, etc.

manomaya kosha (manomaya koṣa): Mental level (sheath) of consciousness.

mano vyakaranatmakam (mano vyākaraṇātmakam): Analytic and discursive function of mind; vi-ā-√kṛ—to analyze.

mantra: A product of spiritual mentation; √man—to think, spontaneous revelation; √man + trai—to save > that which liberates.

mantra maheshvara (mantra maheśvara): The great lord of the mantras.

mantreshvara (mantreśvara): The lord of the mantras.

manushya (manuṣya): (The fire) of mental illumination, one who has that, i.e., man.

manvantara: Universal thought-cycles, the period of transition (antara) between two Manus.

ma shuchah (mā śucaḥ): Do not grieve; √śuc—to grieve.

matrasparsha (mātrāsparśa): Sense-object contact.

maya (māyā): Divine Wisdom and creative power.

medha (medhā): Force of penetration, intelligence.

mimamsa (mimāṃsā): Dissertations, an intensive exercise of the mind; √man—to think, reflect, a logical development of the ancient *oha*.

moha: Delusion.

mokshabhiti (mokṣabhīti): Fear of liberation.

mokshadharma (mokṣadharma): The way of liberation.

mokshashastra (mokṣaśāstra): Scriptures on liberation.

mrityu (mṛtyu): Death.

murti (mūrti): Idol; material form of God.

nada (nāda): Thrill of joy; √nad—to vibrate + √nand—to be pleased, delighted.

nairyogakshema (nairyogakṣema): Living above the hankering after having (yoga) and keeping (kṣema).

namayajna (nāmayajña): A sacrifice only in name.

nanyad astitvadah (nānyad astitvādaḥ): Determined refusal to look beyond, the stand (vādaḥ) that (iti) there is nothing else (na anyad asti).

nara: Man, hero, fighter, following the path of Reason (oha).

narottama: Supreme Man.

na sat nasat (na sat nāsat): Neither existence (sat), nor nonexistence (asat).

nastika (nāstika): Nonbeliever. *See* astika.

nidah (nidaḥ): (pl. of nid) Detractors. *See* devanid.

nididhyasana (nididhyāsana): Profound (ni) and repeated meditation. √dhyai—to meditate.

nidra (nidrā): Sleep, drowsiness of the spirit.

nidra samadhi sthitih (nidrā samādhisthitiḥ): Sleep as a poise of samadhi.

nihshreyas (niḥśreyas): Most excellent, highest good, final beatitude, or knowledge that brings it.

nimesha (nimeṣa): Lit. closing of the eyelid, dissolution of the world, absorption of shakti in shiva (self).

ninya vachamasi(niṇyā vacāṃāsi): Words rising from the depths; niṇya—interior, hidden, mysterious.

nirguna (nirguṇa): Transcendent aspect of existence and power; nir—without, guṇa—quality.

nirlepa: Nonattachment; √lip—to smear, pollute.

nirodha-samskara (nirodha-saṃskāra): Habitual ingathering of forces leading to nirodha.

nirodha-yoga: Yoga of self-control; √rudh—to restrain.

nirriti (nirṛti): Opposite of rita, disorder, chaos.

nirvana (nirvāṇa): Blowing out, cessation, extinction, Void.

nityasattva: Immutable essentiality, also known as shuddhasattva.

nityatva: Eternality.

nivid: Ancient formularies containing epithets or short invocations of gods, knowledge of the depth, called "embryo of shastras" by Aitareya Brahmana; √vid—to know, ni—depth.

nivritti (nivṛtti): Withdrawal, introvert movement, ingathering of forces.

nyagrodha: Banyan tree; √ruh—to grow, nyak—downward.

oha: Reason, the path of reason, later known as tarka; √ūh—to infer, reason.

ohabrahmanah (ohabrāhmaṇāḥ): Men who have attained brahma-consciousness through oha.

Om (Oṃ): *See* Aum.

paragatih (parā gatiḥ): Supreme movement.

parah purushah (paraḥ puruṣaḥ): The Supreme Person.

parah sanatano bhavah (paraḥ sanātano bhāvaḥ): Transcendent eternal existence (light).

parama gati (paramā gati): The highest state.

para prakriti (parā prakṛti): Supreme Nature, the matrix of pure individuality.

pararthya (pārārthya): Purposiveness, having an ultimate (para) purpose (artha).

para vairagya (parā vairāgya): Supreme detachment.

para vak (parā vāk): The Supreme Word.

Parjanya: Vedic god, the shower of determinate cosmic powers.

pashu (paśu): Animal, the unregenerate vital impulses in man, the empirical individual bound by avidya (spiritual nescience).

pashyan munih (paśyan muniḥ): Silent seer.

phala: Fruit, definite result.

pippala: Berry of the sacred fig tree symbolizing sensual pleasure.

pippalada (pippalāda): One who eats pippala, i.e., transmutes the variety of experiences into the stuff of the spirit, radiant ego.√ad—to eat. *See* madhvada.

pita-putriyam sampradanam (pitā-putrīyaṃ saṃpradānam): Transmission (of power and knowledge) from father to son.

prabudh: Awakening.

praja (prajā): Progeny, dynamic march of life.

prajna (prajñā): Spiritual knowledge, wisdom, final illumination.

prajanah kandarpah (prajanaḥ kandarpaḥ): Procreative urge.

prajnavada (prajñāvāda): Sophistications of reason, travesty of wisdom.

prakriti (prakṛti): Nature, Divine Matrix, the Creative Principle, counterpart of Purusha, Purusha's dynamism of will in time.

prakriti-sambhavah gunah (prakṛti-sambhavāḥ guṇāḥ): Wavering modes of phenomenal existence.

pralaya: Dissolution.

pramatripada (pramātṛpada): Levels of consciousness.

prana (prāṇa): The Primary Vital Energy, Life; √an—to breathe.

pranayama (prāṇāyāma): To "stretch the breath out"; disciplined breathing.

prasada (prasāda): Transparency. *See* dhatuprasada.

pratibodha: Awakened perception.

prathamah spandah (prathamaḥ spandaḥ): First thrill (of creation); √spand—to vibrate.

prathamani dharmani (prathamāni dharmāṇi): Primal spiritual laws.

pratishtha (pratiṣṭhā): Basis.

pratyabhijna (pratyabhijñā): Recognition.

pratyahara (pratyāhāra): Withdrawal of senses from objects.

pravritti (pravṛtti): Extrovert movement.

preti-ishani (preti-īṣaṇi): Adjective of Agni (mystic fire) who impels onward; √iṣ—to impel.

priti (prīti): Satisfaction of the heart.

priyah priyayah (priyaḥ priyāyāḥ): As the lover (bears) with the beloved.

puja (pūjā): Worship.

purusha (puruṣa): Person, the principle of witness-consciousness (sākṣicaitanya), a universal form of being gathering in itself the past and the future, the timeless, the immobile, the seer and yet an ingathered totality, the conscious Being.

pururushartha (puruṣārtha): Aim of human life.

purushavishesha (puruṣaviśeṣa): The Universal Purusha.

purvapaksha (pūrvapakṣa): Challenge, objection.

raga (rāga): Attachment; √rañj—to be affected, excited, delighted.

rahasyam: Esoteric meaning.

rajadharma (rājadharma): Duties of a kshatriya, of a king.

rajas: Principle of motion, activity, and disharmony; one of the three constituents of prakriti, the other two being sattva and tamas.

rajasa (rājasa): Type in which rajas predominates.

rajasika (rājasika): Same as rajasa, vital (nature).

rasa: Flavor, the first part of anything, emotional content.

raso'pyasya param drishtva nivartate (raso'pyasya paraṃ dṛṣṭvā nivartate): Even (apī) the relish (rasa) turns away (nivartate) from one (asya), after one has seen (dṛṣṭvā) the supreme (paraṃ).

rathi (rathī): The self or the divinity within, who is the traveler in the chariot (ratha) of the body.

rijuniti (ṛjunīti): Straight movement, same as adhvaragati.

rishi (ṛṣi): The indefatigable traveler who pierces into the Mystery and sees the Truth, Seer; √ṛṣ—to go, to see, to pierce.

rita (ṛta): The universal moral order, cosmic harmony, rhythm, dynamic unfolding of Truth in rhythmic Time-order, predestined cause of becoming; √ṛ—to go.

ritayu (ṛtayu): One yearning for rita.

ritu (ṛtu): Season, life's seasons, the rhythm unfolding itself through life's seasons.

rupa (rūpa): Shape, form.

sadashiva (sadāśiva): Ever-benign Divinity.

sadbhava (sadbhāva): A real idea.

sadhana (sādhanā): Spiritual practice.

sadhu (sādhu): Holy person; saint; a monk or ascetic.

saguna (saguṇa): Phenomenal aspect of existence and power; sa—with, guṇa—quality.

sahaja: Integral simple (perception), innate essential nature.

sahajasamadhi (sahajasamādhi): Natural samadhi, pure divine consciousness in which mental consciousness ceases.

samadhi (samādhi): Concentration, both comprehensive and exclusive; √dhā—to fix, ecstasy.

samanayana (samānayana): Bringing together, assimilation.

samanvaya: Harmonization, synthesis.

sama rasya (sāma rasya): Mutual absorption, unison of Shiva and Shakti, identical state in which all differentiation has disappeared; < sama—equal, rasa—delight.

sambodhi: Same as bodhi.

Samkhya or *Sankhya (Sāṁkhya* or *Sāṇkhya)*: A school of dualist philosophy; metaphysical calculation.

sammoha: Ignorance, illusion of mind.

samoha: Reason. *See* oha.

sampradaya (sampradāya): School, tradition created by transmission of knowledge from one teacher to another, giving completely without reserve; √dā—to give; sampra—without reserve.

samprasada (samprasāda): Light of the clear void.

samsari (samsārī): A moving entity; √sṛ—to move, saṃsāra—world-process.

samskara (saṃskāra): Tendency, impression from a former state of existence.

samvega (saṃvega): Urge.

samyak drishti (samyak dṛṣṭī): Right vision, integral view of life.

samyama (saṃyama): Self-control; dhāraṇā, dhyāna, and samādhi combined; √yam—to control.

sanga: Emotive association.

Sankhya: *See* Samkhya.

sankhyabuddhi (sāṇkhyabuddhi): Path of introspective analysis.

sankhyayoga (sāṇkhyayoga): Way of realization through Sankhya.

sannyasa (sannyāsa): Definite entrance into monastic life, with the vows entailed.

Sarasvan (Sarasvān): Vedic god, consort of Sarasvati.

Sarasvati (Sarasvatī): Vedic goddess, stream of divine consciousness, name of river.

sarathi (sārathi): Charioteer, symbolizing buddhi. *See* rathi.

sarga-pratisarga: Creation and dissolution.

sarvani bhutani (sarvāṇi bhūtāni): All beings, totality of the Spirit's Self-becoming.

sarvatati (sarvatāti): Expansion into all-consciouness. *See* devatati.

sarvatma bhava (sarvātmā bhāva): The experience of all (sarva) becoming the self (ātmā).

sat: Pure existence.

satpati: Lord of Existence.

sattashuddhi (sattaśuddhi): Purification of the essence, one of the daivi sampads; √śudh—to purify.

sattva: Essence, consummation of mystic experience, psychic entity forming the core of personality, light, and harmony; a constituent of prakriti.

sattvapatti (sattvāpatti): Fourth jnanabhumika, first level of Brahma-realization; āpatti—attainment; √pad—to go, stand fast as fixed.

sattvaprakasha (sattvaprakāśa): Same as nityasattva; prakāśa—manifestation, light; √kāś—to shine.

sattvashumshuddhi (sattvasuṃśuddhi): Same as sattashuddhi.

sattvika (sāttvika): Type in which sattva predominates.

satya: Truth, truth as Existence.

Savita: Vedic god, the luminous Impeller; the Sun of divine impulsion; √su—to impel.

savitri (sāvitrī): The famous verse to Savita, RV 3. 62.10. *See* Gayatri.

Savyasachi (Savyasācī): Name of Arjuna, one who can wield weapons with the left (savya) hand too.

sayujya (sāyujya): Spiritual communion; √yuj—to join.

shakti (śakti): Potency, power of Shiva to manifest, maintain and withdraw.

shaktipata (śaktipāta): Descent of power from above.

shaktisanchara (śaktisañcāra): Transmission of power.

shamatva (śamatva): Equanimity, self-poise.

sharira (śarīra): Body, fluxional embodiment of the psychic entity; √śṛ—to disintegrate.

shastra (śāstra): (Revealed) scripture.

shastra (śastra): Laudatory hymn; √śaṃs—to praise.

shashvata (śāśvata): Eternal.

shattarka (ṣaṭtarka): Six rationalist schools.

shayuh katidah (śayuḥ katidhā): (The spark of Fire) lying in so many ways; √śī—to lie down.

shitoshna (śītoṣṇa): Śīta and uṣṇa, cold and heat.

Shiva (Śiva): The Benign Divinity, the Absolute, Transcendent Divine principle.

Shiva-Shakti (Śiva-Śakti): Shiva and Shakti, the Absolute and his power, the Primal Androgyne.

shodashakala-purusha (ṣoḍaśakalā-puruṣa): Perfect Person, purusha of sixteen phases (kalā).

shoka (śoka): Grief; √śuc—to burn.

shrad (śrad): Heart, the shining core within the individual which contains the luminous Void. *See* hrid.

shraddha (śraddhā): Faith, intuition of the Beyond.

shraddha-tapas (śraddhā-tapas): Faith and austerity.

shri (śrī): Fundamental harmony.

shruti (śruti): Revelation, "Heard" (revealed) Word; √śru—to hear.

shubhashubba (śubhāśubha): Good (śubha) and evil (aśubha).

shuddhasattva (śuddhasattva): Pure essentiality, also known as nityasattva.

shuklapaksha (śuklapakṣa): Bright half of a lunar month.

shunam (śunam): The zero.

siddha: A perfected being who has achieved release.

siddhi: Attainment, realization, success.

siddhyasiddhi: Siddhi and asiddhi, success and failure.

smriti (smṛti): Memory, reminiscence, the whole body of sacred tradition as remembered by human teachers, in contradistinction from shruti revelation; √smr—to remember.

soma: Juice of a plant (soma-latā) symbolizing bliss; also a vedic god.

spanda: Vibration, creative pulsation; √spand—to vibrate.

sphota (sphoṭa): Bursting, expansion, Self-manifestation; √sphuṭ—to burst, blossom, blow.

sthirabuddhi: Firmly established in buddhi, equipoised, stable-minded.

sthitadhi: Same as above.

sthitaprajna (sthitaprajña): Same as above.

stuti: Eulogy, prayer, an ecstatic attunement with the Superconscious.

sukha: Pleasure, happiness.

sukha-duhkha (sukha-duḥkha): Pleasure and pain.

sukrita-dushkrita (sūkṛta-duṣkṛta): Good and bad actions, right and wrong.

sukta (sūkta): Vedic hymn, spontaneous, superb (su) uttering (ukta).

sushupti (suṣuptī): Sound (su), i.e., dreamless sleep; √svap—to sleep.

sutra (sūtra): Thread, a (shining) strand (of inner truth), aphorism.

svabhava (svabhāva): Individual nature, inherent nature.

svadha (svadhā): Self-position, self-poise, self-laws, an exclamation used in making oblations for the ancestors.

svadharma: one's own dharma; one's proper path.

svaha (svāhā): An exclamation used in making oblations to the gods; √su—well, √āha—said.

svaprakriti (svaprakṛti): (Supreme's) own nature.

svar: Light-Word, Realm of Light.

svarjyotih (svarjyotiḥ): The Light Beyond, Light of Svar.

svarupa-shunyata (svarūpa-śūnyatā): Status of the Void, experience of one's own self (svarūpa) as Void (śunyatā).

svarupavasthanam (svarūpāvasthānam): Status of selfhood.

svantantrya (svātantrya): Freedom, self dependence; sva—self, tantra—depending on.

tama asit tamasa gudham (tama āsīt tamasā guḍham): Darkness (tamaḥ) was (āsīt) covered (guḍham) by darkness (tamasā).

tamas: Darkness, principle of inertia and delusion—one of the three constituents (guṇa) of prakriti.

tamasa (tāmasa): Type in which tamas predominates, material nature.

tamashi dhriti (tāmaśī dhṛti): Tenacity of tamas, blind tenacity.

tamasika (tāmasika): Same as tamasa.

tandri: Drowsiness (of the spirit); √tandr—to drowse, be lazy.

tanumanasa (tanumānasa): Attenuated mind.

tapas: Energizing of consciousness, path of askesis, radiation, penance; √tap—to heat.

tapasya (tapasyā): Same as tapas.

tarka: Reason, logical system.

tarki (tarkī): One who indulges in tarka, logician.

tat: That (Absolute).

tatastha (taṭastha): Standing on a bank (taṭa) or borderland, indifferent.

tatasthya (tāṭasthya): Status of tatastha, supreme indifference.

tejas: Fiery energy, ardor, spirit, brightness, sharpness.

titiksha (titīkṣā): Calm endurance, patience; √tij—to sharpen, bear with firmness.

toka: Offspring > offspring of aspiration, touch, of final beatitude; √tvac—to cover > tvac—skin, the sense-organ of touch.

trayi (*trayī*): The triple sacred science, used for reciting, performing, and chanting the Vedas, embodying the spiritual realization of the seers.

turiyam (turīyam): The fourth state of consciousness beyond the states of waking, dreaming, and deep sleep, and stringing together all the states.

upadrashta (upadraṣṭā): Witness-consciousness; √dṛś—to see.

upakrama: Starting, setting forth; √kram—to sleep.

upalabdhi: Awareness, understanding.

upanayana: Investiture of the sacred thread; a social sacrament which admits the child formally to the spiritual heritage of the community; √nī—to lead, upa—near.

upanishad (*upaniṣad)*: Knowledge gained through close communion with the Divine; knowledge that destroys ignorance and liberates (Shankara), knowledge gained by sitting near the guru, the end-portion of the Veda, also called Vedānta; upa—near, √sad—to sit, √sad—to kill.

upanishad-rahasyam (upaniṣad-rahasyam): The mysterious and mystical esoteric meaning.

upasamhara (upasaṃhāra): Winding up.

upaya (upāya): Means, the individual's self-reliant endeavor.

upeksha (upekṣā): Indifference.

urdhvasrotas (ūrdhvasrotas): Upstreaming spiritual power.

urvih (urvīḥ): Worlds; uru—vast.

usharbhut (uṣarbhut): Nominative singular of usharbudh.

usharbudh (uṣarbudh): One who awakes (budh) with the dawn (uṣas) of spiritual consciousness.

vach (vāc): (vāk in nom. sing.): The creative word, spiritual expression.

Vachaspati (*Vācaspati)*: Vedic god, divine consort of Vach. See Brihaspati and Brahmanaspati.

vairagya (vairāgya): Dispassionateness, absence (vi) of attachment (rāga).

vaitrishnya (vaitṛṣṇya): Desirelessness; tṛṣṇā—desire.

vak (vāk): *See* vach; rhythm of the vast, eternal urge of self-expression.

varnanupurvi (varṇānupūrvī): Order of letters in a composition.

varta (vārtā): Economics; < ṛtti—livelihood, profession, business.

Varuna (Varuṇa): Vedic god, representing void; √vṛ—to cover, encompass.

vasa brahmacaryam: Live and move about in the atmosphere of the vast; √vas—to live, √car—to move about, brahma—the vast.

vasas (vāsas): Garment, fig. esoteric knowledge.

Veda: Highest Knowledge, sacred ancient text of the Aryas; √vid—to know, to attain, to be.

vedartha (vedārtha): Eternal spiritual truths, meaning of Veda.

vedavada (vedavāda): Cult of occultism—a travesty of the original spirit of Veda.

vedena (instrumental singular of veda): With knowledge.

vena: The (eternal) lover; √ven—to long for, love.

vibhuti (vibhūti): Manifold self-becoming, power; vi—manifold, bhut—self-becoming.

vicharanti (vicaranti): Move on toward the planes of intensive contemplation (vicāra, third person plural of √car).

vidyā: Knowledge; √vid—to know.

vidya-sambandha-krita-vamsha (vidyā-sambandha-kṛta-vaṃśa): Line of descent (vaṃśa) brought about (kṛta) by union (sambandha) with knowledge (vidyā), spiritual descent from teacher to disciple.

vijnana (vijñāna): Knowledge, buddhi, pure dream-state of consciousness, fourth sheath of being after physical, vital and mental, idea-perception.

vijnanaghana (vijñānaghana): Consolidated (ghana) vijnana consciousness.

vijnananatya (vijñānānatya): Infinite consciousness, second of the formless planes in the Buddhistic system.

vikarma: Wrong or unlawful action.

vimoksha (vimokṣa:) Liberation.

vinasha (vināśa): Annihilation (√naś—to be lost); supreme attainment (√naś—to reach, attain).

vinashana (vinaśana): Name of spot where Sarasvati disappears.

vipaka (vipāka): Ripening (of past energies); √pac—to ripen.

vipra: Seer-poet, trembling with emotion; √vip—to tremble.

Virochana (Virocana): Name of an asura, whose glitter is false; vi—false, √ruc—to shine.

virya (vīrya): Vigor, strength, manliness; vīra—(heroic) man.

vishadayoga (viṣādayoga): Yoga of dejection.

visarga: Multi-potent creative urge of the supreme; vi—multi, √sṛj—to create.

vishaya (viṣaya): Objective field.

vishayadhyana (viṣayadhyāna): Preoccupation with vishaya.

vishrishti (viṣṛṣṭi): Self-multiplication, the spirit's outpouring of itself; √sṛj—to pour out, create.

viveka: Analytic (vi) discrimination; √vic—to separate, discriminate, sift.

vrita (vṛtra): Dark forces, veiling the Truth, name of an asura; √vṛ—to cover.

vyanjanashakti (vyañjanāśakti): The power of suggestivity (of language).

vyatha (vyathā): Wavering experiences of dualities; √vyath—to waver, tremble > pain.

vyavasaya (vyavasāya): Determination, resolve; vi-ava-√so—to determine, resolve.

vyavasayatmika (vyavasāyātmikā): (Buddhi) discriminative and definitive function of reason.

vyavasthita: Predetermined and habitual.

vyoman: Sky, security of the Vast; oman—protection, √av—to protect.

vyutthana (vyutthāna): Rising to surface consciousness (jāgrat) from samadhi; ut- √sthā—to rise.

ya evam veda (ya evaṃ veda): He who (yaḥ) knows (veda) thus (evaṃ).

yajamana (yajamāna): Sacrificer, aspirant; √yaj—to sacrifice.

yajna (yajña): Sacrifice, individual and cosmic.

yajnartham karma (yajñārthaṃ karma): Action performed in the spirit of sacrifice.

yajna-tapas (yajña-tapas): Radiant energy of sacrifice.

Yama: God of the dead.

yoga: Harnessing oneself in order to have communion with the Supreme, path or means to spiritual realization; √yuj—to yoke, to join.

yogabuddhi: Cult of practical illumination.

yogakshema (yogakṣema): Acquirement and maintenance > material welfare, prosperity.

yogi (yogī): One established in yoga.

yuktah (yuktaḥ): Same as yogi, one in communion with Integral Reality.

yukta(h) asita matparah (yukta[ḥ] āsīta matparaḥ): Should sit in communion with Me; the Supreme Goal.

Other titles by

Sri Anirvan

Inner Yoga: Selected Writings of Sri Anirvan

Buddhiyoga of the Gita and other Essays